THE Prodigal's SON

CRACKHEAD TO JESUS FREAK

S. E. Tschritter

A NOTE FROM THE EDITOR

"God's got a plan for this story. I can't put into words how God has opened my heart, opened my eyes while working on this manuscript. I know He will do the same when thousands of others read it. Yes, thousands. Even after his death, because of Sam's gorgeous words, Pastor Clint is still pouring into people. To make them better. Stronger. To understand that God still loves us, still uses us even when we fall. People will be inspired by Sam's honesty. Vulnerability. Trust in God. But most of all, how she loved, even during the worst of circumstances. I am honored and grateful to have worked on this project."

—**LARRY J. LEECH II,** Writing coach and editor of award-winning authors

WHAT OTHERS ARE SAYING

"A courageous, Spirit-filled testimony of love, addiction, forgiveness, and faith that will feel personal for every reader. S.E. Tschritter doesn't just tell a story—she invites you to live it. *The Prodigal's Son* is perfect for anyone who's felt too far gone to come home."

—**VINCENT B DAVIS II,** author of *The Man with Two Names*

"Raw. Real. Authentic. Expertly crafted writing. This is one of those stories that stays with you, and you'll find yourself telling others about it."

—**BEN DIXON,** United Kingdom, author of *Vengeance and Honour: A Heroic Quest*

"Binge-read the entire thing!"

—**M.L.,** Canada

"An honest and visceral account of one couple's battle with the cruel ravages of addiction, recovery, relapse, and cancer. Its greatest impact, and perhaps its greatest attribute, will be the reader's profound realization that we are all God's prodigals."

—**TIM EICHENBRENNER,** author of *To Live in the Light*

"The powerful message will inspire everyone who reads it. The themes of recovery, relapse, and redemption apply to all types of addiction. I won't be surprised when *The Prodigal's Son* hits the *New York Times* best-sellers list. Oprah Winfrey, this one."

—**M.P.**, Hot Springs, Arkansas

"In my years serving as a chaplain, I have witnessed countless stories of restoration emerging from crisis. Clint's raw, inflicting journey from addiction to grace mirrors the transformations I see regularly. This powerful story offers hope to those drowning in shame. A valuable read for ministry professionals and hurting souls."

—**RAEWYN ELSEGOOD**, Sydney, Australia, Chaplain, Writer, Speaker,

"Reads like a screenplay."

—**M.T.**, South Carolina

"Until I walked away from alcohol, and God's serenity filled my life, I didn't realize how much Satan stole from me. *The Prodigal's Son* depicts a pastor's battle with addiction, a story that is heartbreakingly absent in the current market. Sam is such a beautiful, gritty soul who doesn't look like the typical authors in the Christian publishing space. I'm grateful for the matching dents in our fenders, and for the courage she's lent me to find the heart of God. Sam, may God bless you and this work for the glory of His kingdom. May Clint's life's work, legacy, and unshakable faith reap a harvest one hundredfold."

—**ASHLEY WORRELL**, author of "The Hebridean Shield" series

"I couldn't stop reading. I wept. I laughed out loud. Who is this book for? Anyone, everyone! Me!"

—**S.F.**, Minnesota

"This book is spiritual, but not religious. I'm not a Christian, and I couldn't put this book down. The main character is so well-depicted, I felt like I was sitting across from him."

—**K.E.**, Brooklyn, New York

"I knew Clint personally. I was his bishop. He was an addict and a felon. And he was a gregarious lover of people. He was an exceptional pastor— one of most authentic conveyors of God's love and grace I have ever known. Samantha knows—lived—Clint's tangled, messy story inside-out. *The Prodigal's Son* is a poignant, unvarnished, account of Clint's journey through the hell of addiction to resurrected life in Christ.

And, Clint's story is our story. We are all created by God with a space— a Hollow—that only God can fill. Until the Hollow is filled by God's unconditional (you don't have to earn it) love, we seek to fill the space with whatever deadens our sense of estrangement, unworthiness, shame, anger. Clint used drugs and alcohol to fill his Hollow. Many of us have our own addictions. Clint would want us to be honest.

Like me, you will be moved to tears when Clint, at last, utters, "I think I finally love myself." Ultimately, *The Prodigal's Son* is a love story—the story of God's unrelenting yearning and pursuit to fill us with His extravagant love. I thank God that Samantha has displayed such vulnerability and courage in her response to God's call to tell Clint's (and her) story. *The Prodigal's Son* is a must-read for all who hunger and thirst for God redeeming, reconciling love."

—BISHOP BRUCE R. OUGH, Former President of The United Methodist Church Council of Bishops

This book is dedicated to spiritual misfits. And to Alex.
There will always be room for you at the table.

AUTHOR'S NOTE

I believed the lies.

I'm not good enough.

I'm not worthy.

Even now, Legion—that's what I named our enemy—is messing with me, tryin' to tell me that people won't want to hear this, my story won't matter. Because he knows if I expose the truth of my victory then you'll believe there's hope for you too.

You and I both know, on the days we're tryin' our best to sober up, if only one voice taunted us to drink, we could silence one demon. But a Roman Legion—five thousand foot soldiers, plus commanders, plus cavalry? That's what you and I are up against—the population of a small city—and Legion's got you chained in the Lazarus pit at the dead center of his army. He's pinned you with the exact same lies.

You are not good enough.

You are not worthy.

You believe the lie, but I wish you wouldn't. If God sees worth in someone as flawed as me, then He sees worth in you too. If God can use a screw up like me, He can use anyone. God's greatest glories shine in the fiercest darkness.

Dear God, open prison doors with this book. Batter down judgmental hearts. Your grace is sufficient for all. Not just the addicts and sinners. Amen.

With Love,
Clint, November 2018

For those who are not familiar with the story of The Prodigal's Son:

The Parable of the Lost Son

LUKE 15 NIV

Jesus continued: "There was a man who had two sons. The younger one said to his father, 'Father, give me my share of the estate.' So he divided his property between them.

"Not long after that, the younger son got together all he had, set off for a distant country and there squandered his wealth in wild living. After he had spent everything, there was a severe famine in that whole country, and he began to be in need. So he went and hired himself out to a citizen of that country, who sent him to his fields to feed pigs. He longed to fill his stomach with the pods that the pigs were eating, but no one gave him anything.

"When he came to his senses, he said, 'How many of my father's hired servants have food to spare, and here I am starving to death! I will set out and go back to my father and say to him: Father, I have sinned against heaven and against you. I am no longer worthy to be called your son; make me like one of your hired servants.' So he got up and went to his father.

"But while he was still a long way off, his father saw him and was filled with compassion for him; he ran to his son, threw his arms around him and kissed him.

"The son said to him, 'Father, I have sinned against heaven and against you. I am no longer worthy to be called your son.'

"But the father said to his servants, 'Quick! Bring the best robe and put it on him. Put a ring on his finger and sandals on his feet. Bring the fattened calf and kill it. Let's have a feast and celebrate. For this son of mine was dead and is alive again; he was lost and is found.' So they began to celebrate.

"Meanwhile, the older son was in the field. When he came near the house, he heard music and dancing. So he called one of the servants and asked him what was going on. 'Your brother has come,' he replied, 'and your father has killed the fattened calf because he has him back safe and sound.'

"The older brother became angry and refused to go in. So his father went out and pleaded with him. But he answered his father, 'Look! All these years I've been slaving for you and never disobeyed your orders. Yet you never gave me even a young goat so I could celebrate with my friends. But when this son of yours who has squandered your property with prostitutes comes home, you kill the fattened calf for him!'

"'My son,' the father said, 'you are always with me, and everything I have is yours. But we had to celebrate and be glad, because this brother of yours was dead and is alive again; he was lost and is found.'"

Part One

The righteous cry out, and the LORD hears them;
he delivers them from all their troubles.
The LORD is close to the brokenhearted
and saves those who are crushed in spirit.

Psalm 34:17-18 NIV

CHAPTER ONE

Dear Clint,

I bumped into your news story about your recent trouble. I am praying for you in this time.

When I was twenty-seven and early in my ministry, my life was a trainwreck. I remember feeling like I was living in Good Friday. And then it was the silent Saturday of grief for a long, long time. Eventually, I got glimpses of Easter—not at once, not like one glorious dawning—but bit by bit. A peek here and there, until I realized Jesus was walking with me all along.

These days made me a better pastor and a better person, and I now cherish my life and my faith in a way I don't take for granted.

So, I am praying for you through the Good Friday. Praying for you through the silent Saturday. Praying you awake into the dawn of new life. However healing needs to take shape in you. And may you know the presence of the Living Christ every step of the way.

God's peace, which surpasses human understanding be yours.

Michelle

SAM, SATURDAY, SEPTEMBER 30, 2017
SLEEPY EYE, MINNESOTA

He said 6:00 p.m., so for two hours I battled every X-chromosome in my body screaming, "Are you on your way home?" "How close are you?" "Why are you so late?" Nagging wife melded with mom brain. "Maybe he made new friends. ... Oh, that would be awesome."

Okay, if he isn't home by the time I get the girls to bed, I'll call. The Little Mouse ate up his red, ripe strawberry a mite faster. The slow, sweet bedtime song galloped at a "William Tell Overture" pace. Rushed kisses camouflaged as "silly." Good nights and air hugs. A closed door. A sigh of relief.

I stumbled into my bedroom and dialed my husband's number. No answer. I tried again. No answer. I checked the ringer volume on my phone, so I would hear when he called.

I pressed my thumb to the green circle on the screen. Again. No answer.

I made sure my phone wasn't set to Do Not Disturb. 10:00 p.m. came and went. No answer. Dread crept in. I checked for missed calls on the phone glued to my palm.

And brushed my teeth. Took my contacts out. No answer. Went to the bathroom. Changed into pajamas. Still no answer. Zombies attacked the main characters on the TV screen, but I barely noticed. My husband had thirty-eight missed calls from me. I hit send again. Just for the heck of it. Thirty-nine. Forty.

At 11:11, I wished not to kill him when I spoke to him again. At 11:30 I pretended the forty-one different emotions churning in my stomach wouldn't keep me awake. At 1:30 a.m. Sunday morning, the sound of my ring pierced the darkness.

"Clint?"

"Mrs. Evans?" A man's voice, but not my husband's.

"This is."

"This is a sergeant from the New Ulm police department. There's been an accident. Your husband's alive, but he's been taken to the hospital."

My heart screeched to a halt. *Please tell me I'm wrong.*

"Was it alcohol?"

"I'm sorry, ma'am. I can't say for certain. But he's all right."

Anger sideswiped fear. I rolled my eyes. "Not when I'm done with him."

"Excuse me?"

My eyes widened, realizing what I'd said and to whom. "Never mind." The inappropriate, poorly-timed joke wouldn't be my last.

"Mrs. Evans, your husband will be arrested upon discharge from the hospital. He …" I heard "fled from officers," "side swiped a car," "hit a utility box…" but the sergeant continued.

So, yes, alcohol, then. Pain stabbed my heart. *No, no, please, no. I can't live through another Chicago. And we have so much more to lose now.* "Oh, my God. Please."

The call ended. It must have, because I wrote this seven years later and we're not still on the phone, but I have *zero* recollection of a "goodbye."

I stared at my closed bedroom door, where just beyond girls five, four, and two years old dreamed in blissful innocence.

Church tomorrow. Today. I groaned and rolled my eyes. "Really. On a Saturday night?" I calculated how much time I'd need to get the girls ready. I hoped I'd fall asleep more easily, knowing where Clint was. Every time I nearly fell asleep, my brain blasted me with another implication of loss as a result of the accident.

I woke up to the alarm at 7:30 a.m. I catapulted out of bed, rehearsing the words I'd share with the congregation. At 7:45, while I rinsed conditioner from my hair, the phone rang. I dried my hand on a towel in route to the phone. "Sergeant Reid?"

"Mrs. Evans?" A female voice.

"This is."

"I'm a nurse calling from the hospital. The doctor found something on the CT scan. You need to come in right away."

Conditioner coated my hair. Water puddled at my feet. Six hours prior, Sergeant Reid's call thrust me into survival mode. Already running on adrenaline, already navigating damage control, already in shock, my brain did not have enough storage space to compute her words. Three children suddenly felt like extraneous puzzle pieces. "The soonest I can get there is 11:30."

Silence stretched on the other end. "Mrs. Evans, we can't talk to him without you here."

That didn't feel true. *What do you do with single people? Wait for their spouse?* But, okay.

"You need to get here as soon as possible," she repeated. "Don't bring your kids."

The hospital was fifteen minutes away. "I'll be there in thirty minutes."

I hung up. Rinsed the conditioner. Phoned Janet from the leadership team. "Clint was in an accident last night. I was going to make an announcement this morning, but they found something in the CT scan. Can you let Faith United Methodist know, please? ... Thanks."

Without hesitation, I scrolled to Erin's number.

Years prior, Erin battled a heroin addiction and broke free, by the grace of God. People who've been in it don't pass judgment. And don't need explanations.

"Clint was in an accident last night. I think alcohol was involved."

"Bring the kids over."

My girls might have been barefoot when I left them with Erin, for all I remember.

CHAPTER TWO

Dear Clint, Sam, and family,

I thank you for your faithfulness to the Lord, and in your service of the Lord, both as prophet and priest—from the people to the Lord and the Lord to the people. I pray blessings from God over you as a covering, and under you to support you. Roger always said, "to understand someone, stand under them, supporting them. We love you and pray for you many times during the day, every day.

Helen Melquist, a pastor's widow

CLINT, SUNDAY, OCTOBER 1, 2017
NEW ULM, MINNESOTA

I opened my eyes. White walls, beeping machines. A long window formed the wall between my room and the hallway. Nurses with clipboards flitted to and from computers and phones at the station just beyond the window. A dark, blank spot where memories of the last twelve hours should have been. I noted my wife's set jaw and sparking eyes when she rounded the glass and stepped into my room. The last time we found ourselves in this scenario, ten years prior, she told me it would be *our* last time.

"Whatever you decide about our marriage," I blurted. "I won't fight you."

She grunted a non-committal answer and stormed over to the seat farthest away from me— a plastic commode against the window. With all the crap I'd put her through, the metaphor fit. Her head sunk into her hands and she stared at the floor.

Minutes of silence passed. The absence of words clued me in to the depths of her fury.

"What happened last night?" I asked.

Pure wrath stared back at me. "You were too drunk to give them my phone number." She catapulted from the commode and stormed into the hallway.

Reassurance vanished with her. Thick cobwebs replaced concrete thoughts. *Sunday morning*, I realized. *Oh, no.* Missing church on Sunday from time to time isn't a huge deal unless, like me, you're the pastor paid to preach the sermon.

Shame flooded through me.

My wife strode in with the doctor. The doctor stepped toward a rolling cart against the wall with a laptop resting on it and scanned his security badge to access the computer. While Sam reseated herself on the commode, the doctor clicked through apps until my files appeared on his screen. "Well, your liver is four times larger than it should be and your Blood-Alcohol Content was .25. But Mr. and Mrs. Evans this, *here,* is what worries me." He brought up an image of my lungs. "You have a lesion here. We'll need to biopsy right away."

"Cancer?" My heart plummeted like I was riding The Giant Drop at Six Flags. My voice cracked like a throwback to seventh grade.

"I can't say for certain."

My wife and I stared eye-to-eye, the implication of the doctor's words setting in. A thousand moments flashed before my eyes. The day we met at a Christian music festival. Throwdown arguments about my addiction. The births of our three daughters. Years of church ministry together. I know I screwed up, but God, I'm not ready to say goodbye. "I have cancer. I'm going to die."

Sam pinched her lips together. "It's not cancer until it's cancer."

The doctor left and a policeman appeared in the hallway on the opposite side of the glass. The fluorescent lights from the hallway glinted off the metal cuffs secured to his thick, black duty belt. My wife, nonplussed by his appearance, hopped to her feet and dashed out like the room was sinking.

A female nurse entered with a pair of canary yellow socks. On the bottom, white, rubber dots surrounded a giant, white, smiley face. *Great.*

When I reached for the socks, pain lit up my body like an internal explosion. I gritted my teeth and leaned back into the pillow.

"I can help you, Mr. Evans," the nurse said.

Waves of humiliation relentlessly crashed into my chest. A thirty-six-year-old man shouldn't need help to pull socks on. Over the nurse's shoulder, my wife and the officer spoke in hushed tones. My life was happening to me, about me, but I was only a bystander.

"I can get the second sock, if you want to get his things," my wife, entering the room. She stalled at the sight of the bruises on my legs and shimmied my second foot into the left sock without looking at my face. "You're being arrested. I told the officer you'll go willingly, and he doesn't need his cuffs."

The officer didn't say a word. We followed him past hospital rooms. One patient in a bed with hair matted to her face, watched us walk by. Nothing moved but her eyes.

At the elevator, Sam said, "So, what happens next?"

The officer's gaze scanned nurses flitting by, a custodian, and open doors to various patients' rooms. "Let's wait." He didn't speak again until we stopped in a café located at the side entrance of the hospital.

The lights were off and chairs rested atop the tables. *Closed.*

Because it's Sunday morning. My stomach rolled. I couldn't tell which thought made me more nauseous, my congregations speculating about their absent pastor, or the cancer diagnosis. I wanted to lie down and never stand again.

The officer studied our surroundings. Satisfied, he offered a straight-forward explanation of the next steps and invited us to ask questions.

Sam's words came then. All of them. She asked questions and repeated the same questions different ways.

My ears buzzed, my head thrummed. *God, Clint, you're so worthless. Why couldn't you have died last night and put everyone out of their misery?*

Most people go their whole lives without having Miranda Rights read to them. This was my *third time? Fourth?* I didn't remember leaving the café. The sky spewed piercing October rain atop my bald head. I didn't feel the cold. The officer opened the back door of his SUV. I angled my feet and crammed them into the miniscule space in front of me. The seat reminded me of a cheap waiting room chair.

Sam's eyes scrunched, confused. Why plastic? I watched comprehension dawn. It's easier for officers to clean blood, puke, and urine off plastic—a detail pastors shouldn't know from personal experience.

Sam kissed the top of my head. "I love you."

The officer shut the door between me and my wife.

She shivered from the cold in her paper-thin, black leather jacket. "Five dollars at a garage sale, Clint," she'd exclaimed several years prior.

Sam deserved better than life's cast offs. *Go inside, sweetheart.* But she wouldn't. She would stand in the cold, in the rain, until the SUV was out of her sight. Despite anger and resentment, Sam would follow me as far as possible so I wouldn't be alone.

The weight of the car shifted, and the officer closed his car door. "I'm sorry, Mr. Evans."

"Yeah. It sucks." I glanced out the window. He'd parked near a loading dock, out of sight from the main parking lot. I was as new to receiving respect from police officers as Sam was to seeing the back of a squad car. "Thank you for concealing my arrest."

"Least I could do."

Darkness seeped in for my wife that day. Shattered trust. Shattered dreams. A chasm formed between us that I hoped we would have time to mend.

For me, the darkness started years prior. No kid wakes up and thinks, "I'm going to be a bully today." The bullied becomes the bully.

No teenager thinks, "I hope this drinking turns into a lifelong battle that steals relationships and opportunities and joy." But when tolerance kicks in, numbing the pain requires higher quantities of your drug of choice.

Becoming an alcoholic pastor doesn't happen overnight. Self-loathing took years to perfect, but childhood circumstances laid the groundwork. I remember the first time I told a lie. More dangerous, though, was the lie Legion told me. The lie that became a death sentence when I believed it.

I don't remember a time without Legion. He always seemed to be close. Even in the good times. Watching. Waiting. Then he'd speak. Whittle away at my confidence. Cast doubt. "You're not good enough." "You're scum." "No one likes you." And I'd believe him. I didn't recognize who the voice belonged to as a child, but his words shaped and cemented my identity.

CHAPTER THREE

Pastor Clint,

I have been delaying sending you this email for quite some time because I wanted to give you all the space and privacy you deserve. The joy, excitement, and love you bring to our church has been missed dearly.

My heart hurts when I think about your cancer. As I write this email, my children are running around the living room playing together. We are close to the same age and the reality of you dealing with this horrible disease—is scary. It reminded me never take the little things for granted. Continue to give your fear to God and know his plan is never wrong.

In regard to the legal issues, forgive yourself. Every day I deal with good people who make poor choices. As a deputy I am expected to skirt a line close to perfection and I know you can relate. When I think of you, I remember a loving man who helps my family grow closer to God. I owe you a great deal and if you ever need help with anything, I am a phone call away.

God bless you and your family.

A Congregation Member

SAM, SUNDAY, OCTOBER 1, 2017
NEW ULM, MINNESOTA

My favorite writing spot in Sleepy Eye, Minnesota, was the back table at the local Hardee's. From my chair, I could see the library across the street and an abandoned movie theater that a family restored into a trendy coffee shop after I moved away.

I lost weight eating at Hardee's by ordering the low-carb combo with a side salad. I thought of the teenage boy behind the register as my conscience. Every time I tried to say, "Frisco and fries," my conscience, wearing a nametag that read "Josh," said, "low-carb combo with a side salad. Coming right up."

Those interactions began two years prior to Clint's accident and the two worlds felt like alternate realities. While I watched the officer emerge from jail, I thought about stopping at Hardee's on the way home. *I hope Josh isn't working, so I can eat all the carbs.*

In my Trailblazer, I followed the officer's squad car to a part of town I didn't know existed. He unlocked the tall, chain-linked gate of the impound lot. I idled—my SUV through the gates behind him.

He stopped his car at a two-story, windowless shed. Gears whined when the metal door retracted into the ceiling, exposing the inside of the garage inch by moaning inch. I craned my next to see beyond my hood. The front fender of Clint's gray sedan came into view first. The garage door revealed increasingly more. My breath jammed. The plastic grill was missing. Leaves stuck out from behind the bent license plate. A crinkled, concave depression in the hood looked like a large animal fell out of the sky and landed on the car.

If the damage stopped there, and I knew nothing of the backstory, the driver might have hydroplaned, swerved off the road, and hit a tree. But that's not what happened.

I parked to the left of his car. From my driver's seat, I stared at the front passenger side wheel—rather, the space where the tire should have been. The bent rims suggested he drove on bare metal for awhile before police used their SUVs to barricade his vehicle. That reminder drew my attention to a police SUV with a bent bull bar. *The vehicle that stopped him?* Clint tore through the town like a nightmare game of pinball.

I forced my cement legs to exit my Trailblazer. The officer stood on the driver's side of Clint's car and watched me. I circled the car starting toward the trunk. Dents and scars made me want to vomit. *This isn't my mess.*

How could he do this?

Oh, God, how do I do this?

I walked past the officer. On the driver's side, a dent and streak of white stretched across both doors. Then I saw the driver's window. My throat went dry. I stared. My gaze flitted to the officer. *Did he strategically position himself to protect me?* I steeled myself and turned back to the blood smeared across the window. Clint's blood. One tomato-sized circle of crimson colored the glass like sponge paint, and three trails of red had dried while they dripped downward. *Where they pressed his face into the glass to cuff him?*

God, pick someone else. This can't be my life.

The officer shifted his weight. "Let me know how you're holding up."

"Every part of this feels like someone else's life." I inched closer to the car. "Am I allowed to touch the car?"

"Yes. Take anything you need."

I reached for the handle and retracted my hand. Blood coated the handle. Blood on the door. Blood on the fractured side mirror. I felt the officer studying me and shoved panic aside. I knew somehow, through the static of shock, I needed to empty the car myself to heal from a grief that hadn't reached me yet.

Metal crunched when I forced the dented driver's door open. Blood on the dashboard, the A/C and radio knobs. Blood on the gear shift and steering wheel.

On the passenger side floor, open cans and bottles of alcohol lay strewn beside a brochure for a spiritual retreat Clint intended to attend. Reality flayed me and I simultaneously felt nothing. I opened each door one by one as fast as my sluggish body would allow. Removing Kelly and Trinity's car seats required me to kneel in the chair to release the buckle. I huffed and grunted and nearly cried in frustration as the seat outmaneuvered me.

I felt cold air on my bare back and yanked my hoodie down. No need to add indecent exposure to the list of the Evans' weekend activities. I shifted my backside out of view and continued my losing battle with the car seat gods. Just as the officer offered assistance, I released the latch for the last car seat. Board books lay on the floor of the car. *I have nothing to put those in.*

I tossed the car seats in the Trailblazer and popped Clint's trunk open. An unzipped, black duffel held his dirty football gear. A leather communion kit rested next to the bag. I tossed the communion kit and the kids' books into the football duffel, sluffed through random papers and empty diet Mountain Dew bottles, and declared myself finished.

I left the impound lot and sped past thirteen miles of cornfields toward home—and Hardee's. When I lagged into Hardee's, Josh stood behind the counter. *Shoot.*

"Wow. Sam. You look awful."

I sighed. "You have a way with women, Josh."

His cheeks pinked. "Sorry."

Something inside me deflated, surrendered. "My husband's in jail, and he might have cancer." I shrugged, like I'd said something as ordinary as "my cat vomited on my favorite rug."

Josh touched the screen in front of him. "Frisco it is. I'll even let you eat fries today. Do you want fries or a side salad?"

The simple choice overwhelmed me. "I don't know."

The teenage boy reached into his back pocket and withdrew his black billfold. "My dad's been in and out of jail." He completed the order. When the drawer slid open, Josh slipped bills from his own wallet into the register.

Fifteen minutes later, I pulled up in front of my house, surprised to see my in-laws' car. I vaguely remembered calling Chuck on the way to the hospital. I glanced to my right and tilted my head with the ghost of a smile when I saw the dining room table. Hardee's bags, abandoned chocolate shakes, half-eaten cheeseburgers, and the dehydrated fries no one eats littered the surface.

Dawn sat in the living room to my left. Her weary gaze met mine. I followed the sound of my daughters' chittering. Two steps in, their Barbie-and-Duplo-and-Little People minefield came into sight.

I knelt to greet them with hugs, mustering casual cheer. "Daddy was in a car accident. He's okay." I stared over their heads at my in-laws.

"Daddy should be able to come home from … the hospital… Tuesday, we hope."

The girls' attention returned to the imaginary world they'd created.

Crisis averted, I maneuvered through Barbies toward the dining room. I swept the girls' lunch debris to one end of the table, creating space for myself, sunk into a chair, and opened the Hardee's bag Josh packed for me. Inside, I found a Frisco burger, fries, *and* a side salad. With Josh's thoughtful gesture, the tears finally came.

CHAPTER FOUR

Dear Clint,

I admire your strength, faith, and concern for others, even as you deal with your own illness.

Laura

CLINT, 1987
SAN DIEGO, CALIFORNIA

Five inches of bare ankle showed between the top of my frayed sneakers and the bottom of my new, Goodwill jeans. I tugged at the faded Hulk Hogan and Mr. T on my stretched-out T-shirt—to the pace of my locomotive heartbeat. *I'm not dressed right. This is my third school in eight months.*

I hated the Navy, and I hated the dumb school I attended on base. *I want to go home to North Dakota. I wish I'd eaten more Fruity Pebbles this morning. I'm still hungry. Why did Dad have to join the Navy?* I glanced past the laminated February calendar, out the window. *Palm trees.* I was still mad about December without snow.

The kid to my right frowned at me. The bold blues and greens on His shirt fit him like a glove. *Why is he looking at me? How much would a shirt from a real store cost? I wish my hair looked like his.*

"Clint," a woman's voice said.

I feel dumb. I'm not dressed right.

"Clint, right?"

Oh, the teacher is talking to me.

The young woman touched my desk. "Clint? Why don't you tell us something about yourself?"

"Um…" *I'm not good enough.* To my right, Perfect Hair waited to hear what the new kid in sloppy clothes could possibly have to offer. I ran my hand across my frizzy, brown hair. "My family moved from Texas. We lived with my grandpa on his horse ranch. I left my horse there. I miss her a lot. Her name is Black Beauty."

"Wow, Clint," said the teacher, moving toward the front of the room. "Sounds like you'll have some great stories."

Beside me, Perfect Hair nodded. His approval lit me up inside. *If I can be what other people want, people will like me. I wonder what lunch will be today.* Thoughts mercilessly whizzing through my brain created constant static. *I wish I'd eaten more Fruity Pebbles. What was my horse's name again? Hogan versus Piper's coming up!*

"Psst. Clint." Perfect Hair glanced at the teacher, who wrote "2+5=" in perfect penmanship, on the dark green chalkboard. Perfect Hair punched me in the arm. "Hey, Clint. A bunch of us are fighting Class Six at recess. Wanna come?"

My first invitation. Thank you, Black Beauty. "Is Class Six mean?"

"Nah. We fight for fun. They're the heels and we're the heroes."

I beamed at the wrestling reference.

"Devlin." Scolding my new friend with a single word, the teacher didn't turn around or skip a mathematical beat.

I grinned at Devlin and whispered, "I'm in."

For the next hour of class, I replayed my favorite wrestling match in my mind. Hulk Hogan in his gravelly voice threatening the safety of Andre the Giant while pointing to the World Heavyweight Title around his waist. I tightened my stomach, throwing ghost undercuts at my desk and watched the minute hand crawl from number to number. I imagined the bell ringing and shouldering my classmates like the mob of spectators at Madison Square Garden.

One minute before the bell rang, the teacher swished her hands together. Chalk dust flitted to the floor—the closest I'd come to a white

Christmas. "All right class, let's show Clint how well we line up in a quiet, single, file line."

The metal feet of my chair screeched against the floor when I shoved myself back from the desk and joined the line. My teacher drew a finger to her lips, reminding us to be silent. My whole body vibrated with energy while we wound through ten miles of hallways to get to the playground.

Then, with a quick slam of the exterior doors, freedom.

"Clint, this way. Devlin sprinted toward the far end of the playground.

Beyond the shadow of the school, yellow sunlight soaked into my skin. Rubber soles against concrete and heavy breathing drowned out the distant shouts and squeals of the other kids on the playground. Two by three, more boys gathered.

After a couple one-on-one brawls, Devlin grabbed my hand and thrust it into the air. "This is Clint, the new kid. Who wants to fight him?"

A few weeks later, in the same spot on the playground, Duke from Class Six and I stared one another down. My favorite WrestleMania shirt was torn and smeared with residue from the blacktop. My cheek stung.

Duke's palms slammed into my shoulders, and I toppled onto my butt. Classmates cheered. I hopped to my feet and brushed away the gravel embedded into my palms. I plowed into Duke, head-first, banding my arms around his sweaty waist. He landed on his back. The glare in his gray eyes told me we'd both stopped pretending. I straddled his body and punched him. My knuckles connected with the soft, fleshy part of his nose. Bone caved beneath my knuckles. Bright red blood spurted from his nostrils.

Duke screamed and grabbed his face.

Boys shouted.

Adult hands gripped my arms and yanked me off Duke.

My teacher's sweet smile faded when I appeared in the classroom doorway after returning from my suspension. "Take your seat, Mr. Evans."

I'd never heard the mechanical buzz of the fluorescent lights before. The room had never been quiet enough. My classmates' gazes followed me while I walked to my desk and made a joke. Several classmates laughed.

The teacher pointed to the back of the room. "Maybe the coat closet is a better place for you for now."

Sitting in the fleece-lined prison, I picked at a loose thread in my jeans.

"Devlin," my teacher said, "eyes front."

I glanced up and met the gaze of Rose. Her long, blonde ponytail hung straight down the middle of her back. The red, plaid bow at the top matched her dress.

"I'm sorry," she mouthed and spun in her seat before the teacher spotted her.

I leaned my head against the wall. My face burned, but this time, not from the road rash on my cheek. "Don't cry. They'll think you're a baby." Rose never got in trouble. Everybody liked her. Why couldn't I be more like Rose? *I want to be like Rose.*

I felt different, like people saw a stain on me. *I am always the one in the corner.* I felt like a good person, but I couldn't stop getting into trouble.

⌁

I dropped my backpack inside the front door. "Mom?"

"In here."

I followed the sound of her angry voice to the bedroom hallway and stepped over a heap of my clothing to get to the door. I rolled my eyes before she could see me.

"Your teacher called, Clint. I just," Mom shoved a large bin of my little brother Darry's toys across the floor, "don't know what to do with you."

With three boys in a three-bedroom house, my brothers and I took turns having our own room. Losing my room was my penalty for the fight and the suspension. "I try, Mom."

Her voice softened. "Oh, Clint. I know. Tell you what. If you can go two weeks—two weeks—without getting in trouble at school, I'll buy you the remote control car you've been staring at in the window of the drug store."

"Really?"

"Really."

I held my breath for two weeks, and Friday, my teacher sent a note home:

> Clint's behavior has been incredible these last two weeks. He's worked really hard and set a great example for the other students on how to be a good listener. You should be very, very proud of your son.

I don't think my mom expected me to succeed. So, I'm sure the money for the car likely came out of our grocery budget that week. But Mom kept her promise.

The next Monday I was relieved to get in trouble at school.

CLINT, PRESENT DAY

Few people had the patience for my ceaseless energy. My teachers tried, but I exhausted them. I had severe ADHD before anyone understood the diagnosis. Studies at the time believed stimulants counteracted the effects of hyperactivity. My mom fed me tons of Mountain Dew and caffeine because she didn't know any better.

I didn't understand money, but I understood we never had enough of it. My brothers and I joke about trips to Denny's because my dad would point to a certain place on the menu and say, "you can order from this section." We laughed, but as a child I believed I was only worth the items in the box.

I don't blame my parents for mistakes they made with me. They did their best. My parents' parents set lousy examples. My mom's dad passed out drunk every night in the living room chair. Her mom pretended that was normal and scolded the children whenever they raised questions. "Emotion" was a dirty word.

My dad's parents disappeared for two months at a time, leaving five teenagers and elementary-aged children in a trailer home to fend for themselves. Uphill both ways, barefoot in the snow, wasn't far from the truth for my dad, who lived miles beyond town. If he wanted to participate in extracurricular activities, he had to walk there and back himself.

A seven-year-old can't see the road map of choices. I didn't realize innocent fights on the playground would result in a bad reputation. The shame hovering over me darkened. First Grade Fight Club fights led to real fights, which I avoided for as long as possible.

Then, in ninth grade, I hit back. And once I started hitting, I didn't know how to stop.

CHAPTER FIVE

Dear Clint,

Sorry it took me so long to share my support and thoughts. You are missed and thought of often. Remember you are loved by many. No one is perfect. We all break at a certain point. My daughter asks for you daily. She sends greetings and dino-hugs. You are a great person. Please never forget that.

Erika

CLINT, SUNDAY, OCTOBER 1, 2017
NEW ULM, MINNESOTA

The officer turned left out of the hospital parking lot onto 5th Street and then right at the first stop sign. Rain dripped onto the car windows and any minute the pale gray sky would burst with a storm.

Cancer.

Did Sam say she would call my parents?

What will people at church think? God, I am such a hypocrite.

A park with a tall tunnel slide and a taller twisty slide came into view. *The girls love Harman Park. Oh, God. The girls. Sam. What is she going to tell them?*

The officer rode his brakes down the steep grade of Center Street. The four-story county jail faced Turner Hall, where the girls attended gymnastics classes each week in their cute, little leotards.

I'm such a piece of shit. The girls deserve so much better. Sam deserves better. Good thing I have cancer. Maybe it'll be quick.

A line of six single-stall garage doors blended into the backdrop of the building. Tan on tan. The officer stopped in front of one of the garage doors.

I don't want to die. I want to be there for my girls. I want to watch them grow up. I don't want them to grow up without a dad around like I did. God, please.

To the left of the door, a sign read: "Sally Port. Door 5." The metal garage door creaked upward.

Stark fluorescent light within the building blended with the hazy gray sky outside. The sally port looked like an empty garage. The low ceiling made of cement met with cinderblock walls painted tan.

The officer waited for the garage door to touch the concrete floor before opening my door.

"Hold your hands out, Mr. Evans."

"Thank you for not cuffing me in front of my wife."

"Everyone makes mistakes, Mr. Evans. We do our best to treat people with dignity here." He spanned his hand across my bald scalp and secured his other hand beneath my left armpit to help me stand. "Watch your head."

The room smelled like car exhaust and faintly of a nasty odor I couldn't quite place. A loud heater in the corner blew back the chill of the wet, autumn day.

I can't believe I'm going to jail. I want to die.

Two officers joined us—a man with dark hair and a woman about a head shorter than him, with short, blonde hair. Their badges were sewn onto their uniforms.

So, no one can use their badges as a weapon.

My gaze fell to their duty belts, expecting to see a gun. No gun, no taser, no stick. Only cuffs, leather gloves, and a ring of keys that rivaled the church janitor's set.

The female guard buzzed a door for entry, and the three officers escorted me to a box-sized room just off the sally port.

The bitter smell I couldn't place in the sally port permeated the walls. *Vomit and stale piss.* Still not quite sober, my stomach rolled over. I gagged. *Don't add to the smell.*

Two black foot silhouettes were painted on the floor, along with two black handprints, on the wall at chest height.

"Please place your hands and feet on the designated spot. Remove your shoes," the woman said. "Lift up one foot ... Now the other."

"Are you carrying any weapons?" The male intake officer asked.

"No, sir."

His hands started beneath my arms. He patted my waist and hips. His search slid down to my ankles and up toward my inner thigh. The hem of my boxers bunched beneath the burgundy scrubs the hospital provided.

Nurses had dressed me the previous night, in clothes that were not my own. *What underwear am I wearing?*

I closed my eyes against stinging tears, wondering when the humiliation would end. Not any time soon. "I want to die."

"What did you say, Mr. Evans?" the female officer asked.

"I have Stage IV cancer. I want to die."

"Well, we're not going to let that happen here."

"Oh, I know. But my wife doesn't need to watch me die."

They finished patting me down. Turning up nothing in the search, the arresting officer uncuffed me, and the three officers and I entered a small elevator.

The doors parted, revealing a larger room with the same tan walls.

Cautiously, I inhaled. *Dirty socks.* The air smelled better, not great.

The officers motioned for me to sit in an office chair on one side of a table. My arresting officer sat opposite me, glancing at a computer screen.

Cancer. I can't be here.

"Mr. Evans," he said.

I have to figure out the cancer. I can't abandon my family. God, I'm so sorry. A sob escaped against my will. I choked it back.

"Mr. Evans ... Mr. Evans, would you like me to call a pastor to come speak with you?"

I guffawed at the irony. "Yeah, probably."

"I can call if you'd like," said the female officer. "When we finish booking."

My arresting officer glanced at her. "Thanks." Then he refocused on me. "Have you ever been to state or federal prison?"

"No."

"Have you ever been to jail?"

"Yes."

"Are you now, or have you ever been affiliated with any gangs?"

"No." *Tried once. It didn't take.*

"What is your current profession?"

I exhaled. "Pastor."

"Mr. Evans, are you suicidal?"

My breath shook. *Sunday morning. I'm a pastor in jail. I have Stage IV cancer and shame so insurmountable not even the Hulk could escape from it.*

Legion dropped down in the seat beside me, folded his arms across his chest, and leaned back, sneering. "The world would be better off without you in it."

"Mr. Evans, are you suicidal?"

"I might be."

I looked between the officers. I felt tears collecting at the rims of my eyes. "I'm sorry. I couldn't take it anymore."

"We'll get through this," said my arresting officer. "Everyone here wants the best for you."

Shame compressed my head and shoulders like a building worth of cinder blocks. I pressed my hand against my mouth. "Okay."

"Just a few more questions, and they'll get you squared away."

Anxiety speared me. "Please don't put me with other people right now."

"Not a problem," said the female officer, "Mr. Evans." The arresting officer asked, "Do you have any medical conditions we should know about?"

We'd told him about the diagnosis at the hospital, but duty required him to ask the question. "Yes. I found out this morning I have Stage IV cancer."

The female officer's jaw dropped. "As soon as we finish here, I'll find you a local pastor."

Good luck. They're all where they're supposed to be this morning—behind the pulpit.

"Thank you."

After I got fingerprinted, I showered. *At least the shower stall is private.* I dropped my guard behind the curtain and felt safe enough to weep. I whispered, "Oh, God, I'm so sorry. I've made a fool of you." And sobbed. "I'm such a hypocrite."

I toweled off. My shoulder blades reminded me I'd been in a car wreck the previous day while I wove my arms through the holes of the bright orange T-shirt. I shook my head. Orange socks, orange underwear, and a thicker version of scrubs, grayish-blue in color.

The male correctional officer held a mesh bag. "Place your belongings in here."

I dropped the burgundy scrubs and yellow socks into the bag. Nothing I wore into the jail, except my boxers belonged to me.

"Naked I came from my mother's womb and naked I will depart" (Job 1:21).

I felt God stripping me of my entire identity. *I am nothing.* I slipped into the jail's version of blue Vans and stood against the wall for my mug shot. *Everyone will see this.*

The officers produced two tan blankets—the kind dry feet catch on— at the bottom of a stack of blue sheets, two hand towels and a wash rag. They supplied a spare change of clothes and shower shoes and led me through a narrow hallway to the holding cell on the lowest level.

"No inmates will see you here," the female officer said. "My pastor is on her way." Her brow creased. "She hung up before I finished talking."

"Who's your pastor?" I asked.

"Pastor Taylor."

Adrenaline reverberated through every cell in my body. *"Jo Anne Taylor?"*

"You know her?"

My stomach rolled again, not from alcohol or foul stink. Jo Anne and her husband hosted me, Sam, and the girls for dinner over the summer. I'd personally wished her a "Happy 29th birthday" for the past three years. Continuing education classes, youth retreats and events. Jokes no one else understood. United Methodist pastors formed a quirky extended family, complete with drama, trauma, and beauty, and Jo Anne and I were part of that same family.

Dread doused me at the thought of having to face her. "I know her."

The male officer spoke into the mic on his shoulder and the holding cell door clicked open. The room held a single bed. A metal one-foot by two-foot table and chair were bolted to the wall, near a metal toilet and sink in one. A shelf that might hold the weight of a book.

"We'll be checking on you every fifteen minutes," said the male officer.

I learned later that correctional officers made rounds every thirty minutes— unless they place someone on suicide watch.

The bomb-proof metal door slammed behind me, trapping me with my worst enemy. Me. *This world would be better off without me in it.* I laid on the flimsy mattress.

The door buzzed.

I shot up from the bed. "Awake. I'm awake."

"Mr. Evans," said the correctional officer, "Pastor Taylor is here to see you."

Officers escorted me to the Intoxalizer Room and sat me down at a steel table. Jo Anne entered. I tried to look at her, but my gaze dropped to the table.

She sat. "So. ... What's going on?"

Her question popped the cork of a champagne bottle. "I drove home after football and stopped to buy vodka. I couldn't take it anymore. I drank the whole thing before I hit New Ulm ..." I rocked back and forth in a rhythmic motion while I spoke, helpless to the ADHD and shame that churned my thoughts.

Garbled words tumbled out faster than I could articulate them. I wasn't 100 percent sober while I spoke to her, which didn't help. "Flandrau State

Park … Cottonwood River. I couldn't keep the driver's door closed. This morning in the hospital, they told me I have Stage IV cancer."

Jo Anne heard the story first and the details were a jumbled wreck. To her credit, she just let me blather. From her ministry as a pastor, and working in collections in her previous life, Jo Anne knew how to listen to someone in crisis. When to talk and when not to.

"I'm a pastor, drunk in jail on a Sunday morning, instead of preaching. I'm a thirty-six-year-old man who just found out he has cancer. Instead of crying with my wife, who's furious at me, or hugging my children, or calling friends and family, I am trapped behind bars with a legion of old demons reminding me I am a low-down piece of shit. I ruined everything. Everything is ruined.

With dry humor, she said, "How very Isaiah 6[1] of you."

I jerked my head up and studied her face. Zero anger or disappointment. Her smile didn't reach her eyes, but she was smiling. She still loved me? That confused the hell out of me. *I haven't ruined everything?*

"Clint, you are God's beloved child."

I squeezed my eyes shut on her words, trapping in the truth she spoke over me, aching to believe her.

"Can you make it through the next hour?"

I choked out the words. "I don't know."

Her warm hands grasped my wrists. "Promise me you'll make it through the next hour. I'll call Fred. He'll come."

Fred, our boss, but part of that same quirky family.

"He cares about you. He'll come. God is doing something crazy here, Clint. He isn't done with you yet. You're still alive and there's a reason for that."

"I didn't hurt anyone last night."

"There's a reason for that too."

"Let's pray," said Jo Anne. "Dear God, thank you for sparing Clint last night and for showing us the potential cancer. We trust you will

---

1 "Woe to me!" I cried. "I am ruined! For I am a man of unclean lips, and I live among a people of unclean lips, and my eyes have seen the King, the LORD Almighty." *Isaiah 6:5 NIV.*

work all things for your good. Be with Clint in these moments. Grant him peace and strength beyond his wildest understanding. Help him look forward to how you're moving, with eager anticipation. All this we pray in your name. Amen."

"Amen." My voice cracked with emotion. "Thank you, Jo Anne."

"Anytime, Clint."

We both stood.

"Well, I'll try not to make a habit of this situation."

"Probably best."

I saw her for the first time. Dirt smudges covered the front of her T-shirt and shorts. Dark residue coated the undersides of her fingernails. She'd recklessly abandoned whatever project she'd been working on and rushed to jail.

Because it was me.

⌖

Tuesday morning, correctional officers escorted twenty of us to the courthouse connected to the jail. We sat behind a partitioned wall that formed a hallway along the courtroom.

The officer hooked his thumbs on his belt. "You'll be summoned one by one. The judge typically goes in alphabetical order from A-Z."

Evans. I'd be one of the first. I shoved my anxiety away. Tried to, anyway.

"Hey, man, Clint, right?" said the guy across from me. "Your words saved my life yesterday. You're the only one who's ever helped me believe this world might be better with me in it. I'll keep my promise to you. I ain't gonna take my own life."

"Keep it down, gentlemen."

The officer sounded reluctant to enforce the rule.

"Zimmerman," called the bailiff.

One officer raised his eyebrows. "I guess were going Z to A today."

Zimmerman shot to his feet. "See ya later, suckers."

"Clint Evans?" We all turned toward the sound of my name. A large man in a sharp suit entered the hallway from the courtroom.

I raised my cuffed hands. I wouldn't have been more surprised if Jesus Himself called my name. "I'm Clint."

He walked down the short hall. "My name is Greg. I'm your attorney."

"Dude, how'd you get a fancy, shmancy lawyer already?" the guy across from me asked.

I couldn't have answered if I wanted to. A powerful surge of emotion rushed through me. Confused me. Hope felt out of place considering my situation, but it thrummed against my chest all the same.

The other inmates cast sidelong glances.

"What makes him so special?" another guy asked.

All my life, people banished me to spaces where they wouldn't have to deal with my obnoxious behavior. Before Jo Anne two days prior, I couldn't recall a time someone stepped beyond the margins looking *for* me. *Someone's in my corner?*

Greg lowered himself into the chair next to me. "We don't have much time. Your wife—beautiful person, by the way ..."

Again, I felt the jealous stares of the others.

"Told me your last offense happened in 2006, eleven years ago, but you weren't driving. You'd pulled over to sleep it off. Correct?"

"Uh ... yeah."

One by one, inmates disappeared. I heard the judge speaking with them on the other side of the wall, but I paid little attention and had no concept of time.

"The judge is calling for Clint Evans," the bailiff said.

Greg rose and waddled toward the bailiff's summons.

Five minutes later, Greg returned. Beads of sweat dotted his forehead. "I bought us some time." He dove into the contents of my file.

When I was the last inmate in the narrow hall, the bailiff called my name several times, each time with growing impatience.

Greg and I stood and scurried past the wall into the courtroom. My gaze flickered to the court spectators, and my steps faltered.

Not one *in my corner. Many.*

Part Two

But Joseph said to them, "Don't be afraid. Am I
in the place of God? You intended to harm me,
but God intended it for good to accomplish what
is now being done, the saving of many lives.

Genesis 50:18-20 NIV

CHAPTER SIX

Pastor Clint,

We're sorry to hear about your health problems and pray treatment is successful. We also pray for leniency in your legal matters.

Thank you for all you did for my mom through all her health issues. It meant so much to us, and I know she always appreciated your visits to her apartment for communion.

I pray for you and your family and a fair and speedy resolution so you can move on and into what God has planned for you next. We have *all* fallen short, and I pray your church families remember this and support you to the conclusion.

Thanks again for taking such good care of my mom.

G&J

SAM, SUNDAY, OCTOBER 1, 2017
TWO DAYS PRIOR TO CLINT'S COURT APPEARANCE

Sunday night, after I'd gotten home from the impound lot, my cousin, Debi, called again. I stepped outside and wandered around the back lawn. The cold grass felt refreshing on my bare feet.

"I prayed the church services will go well this morning," she said, "and the church will support Clint."

I headed a dead rose. "Oh, the services are over, and they did, and they are."

"Great. I'm also praying he'll get the legal support he needs."

"He does. One of the men from our church is a retired prosecutor. He has all sorts of connections."

"I'm also praying jail won't interfere with the medical help he needs."

"The officers assured us this morning, it won't."

"Well, then what the heck am I wasting my time praying for? I could be watching TV."

I grinned. "Thanks."

"You're welcome."

My friend, Jo Anne, called a few minutes later. "A woman who works at the jail is a member of my church. It's not odd, Sam, for her to call me and let me know when someone needs a pastoral visit."

Pastors have VIP passes to jails and hospitals. I couldn't see my husband in jail until Monday morning, but visiting hour restrictions didn't apply to most of Clint's friends.

"I'd been in the backyard, barefoot and gardening," Jo Anne said. "My church member said, 'We have a Methodist man from Sleepy Eye here requesting a clergy visit.'"

"Oh," I told her, "well then he needs to talk to Clint Evans. Let me get you his number."

While I scrolled through my contact list, she said, 'The man in jail *is* Clint Evans. He ...'

"I paused for a heartbeat. 'Don't explain. I'll be right there.' I ran into the house shouting Bruce's name and yelled down the stairs into the basement. 'I gotta go. Clint's in jail!' I'm not sure if he heard me because I didn't wait for an answer." Her tone blended humor and gentleness. "Sam, I have never put my shoes on so fast."

We laughed together, a gift. Then I asked, "How was he?"

"Broken."

She described rainbow bruises forming beneath his eyes, his silence, his sagging posture.

I wanted to ask her what he'd said, but she'd never breach his confidence.

"Sam, we'll get through this. You are not alone."

I received so many calls throughout the day. And texts. And social media messages. And emails. So much love from family and church members that I powered off my phone.

The church had been instructed by the district superintendent not to speak to our family until the legal matters were settled. Two women went the "ask forgiveness rather than permission" route.

Erin, who'd taken the girls to church that morning, came to the house long enough to hand me a tub of cheesecake filling and a can of whipped cream. Then she left.

Another church member knocked on the door while the girls and I ate dinner. The interruption annoyed me. I didn't want to talk. I didn't know what to say. She wrapped her arms around me in a giant hug, told me she loved me, and left. Best. Hug. Ever.

I asked Clint's mom to spend the night. After I tucked the girls in, I sunk onto the couch beside her. She spoke on the phone with Clint's younger brother, Korey, in Brooklyn. I'd told the family, "When the doctors scanned for internal bleeding from the accident, they found potential cancer."

"Here. Talk to Sam." She passed me the phone.

"Clint has internal bleeding?" Korey asked.

"What? No." I pinched the bridge of my nose. "Who told you *that?* Doctors scanned for broken bones and internal bleeding but found nothing. And if he does have cancer, then this accident saved his life."

"Right, because who says, it's Friday, I think I'll go get a CAT scan."

"Right." I liked Korey's joke, so I planned to use it later.

My phone dinged with a notification. I stared at the screen.

Sam. Are you okay?"

Nope.

I knew this friend through a mom's group, not our church. No news stories linked Clint to the incident—yet. I thought I had another day before the news went public.

How did you find out?

> Someone tagged him in an article
> about the accident. The article didn't
> have his name, but after I saw the
> tag, I checked the jail roster.

Checking the jail roster—that's a thing? Embarrassment ignited every red blood cell in my body. Did people in small towns read the jail roster for fun? *So-and-so hasn't called me back in two days. It couldn't be because she's avoiding me because I was rude. Something bad must have happened. Oh, wait. I know. Let me check … the jail roster.*

My sarcastic thoughts gave way to static. *Buffering…. buffering.* The words finally computed and despair coursed through me.

> Please don't say anything to anyone.

> Oh, no Sam. I wanted to see if you
> were okay.

I imagined her standing before a gilded treasure chest with the glittering fortune of gossip. My insecurity heard her telling other people, "I figured it out right away. I checked *the jail roster.* Then I texted Sam to check on her."

I bowed out of the conversation with her, called a friend from church, and told her about the tagged article. While we spoke, she investigated. "'It's a fake account."

"What?"

"It's a fake Facebook account. This person's Facebook name is 'Aunt B.' There is no profile picture and no friends listed. And the bio information—born in, works at, is from—is all from different states."

"So, someone set up a fake Facebook account to tag Clint in the article?"

"I think so."

"How could someone be so malicious?" I snorted. "Maybe Satan set up the account. Aunt Beelzebub."

She laughed.

An unjustifiable peace rushed through me. "The accident didn't kill him," I said. "And he didn't kill anyone else. The alcohol didn't kill him. And we found out about the potential cancer. Satan's scrambling to see what else he can do."

"I'm going to report this acco—"

The line went dead.

I tried to call her back, but the call went to voicemail. I attempted several more times with no answer.

An hour later, she called me back.

"There you are," I said.

"The second I tried to report the bogus account, my phone died. I couldn't get it to charge beyond 1 percent for twenty minutes."

What is going on?

I slept soundly until 3:00 a.m. when Trinity woke up screaming for water. But I'd only received two hours of sleep the night before, so, cheers to progress.

The next morning, Monday, Heather texted. She often crashed our Methodist gatherings. "Am I your favorite Catholic, Clint?" she asked once.

"You're my favorite *living* Catholic," he said.

Clint devoured works by Henri Nouwen, St. Francis, Augustine, Thomas Aquinas, and Pope Benedict XVI, which always made me laugh. His bio would read: "Interests Include: football, ESPN, professional wrestling, and books by Catholic theologians.

I told Heather about Aunt Beelzebub and our friend's phone dying. Her response:

> Wanna hear something freaky? Last night I dreamed about the devil. I never dream about the devil.

Regardless, I called Erin. "You're not gonna believe this …" except I knew she would. I thought she would. Her silence after I told her about the Facebook account scared me. "Erin?"

More silence, then finally, "Um, Sam. Satan sat behind the wheel the night of the accident."

I swear to you on the life of my firstborn child, I am not making this conversation up. At least if the judge institutionalized me for insanity, Erin and I could room together. "Ok, Erin. Maybe a couple more details."

"When I thought about the car accident, I got this vision of Satan behind the wheel. As soon as the cops stopped him, while they cuffed him, Satan jumped out of the car and laughed and pointed at Clint and mocked him in a sing-song voice."

I took my turn with silence. I never repeated the conversation to Clint. I kept that detail from the judge, as well. I didn't foresee "Satan did it" holding up in court. "Your Honor, my husband is innocent of all charges after all."

Yet the conversations about Aunt Beelzebub's Facebook account, Heather's dream, and Erin's vision synched together like puzzle pieces.

A battle waged beyond the scope of what we saw. In addition, Erin's vision granted me a vivid portrayal of the battle every addict fights against demons. And my grace grew for the addict.

CHAPTER SEVEN

Clint,

    I love you dearly. I am so proud of you and all you accomplished. You know your dad and I have always loved you, but in our younger, mixed-up years, we failed you in a lot of areas. When I think about how my father went into alcohol treatment sixteen times, I'm grateful for how far I've come and know I have a lot more work to do toward healing. You're a great son to have and I am so very glad God chose me as your mother. I'm so glad for all the healing taking place in our lives.

    Love you with all my heart,

Mom

CLINT, 1990
SAN DIEGO

Mom yelled from the kitchen. "Clint. I'm going to be late for work."

"Peeing, Mom." *'Cuz I'm gonna have to hold it for eight hours today.*

"You better not get any on the toilet seat. Hurry!"

I rolled my eyes. *It's not like I can control the speed.* I ran a piece of toilet paper across the seat, just in case. I flushed the toilet, ran water over my hands, and zipped up my fly on the fly. In the car, I needed every one of my nine-year-old muscles to wrench the door shut on my parents' light blue Plymouth Acclaim.

"It's gonna be a late night at the sitter's tonight," Mom told my two younger brothers and me, careening a corner on two wheels. Our bodies jerked to the side.

I'm not sure Mom ever took a driver's ed course. I think one day she just got behind the wheel of a car. *Wait.* My heart skipped a beat. *Late night? Oh, no.* "Can you please come get us early?"

"Clint, stop. Your dad's ship is gone for another three months. I'm doing the best I can."

I know. That's why I haven't told you.

My heart pounded when the car turned up Jo's block and picked up pace when we slowed to a stop in front of her house. Jo, a scant woman with a cropped head of brown-and-gray curls, stood by her front door and squinted against the early morning sun. Her puckered lips reminded me of Cruella de Vil. She pinched a cigarette between two fingers. Smoke clouded around her face.

The car jerked to a stop.

"Okay, boys. Out. I love you. Behave."

The tires screeched, and Mom's car vanished around the corner.

I trudged toward the front door behind my brothers. My shoelaces dragged on the sidewalk. She let them walk into the house but grabbed me by the arm. "What? Aren't you going to say hello?" She squeezed enough for it to hurt.

"Hello, Jo."

"Rude little boy," she muttered. "If your brothers misbehave today, you'll be punished."

I shook my arm free, weaved through the house, and wandered out into the backyard. The fence loomed over me on all sides, casting a shadow over a large portion of the yard. *Only twelve hours to go.*

I imagined the wooden fence as the rubber ropes of a wresting ring and ran full speed toward the fence. Right before impact. I bounced off the ropes and came chest to chest with "Macho Man" Randy Savage. In three quick moves, I leg-dropped him and pinned him to the ground. Spectators' applause filled the arena, and they cheered for me by name. I jumped to my feet and ran at the ropes. *Only 11 hours and 55 minutes to go.*

After winning the WWF Heavyweight World Championship, the

backyard transformed into Candlestick Park, home of the San Francisco 49ers. I entered the field and pumped one fist into the air as cheers erupted and melded into a familiar roar. With the bright, white "16" on my burgundy jersey, I was invincible.

"Bang. Niner Gang. Bang. Niner Gang," fans shouted. Suddenly transported to the opponents' two-yard line following a long kickoff return, I curled my fingers into natural grass, reviewing the first play of the game.

I refused to look at 'the man with the hands.' I wouldn't give the Rams glaring down Jesse Sapolu and the rest of the O-line any indication. But I knew Jerry Rice wasn't looking at me, and I nodded straight ahead. All-Pro Mr. "80" knew I'd throw to him on a fade route to the corner of the end zone. "Hut. Hut."

Sapolu snapped the ball. I shuffled three steps backward, slanted right, released the ball, and watched it sail through the air.

"Clint, are you coming in for lunch, or not?"

The stadium evaporated. For the first time in hours, the yellowed grass reappeared. I hung my head. "Yes, Jo."

Inside, the air conditioning felt like heaven.

A Capri-Sun waited for me. *If I drink, I'll have to pee.* But my mouth felt like cotton. I stared at the sweating drink. Thirst won over. While Jo patiently poked the straws through my brothers' drink boxes, I struggled to poke the straw through the foil hole. I shoved really hard. The foil give way. *Pop.* Juice spurted everywhere. *Shoot.*

"Clint," Jo shouted, "you're nine years old now. Can't you do anything right?"

I grabbed a paper towel and swiped up the mess. *Stupid. Stupid, stupid, stupid. You're so stupid, Clint.* Finally at the table, I inhaled my generic macaroni and cheese and hot dog at the speed of light, dumped my dishes into the sink, and disappeared outside. A couple hours later, my abdomen ached. *My pecker's going to explode if I don't pee soon.* I refused to use the bathroom.

The phone rang.

Thank God.

I knew exactly how far the kitchen phone cord reached. I hid in corner of the yard where the house met the fence. Desperate, I whispered, "Come, on, hurry."

The back door creaked open. I shoved it back in my pants and whipped my zipper up.

"Whatcha doin', Gent?"

My little brother Darry couldn't pronounce my name the right way.

"You scared the tar out of me." I took a huge breath. "I was, uh, looking at these rocks. Wanna look at rocks with me?"

"Nah. Jo's givin' us candy. Wan some?"

My eyes widened. "Yeah, I want some."

I burst into the house behind Darry. I'd forgotten. I'd absolutely forgotten how much Jo hated me. "You." The veins in her forehead popped out. "Bathroom. Now."

"It wasn't me." I wrung my hands. "I haven't even been in the house all day."

"Come with me."

She stormed into her precious bathroom and pointed an accusing finger at the toilet seat. "There is urine all over the seat. You wanna tell me how the pee got there?"

"It wasn't me this time, Jo, I swear!"

Her oldest son caught my eye from the hallway beyond her sight and smirked.

"Clean this up and then maybe I'll give you dinner, you filthy slob. No wonder your mom leaves you here all day long. She probably hates you. Hates what you do to her house. You're a pig. You're a stupid pig. You clean up this pee, you pig."

I stared at the floor, forcing tears back.

"Look at me."

I refused.

"Look at me, stupid." She wretched my head up and smashed it against the wall. My ears rang and for a moment darkness clouded my vision. "You will clean this shit up, you piece of shit. We like your brothers. We just don't like *you*."

I fumbled with the cleaning supplies she shoved into my hands. She shouldered past me and knocked me into the wall.

Tears streamed down my cheeks. I knelt on the floor and scrubbed the toilet. When I finished, everyone else sat at the table. I walked toward the empty chair.

"Uh-uh." Jo grabbed my collar and twisted it in her fist. "Not you. Slobs get to face the corner and think about what they've done."

My eyes burned, but I would not give her the satisfaction of tears. When Jo turned her back, someone whipped a chicken nugget at my head. I spun.

Her son's eyes gleamed with arrogance.

"Did I say you could turn around?"

I snapped my head back into the corner. My stomach groaned.

After a few minutes, silverware rattled. Chairs scraped against the floor.

"Alright, Clint. You can eat now."

I turned around. She'd placed only three chicken nuggets and five fries on my plate. She scraped a mound of food from her son's plate into the garbage. "Pigs only get leftovers."

In the other room, the box television with wooden trim sat on the floor and took up most of one wall. My brothers sat cross-legged on the brown shag carpet. Their eyes were glued to *G.I. Joe* on TV, and huge suckers puffed out their small cheeks.

After dinner, I cleared my dishes and sat next to my brothers. I knew better than to ask for candy.

Or use the bathroom.

Or ask for more food.

Or play with her sons' toys.

Jo's husband hated me more than Jo did. When he stomped through the door after work, I knew better than to look at him, or talk to him. Or breathe his oxygen.

At bedtime, Jo dropped sleeping bags and pillows onto the floor in the living room. She turned on *Texas Chainsaw Massacre,* and I knew better than to try to change the channel or adjust the volume.

My brothers fell asleep, but the music blared in my ears. I covered my face with a pillow. *Mom, please hurry.*

Finally, finally, the doorbell rang.

I jumped up, swung the door open and collided with my mother's waist. Her arms banded around me. I slid into the car before my brothers even got their shoes on.

"So, how was it today?" Mom asked.

"Fine, Mom," I said. "Everything was fine."

CLINT, 1995

Jo's abusive treatment of me went on for more than a year before I told my mom. She spoke to that monster Jo, and we never saw Cruella de Vil again.

I found out later Jo told other moms in the community not to let their kids play with me. I found out the hard way. My brothers were invited to parties, and parents specifically excluded me.

My low self-esteem made me an easy target. After three years of watching me get pushed around, my dad had enough. "Clint, you need to fight back." The next day, in sixth grade, a kid harassed me, so I knocked him off the stage. He left school with a bloody nose. I left with a suspension.

In eighth grade, I beat a kid up for mocking my weight. Violent flashes appeared like foreshadows. I'd take the bullying and harassment. Take it and take it—and then explode. By ninth grade, I stopped caring. I skipped more than thirty days of school. Nothing soothed the ache in my chest, the longing to be loved. I wanted to be done. I wanted to feel normal, fit in. Instead, I accepted the fact that I would be a lowdown piece of shit.

By ninth grade, nothing was sacred. Nowhere was safe. The Navy recruitment office transferred Dad to Washington. Before the move, Mom showed us photos of snow-peaked Mt. Rainer and lush green trees for hundreds of miles. The Navy dropped our suitcases in barren, brown Kennewick, Washington, and my joyful heart belly-flopped into my stomach.

My dad's sister lived five hours away, near Portland. But saying, "only five hours away," felt much shorter than the reality of the distance.

Rich kids made fun of the way I dressed. We'd moved from cultured San Diego to gang-infested Kennewick in the middle of the school year and the curriculums didn't align. Other students viewed me as the fat, poor, stupid kid, and I didn't really make friends.

In ninth grade when I dragged my fingertips across the uniform bumps on the surface of a basketball. The desert sun, the only good thing about Kennewick, beat down onto the blacktop. I dropped the ball to the pavement. *Thump.*

It bounced up to my right hand. I pressed it down again. *Thump.*

Left hand. *Thump.*

Right hand.

Left, right. I dodged an imaginary opponent. My legs gained momentum when I dashed toward the hoop.

"Hey, kid. This is our court."

I grabbed the ball and tucked it beneath my arm.

Two boys, with one or two years on my fourteen, stared me down. They wore green basketball jerseys with a yellow "SONIC" stretched across the front. Their black bandannas grabbed my attention. "Kid, you gotta go. It's our turn." One boy wore his bandanna like a headband. The second boy wore his black bandanna around his ankle, above his black high top. *Hispanic gang.*

So, I understood the threat when I said, "No. Go use the net on the other side." I waved toward the empty hoop at the far end.

"We want this one."

I raised to my full height. "No."

The one on the left bumped his chest into mine. "What'cha gonna do, little man? Gonna make us leave?" The second boy stepped closer and sneered.

"Leave me alone."

"Make us."

I'm gonna need both hands. I dropped my ball, lunged toward them, and fisted their smooth, nylon jerseys in each of my hands.

They looked down at my hands and chuckled condescendingly. "Yeah, right, like you're gonna …"

I tightened my grip, narrowed my eyes. I felt myself grow taller. White spit strafed from my mouth and landed on their faces. I gritted my teeth, my voice deeper than normal. "You posers really wanna fight? I'll fight. I'll slam you *both* to the pavement."

Their jaws slackened.

"You picked on the wrong guy."

I glared between them, released their jerseys, and shoved them back. They must have seen in my eyes what I felt shaking my entire body. Rage. Their next steps were backward away from me. I stood resolute until they turned their backs to me and retreated.

Fury coursed through me. The adrenaline. My pent-up breath sounded like a deflating basketball. Sweat tickled my forehead. I jogged toward the fence in the shadow of a nearby spruce and rubbed my fingers along the uniform bumps and the smooth, black spine. *Thump. Thump. Thump.* Imaginary opponents came into focus. I felt ten feet tall, like I could just tip the ball into the net. *No one's ever gonna fuck with me again.*

Thump. Thump. Thump.

One, two steps. My feet left the ground for the shot. Nothing but chain-link net.

CHAPTER EIGHT

I will never, never forget Pastor Clint. His message of love will stay with me forever. His fortitude was amazing.

Janet Rieke

SAM, MONDAY, OCTOBER 2, 2017, TWO DAYS AFTER THE ACCIDENT
NEW ULM, MINNESOTA

He tipped the hunter-orange chair against the brick wall of the jail's waiting room. The lanky stranger gathered his scraggly, rust-colored hair into a ponytail.

"Feels weird to be on this side of things," he said to his girlfriend.

My chair faced a heavy metal door locked by an electronic keypad. *How did I get here?*

The couple sat with their backs to a strip of windows. His girlfriend's shirt squeezed her rounded figure and showcased the outline of her three-sizes-too-small bra.

"I'm here to see my nephew," the man told me. His rust-colored beard came to a point above the collar of his flannel.

I shifted and clutched the handles of my purse with both hands. I felt overdressed in a button-down shirt and business slacks, like the uptight character from a Rom-com light-years from her comfort zone. My haughty judgment deflated on a breath. We sat in the same room at the same time for the same reason. "My husband," I said. *I'm at the jail to visit my husband*—a statement no one should ever have to articulate.

An officer emerged from behind the vaulted door and allowed the man and me to enter.

The bathroom-sized space was constructed of gray, cement walls to my right and in front of me. To the left, Clint and a stranger sat behind a thick pane of plastic, with an officer standing behind them. The flannel-clad uncle took the seat in front of his nephew and slid into conversation with ease.

I lowered into the chair and noted all the people present for my private conversation.

What the heck and I supposed to say? The colloquial "Hey, how're ya?" didn't fit with armed policemen glaring down at me with pinched eyebrows.

I stared at Clint through the glass. Bruises formed beneath his abrasions overnight and his face looked hideous. His posture reminded me of a beaten dog who knew better than to fight back.

What do I say? I thought of the visitor log. "I saw Nip's name on the visitor log."

The head of our church staff relations committee prosecuted DWI's for thirty-seven years in our county. Having retired only two years prior, Nip still had many connections. He'd called me the previous night and said, "You want Greg as a public defender. He even beat me a few times."

Clint brought his fist to his forehead. "Yeah, he walked me through what will happen in the courtroom tomorrow. He said one of the charges—a felony hit-and-run—is pretty serious." Tears choked his apology, and he pinched the bridge of his black-and-blue nose. "I'm so sorry."

Broken. Jo Anne's voice echoed.

My heart filled with pity. "We'll figure this out. One thing at a time. We're not alone. God's in this." I knew the words were true, even if I didn't believe myself in the moment.

I still felt like he cheated on me with alcohol, and a question mark ended my decision about our marriage. So, I stuck to promises I could keep. "I'm right here. And I'll be in court tomorrow."

Before we finished our conversation, a correctional officer declared the visit over. Guards on both sides of the glass ushered everyone out of the room.

I returned home to find my entire living room rearranged. My mother-in-law had draped every tablecloth and placemat she could find over end tables, the hope chest, and even the buffet. A picture I'd displayed on the buffet hung on the wall.

I hung my coat on the hook near the door. I noticed three plastic M&M toys displayed on a shelf above the hooks. I closed my eyes and groaned inwardly. Who rearranges someone else's house? Fury would have required energy. "As soon as you leave, the M&Ms are coming down." *And the tablecloths and holy cow, the placemats-turned-doilies. What is this, the 1950s?*

"They're cute!"

"They're coming down."

"I know." She laughed.

I stepped on the scale that night. I lost three pounds in two days despite eating cheesecake and French fries. We'll count our blessings where we can.

CHAPTER NINE

Dear Mom and Dad,

    I know you wanted the very best for me. I know you did the absolute best you could with the cards you held. As a father, I've learned how difficult adult choices can be. I felt your love for me when I was a child, and I feel it now. Nothing needs to be forgiven. My empathy and grace for others are because of you. I'm grateful to be your son. I pray you'll cherish joy. I love you so much.

Love always,

Clint

CLINT, 1994
KENNEWICK, WASHINGTON

Kennewick sucked.

Low cost was always my parents' main priority in choosing housing. If one place allowed pets and the next place didn't, our parents surrendered our animals.

Nothing sacred.

That's not what happened to my favorite dog, Emmitt, though. I named him Emmitt because he ran like Emmitt Smith of the Dallas Cowboys. Emmitt ran a pattern right into the middle of our busy street and collided with a car speeding by. The impact splattered him all over the pavement. I watched whole thing.

I made friends with a kid named Clint that no one in my family liked. Clint witnessed a murder. Later, he and I played with the body chalk.

Nothing sacred. Nothing safe.

My parents made life-altering decisions on a whim. They moved from place to place and job to job. My dad worked in Wyoming for awhile, chasing income. My mom went from zero religion to "Ninja Turtles are demonic" and threw out our favorite toys.

Mom experienced true Christian community in San Diego, and I honestly don't think she's felt connected to church for more than twenty-five years. Mom and Dad would attend one church. Dad would start making friends and attending men's study groups. After a few months, Mom found reasons not to like the church and stop attending.

When I was a child, though, holy church batman. Every time a pastor made an altar call invitation, my mom forced me to go forward to accept Christ—just to be sure I got it right. Relationship with Jesus is actually a one-and-done thing. I experienced enough prayer to last a lifetime.

Church wasn't Mom's only impulsive decision. My parents decided to separate. They'd split assets and living arrangements. My mom moved me and my brothers back to Minot the summer between seventh and eighth grade, declaring she and my dad were getting a divorce. I trailed Mom into welfare offices while she calculated the costs of single parenting. Then, one day, she said, "Just kidding, we're going to stay together." And she moved us back to Kennewick.

Every time they separated or moved, my mom blamed me. And every time my parents changed course, my brothers and I flapped in the wind, mercilessly in tow. My self-esteem and confidence took hit after hit.

Though this isn't accurate, at the time, I felt like the only time I spoke to my dad when I was in trouble. Dad gave me the "don't smoke" speech with a cigarette in his hand.

My mom never asked, "What do you want to be when you grow up?" or "Where do you want to go to college?" She didn't encourage my future because she didn't expect me to succeed.

When I wanted to escape my life, public transportation offered me the golden ticket to freedom. I figured out which bus stops to get on and off so I could get from one end of Kennewick to the other for ten cents.

I argued with teachers and refused to do assignments. Teachers despised me as much as I despised them and they requested the disgusting, unwanted kid be moved to other classes. My words, not theirs. I collected more referrals than anyone in school.

I hated school and how much focus learning required. I hated the other students. I hated being harassed by teachers and classmates alike.

I'd probably learn better on my own. Then I wouldn't have to deal with all this garbage every day. I could go at my own pace and sit the way I needed to and figure out the problems my way. One day I approached my dad, wheeling the lawn mower to the front lawn. "Hey, Dad. I'm really struggling. I think I want to get my G.E.D."

"G.E.D.'s are for losers, Clint. You're a loser right now. You don't want to be a loser, do you? Something is wrong with you." He released the handle of the lawn mower. "No one likes you. You're not going to amount to anything. You're out of control!"

I knew he was trying to motivate me—in his own way. But each word of his speech broke me and fueled my rage. My entire being shook until I became fury embodied. I overpowered my dad. I straddled him on the front lawn, powerless to my own anger. I threw haymakers at his face and gut while he refused to fight back.

"Clint, stop, please."

I couldn't. I didn't.

"Clint, I'm sorry."

Nothing else, no one else existed. If a tyrannosaurus rex appeared on the front lawn, I wouldn't have noticed. I didn't really see my dad, either. Rage blinded me.

The next morning, in my bedroom, I dropped a pile of size 2X white T-shirts onto the bed beside my ninth-grade portraits. I glared at the photos. *Fat ass.* Then I uncapped a black Sharpie and scrawled vulgar sayings on each T-shirt.

"God hates you, MF."

"STFU."

I pointed at each of them in eenie-meenie-minie-moe fashion.

Someone knocked on my door. "Clint," said my mom. "Are you ready for school?"

Smiling, I opened the door.

Her eyes landed on my big, bold "FU." She put a hand over her mouth and lowered it. "You can't wear a T-shirt with profanity to school."

"Are you gonna stop me?"

Ultimately, the school expelled me. I remember seeing people at the end of the year, happy and hopeful. They asked me where I'd been. I didn't really have an answer.

After my expulsion, my dad spoke the best words I'd heard in years: "We're moving back to Minot."

Thank God.

I pretended not to care that my mom, again, blamed me.

I tried to do better in Minot, in tenth grade, truly. During the first semester, I achieved Bs and Cs. I met my best friend, Travis, when we were both called out of English class by the principal.

In the hallway outside our classrooms, the thin, well-dressed man looked us in the eye—his words gentle, but stern. "You boys have both been skipping a lot of school. Stop, or I'll write you up."

"Yes, sir." I said.

"Sorry, sir," added Travis.

The principal ended his pep talk and showed us back toward class. Travis's hand reached for the door handle.

"Hey, man. You wanna get high?" I asked.

Travis dropped his hand and shrugged. "Sure."

Instead of returning to class, we slipped out the nearest exit. It took all three sentences for the conversation to come around to Bret Hart, the Undertaker and The Ultimate Warrior.

"I call it the Perfect Plex," Travis said, imitating Mr. Perfect.

I grinned and pinched the joint between my lips.

"How does it work? Perfectly," Travis said, in 'perfect' imitation. "As Koko B. Ware will see tonight."

A hazy cloud formed around us. Travis added gravel to his voice and dropped his pitch in imitation of Vince McMahon. "San Antonio's own showstopper, Shaaaawn Michaaaaaels." By the end, our sides hurt from laughing so hard.

For a short period of time, I joined a gang. I quickly decided gaudy, plastic gold jewelry wasn't my style. I felt like the bird in *Are You My Mother?*

Do I fit here? Do I look like them? The answer was always no.

Two of my cousins attended a huge youth group in town and invited me to go with them. They truly cared, and I'll be forever grateful to them. Despite their loving efforts I fell in with degenerates. How's that for a four-syllable word, Mr. English teacher?

By then, I'd owned my identity as a loser and screw up and hung out mostly with smokers and school dropouts. Legion capitalized on every opportunity to remind me I'd never amount to anything, until *you're worthless* became the intrinsic truth at my core. So, it's not surprising I failed at everything I tried. No one believed I'd succeed.

I weighed three hundred pounds of mostly fat and withdrew from the shadows long enough to try out for football. I believed my weight and my love for football would be enough to get playing time. I fantasized about being the team MVP and winning a football scholarship to college. *I'll show 'em. I'll make my dad proud.*

Mostly, I sat on the bench.

No one ever taught me how to workout. No one knew me, or my capability. Dejected, I didn't try out for the team the next year.

Instead, I landed a job at Kentucky Fried Chicken and held my own money in my own hands for the first time ever. No one taught me about finances. I blew all my money on weed like a pro. Marijuana affected my job performance and reliability—imagine that—and before I knew it, I'd worked at six different places within one year. *I'm not worthy of a real job, anyway.*

This all happened around the time I met Travis. Ironically, when I finally found my safe place amongst the most loyal group of guys I'd ever met, my life truly spiraled out of control.

CHAPTER TEN

Even after meeting Clint only a few times, he impressed me. He was such a wonderful man with a strong faith.

Pastor Larry and Vicky

SAM, 2017
COURT DAY

The heels of my knee-high, leather boots clunked along a sidewalk plastered with red maple leaves from the recent rain. My brown tweed skirt bounced in time with each step. The courthouse loomed, casting an immense shadow. I tugged at my brown jacket against autumn's bite. I spoke toward the cloudless, neon blue sky. "All right, angel armies. Are you with me?"

Your prayer isn't aimed high enough. And yes, my angel armies are with you.

"Thank you, Jesus."

I entered the building through an empty, blandly painted hallway. Zero other people. My steps faltered, brow creased. *Is this the right day? The right place?*

Every step of this new saga brought me into uncharted waters. That feeling, of stepping into the unknown, would last for years.

Scanning a black-and-aluminum letter board, I read "courtroom" followed by an upward arrow, beside a tan elevator. When the elevator opened, I sighed at the sight of a familiar face—Nip. I smiled thinly at the man with a cap of stark white hair and small gray eyes. He was dressed even more crisply than he did on Sunday mornings. He nodded approval at my attire.

I'd only been in a courtroom a handful of times, but I'd always wondered how people who show up with stained T-shirts and ratty jeans expect to be taken seriously. If I wanted to be respected by the judge, I needed to show the judge respect.

Nip confirmed my thoughts when he said, "It never hurts to look your best." He placed his hand in the middle of my back and ushered me toward the lockers where I could store my purse and cell phone.

"Hi, Sam." The gentle greeting sounded muffled. *Who else knows me here?* On the other side of the glassed-in, court administrator's office stood a woman I immediately recognized from one of Clint's churches.

She works here? My mouth popped open, and I swallowed my embarrassment. I waved, but kept walking with Nip.

He stopped without a warning. "Oh, there's Greg." Nip pointed, "Greg, hey." Nip turned back to me. "Choose any locker." Then Nip vanished down the hall.

Two more church members arrived, and I wanted to check my whole self into a locker. I plastered on my brave face and pleaded with God to wake up from the nightmare.

So many church members appeared, I wondered if the secretary sent out a church newsletter. *No. There'd be standing room only.*

Nip returned with someone I assumed was Greg—a round man with a gracious smile. Nip and Greg led me to an alcove near the lockers with enough room for a single table and chairs. *Great. The fate of my husband will be determined in a closet.*

"You can stay if you want, Nip," I said.

"Actually, there's someone I want to talk to."

Greg opened a folder with details about Clint inside. The format and wording might as well have been in a different language, but Greg traced his thick forefinger across paragraphs like he was reading a children's book.

Where did the folder even come from?

"Public defenders take turns," Nip had told me Sunday. "It's likely Greg will have to ask another attorney's permission to take the case."

"Were you next in line to take Clint's case?" I asked Greg.

"No, but it wasn't a problem."

Greg summed up Clint's situation for me. Halfway through his explanation, I realized I was supposed to be listening.

Focus.

And I tried. I promise, I tried. But in the end, I knew two things: One, there was a felony charge of fleeing officers that could end Clint's career and life as we knew it. And two, Greg explained everything in German.

Nip, my courtroom fairy godfather, appeared. "They're letting people in."

We stepped up to a line for metal detectors, and the officer waved us through. Nip tossed his keys and wallet into a small tray with the ease of an innocent man. I didn't carry weapons on me, but as the officer urged me forward, I was terrified I ended up with a steak knife in my purse, or a firearm I didn't even own. I stepped through the gray, plastic frame, praying the imaginary machete strapped to my calf wouldn't set off the alarm.

Whew.

"You ready?' Nip asked.

"No," I said. "But my feelings seem irrelevant."

He opened the walnut door, revealing a diamond-shaped room with concentric patterns of lights shining down. The wood paneling around the room and at the judge's bench reminded me of every courtroom scene on every movie and TV show I'd ever seen. Greek-themed murals on the wall depicted impressions of justice. Movie theatre-style chairs waited for us to sit in them.

Four church members rose and greeted me with hugs.

Maybe an announcement had been *mailed out.* I greeted everyone as warmly as a I could with heat flashing across my cheeks "This whole situation is so embarrassing."

There. There it is.

"Oh, Sam," one of them said. "It could have been any one of us."

I tilted my head to the side. *Doubt it.* But I appreciated the sentiment. Shame, like a pounding headache, receded into the background. The church members' pity blended with love. *These are my people. They don't want me to face this alone.*

A dozen family members of prisoners arrived and took their seats. One woman wore a dress. Otherwise, the nicest outfits among them were sweatshirts and jeans. Others wore wrinkled T-shirts. Some made little-to-no effort to brush disheveled, bedhead hair.

Men with business suits, briefcases, and a sense of determination in their strides entered. Nip inclined his head toward a man in charcoal gray with a red tie. "The prosecutor for Clint's case."

Near a side entrance, the judge shrugged into his robe. He looked straight at me and raised his eyebrows. "Hey, Nip. How're ya? Done any fishing lately?" His voice carried. Everyone stared.

Nip grinned. "The wife and I have plans to head up north next weekend. You?"

I stifled a laugh of relief—and disbelief.

Their conversation took flight like a perfect cast. The judge adjusted the V-neck of his robe and nodded at the bailiff.

"All rise."

We stood and waited for the judge to take his seat. A moment later he called court to order, gavel and all. He recited the date and time for the benefit of the court reporter and named the officials present.

At least with alphabetical order, Clint Evans will be one of the first ones called.

"Ah," said the judge, "let's go in reverse alphabetical order today."

Figures.

But as I type this years later, I suspect the judge's choice was not as off-the-cuff as his tone suggested. Because I'm *speculating* the "someone" Nip had darted off to speak with during my meeting with Greg may have been the judge.

I sat back in my chair, annoyed about the wait. *There are less supporters than prisoners.*

One by one, men and women stepped before the judge, known by their offenses more than their names. Third degree assault, breaking a restraining order, DWI.

One man argued with the judge.

I cringed. *You're arguing with the man who decides your fate?*

The judge only settled two cases and assigned lawyers and future court dates to the remaining detainees. Officers escorted several people back to jail. Spectators gathered their purses and jackets and tiptoed toward the back door when their family member's appearance concluded.

Finally, *finally*, Clint's name was called. A round man with a gracious smile responded to the roll call. "Greg, representing Clint Evans. Permission to approach the bench."

"Permission granted. Prosecution, why don't you come up here as well."

"Is this normal?" I asked.

"Shhh," said Nip. "No."

The three men engaged in a literal sidebar conversation. Afterward, the prosecution took his seat, Greg strode toward me, and the judge called the next person in line.

"Come with me," said Greg.

"Can Nip come too?"

"Your choice."

"Yes."

Greg led us behind a wall with a mural depicting a woman in a white gown holding an uneven silver scale. His lungs fought his weight for a deep breath while he cinched hundreds of words foreign to my extensive vocabulary into a few seconds.

"Wait." I stuttered. "What does 'adjudicate' mean? So …"

"I'm sorry. I don't have time."

"Clint Evans," the judge called from his bench.

"Come on." Nip tugged at the sleeve of my jacket like we were about to miss our train. "Stay of adjudication means if Clint commits no offenses for three years, the felony drops from his record completely."

"Oh." *Why didn't Greg just say so?*

Gripping Clint's arm, an officer escorted my husband to the table where Greg stood. Steel cuffs encircled his wrists.

Clint's gaze found mine and flitted to our people behind me. His eyes grew to the size of Greg's figure and his attempted 'thank you' smile failed. He dropped his chin and closed his eyes.

The judge motioned to Clint.

"Does the prosecution have any objection to Mr. Evans's handcuffs being removed?"

"No, Your Honor."

An officer stepped forward. The silence of every person in the room magnified the click and jingle of metal.

Clint rubbed his wrists. "Thank you, Your Honor."

"The defendant should not speak to the judge unless spoken to," said the judge. "And you're welcome."

The court reporter typed the exchange. Her mouth tipped up into a smile.

"Bail has been set at $15,000," said the judge.

"Fifteen thousand dollars seems appropriate," said the prosecution.

With a pending felony *charge?* I furrowed my eyebrows, waiting for more, such as …. *Clint Evans was involved in a highspeed chase under the influence. He endangered the lives of many people and damaged property all throughout the city. In addition to the $3,000 DWI fine, the county holds Mr. Evans responsible for reparations to police vehicles and city property.*"

If proceedings continued as I imagined, court officials would need to scrape me off the floor like road debris when they finished.

The prosecution remained silent as Greg argued for release without bail. "Outstanding citizen … show of great support," he gestured toward Clint's clan, "… professional accountability…"

The judge spouted off Clint's follow-up court date and struck the gavel. "Court adjourned."

Court … wait … what?

Real time resumed for everyone else. Court officials, spectators, and reporters scurried about their day.

In the hall beyond the courtroom, Greg beamed. "I can't believe how many people were smitten with Mr. Evans—the judge, court reporter, spectators. Even the prosecution and the lady in the administration office."

So that wasn't my imagination… Only what Greg referred to as "smitten," I recognized as walking in God's favor. I witnessed God's favor on Clint in the courtroom, but I couldn't comprehend it.

"Thanks for everything," Clint said to Greg, shaking his hand

Greg nodded. "When Nip asks you to do something, you do it. You'll never understand volumes spoke by Nip sitting beside you in court."

I thought about the conversation I witnessed between the judge and Nip. How he hand-picked Clint's attorney and leveraged time for Clint and Greg to speak before facing the judge.

God's favor. Why us?

"Anyone who would be willing to write a character reference would help us," said Greg.

"I received so many encouraging messages this Sunday, I turned my phone off." I laughed.

Greg's face lit up. "Give me all of those messages."

My smile dropped. The task was a blessing in disguise, though, because the hours I spent collecting references meant less time for awkward conversations with Clint.

My heart had stalled at "Mrs. Evans, there's been an accident." Every event following the initial phone call sped past me like a reckless driver evading police. *Husband in handcuffs* immediately followed by *now it's time for lunch* made zero sense.

The situation reminded me of our oldest daughter's birth. Our family walked into the hospital as two people and walked out as three. The nurses gave us a human who'd literally never seen the light of day and sent us to our car. *What now?*

I drove home with Clint, the drunk driving accident strapped securely in the backseat. And no clue what to do next.

CHAPTER ELEVEN

Clint,

I can't believe you'd punch Santa. Then again he was at a hockey game … and he's a BEARS fan.

Thanks for your sweet friendship,

Kyle

SAM, 2017, ONE WEEK AFTER THE ACCIDENT
SLEEPY EYE, MINNESOTA

I grabbed my ringing phone and looked at Caller ID.

Please don't cancel. I set my laptop down and unfolded myself from the couch in the three-season room to step outside.

When pastors go out of town, they hire substitutes to preach. With a degree in youth ministry and Bible, and plenty of experience in the ministry realm, pastors frequently asked me to fill in on Sundays they'd be gone. Often, they'd invite me to set up a table with books I'd written.

Please don't cancel on me.

The phone rang again. A mere thirty feet of grass separated the vinyl-sided parsonage[2] and the brick church Clint's bosses suspended him from. I stood in the shadow of both and greeted my friend on the other end of the phone.

"Hey, Sam," the male voice said. "I'm going to find someone else for the fifteenth. You have enough to deal with."

Do I get a say? But the finality in his tone left no room for rebuttal. I supposed, "Why am *I* being punished?" would sound childish.

....
2   A "parsonage" is a home for pastors located on the church property.

Then he said, "At least the accident revealed possible cancer, right? God works in mysterious ways."

I cringed at the platitude. The call ended. I fell to my knees and stared at nothing. Freshly cut grass poked through my pants.

"At least the accident helped find the cancer" became the most common response when people heard my story. Their words implied we should be grateful for the accident.

But as *the wife? I lost.* I faced repercussions because of Clint's choice to drink and drive. Each consequence hit me like a 350-pound lineman, and before I could process the impact, others around me would say, "Sounds like the accident saved his life."

The doctor, the morning Clint woke up in the hospital, had been the first one. He'd delivered the news of Clint's cancer with a conference room voice—stark and crisp—and I hated it. *This is not an amphitheater. It's a twenty-foot by twenty-foot box and we're the only ones in the room.* "Mr. Evans, have you engaged in alcohol or drug use lately?"

I shook my head no. *Of course, he hadn't.*

"Yes. Alcohol."

"How often?"

"Every few weeks."

My next heartbeat skidded to a stop. I misheard him, right? But the conversation continued without waiting for my thoughts to catch up.

"How long has this been going on?"

"Seven months or so."

Seven months? I replayed moments from the last half-year, seething. Certain details shifted into place. My husband lied to me for seven months or so. For seven months or so, he'd been drinking under our roof. And he never actually came clean. He got busted. Any parent or teacher can explain the monumental difference.

That knife was still slicing me in half when the doctor said, "Well, Mr. Evans. It looks like the accident saved your life."

Less than a week after the accident, at Hardee's, when I walked past a table where two elderly couples sat, their conversation abruptly ceased. Each of their silver-haired heads jerked up like a choreographed cue from a musical. They fixated their gazes at different places in the room. One woman actually looked at the corner of the ceiling. Disgusted, I stopped and stared at them. I stood there long enough to warn them I knew who they were talking about, long enough to make them uncomfortable and ashamed. Long enough to make them feel like idiots staring at the corner of the ceiling. I thought about saying, "You should be ashamed of yourselves," but I didn't need to. I walked away without a word, humiliated by strangers. I did not recognize those couples.

Two weeks later, I sat in the corner at Hardee's and a few tables away, four men conversed. One of them must have neglected his hearing aids, because they spoke loud enough for everyone in the restaurant to overhear. I heard the words "minister" and "can't believe."

My fingers paused on the keyboard of my laptop. "You're talking about my husband," I said in my 'mom' voice. "I'm sitting *right* here."

"It's all public knowledge," one of them said. "You can read about it in the paper."

Heat rushed to my face, fueled more by anger than embarrassment.

"We don't mean any disrespect," another said. "I know your husband. He's done a lot for this community. We're surprised, and we feel bad."

"This could happen to anyone," a third man said.

I turned back to my laptop and dropped my face into my palms. I can't remember ever using tears to manipulate before in my life, but there's a first time for everything. They started out as a show, but then they were real.

Twenty minutes later, the man who made the crack about it being public wrung his farming ballcap in his hands when he approached my table to apologize.

CHAPTER TWELVE

Clint,

You love people regardless of past performance. There are no mind games with you. What you think is what people hear, ready or not. And you're as loveable as a big teddy bear.

Love from Breanna

CLINT, 1996
MINOT, NORTH DAKOTA

I slid into the driver's seat. *Buckle. Even though you'll be going 10 miles per hour.* I gripped and regripped the steering wheel. *They're all staring at me. Don't mess this up. Don't mess this up, loser. Any idiot can drive. Right?*

Mr. Baker, the Driver's Ed instructor, stood in a tower overlooking the track. Classmates watched intently from the bleacher seats below the tower. Backpacks, books, and sweatshirts flung carelessly onto the risers filled in the empty spaces.

Adjust your mirrors. I'd never been behind the wheel of a car, or even an ATV. I turned the key in an ignition for the first time.

"All right, Clint." Mr. Baker's voice boomed over the loudspeaker. "Shift the car into Drive."

Drive, Drive, Drive.

I looked down at the pedals. *The brake is one on the left.* I compressed the brake and shifted the car into Drive. I switched to the gas pedal, and the car lurched forward.

"No!" I heard from the tower.

I slammed on the brake.

Kids in the bleachers laughed.

I'm such an idiot. I gently removed my foot from the brake and eased my foot onto the gas pedal.

"Okay," said Mr. Baker. "All right."

"I'm doing it." I steered the car around the oval-shaped track and waved when I passed Mr. Baker's assistant, Creepy Jerry.

"Easy, easy," said Mr. Baker. "You're going a little fast."

I glanced at the speedometer. 15 mph.

"Okay, now, stop the car and shift into Park."

Okay, okay. Foot on brake. I grabbed the gear shift and shoved it upward. Okay. Park? Park. I eased my foot off the brake, not completely trusting my work. The car didn't move. A grin stretched my cheeks. "I drove. I just drove."

"Okay, Mr. Evans. Show us Reverse."

"Reverse. Okay. That's easy." I stomped on the brake and shifted. When I hit the gas, the engine revved, but the car didn't move.

"No, you idiot!" I heard from the loudspeaker. "Reverse."

"What did I do wrong?" My gaze darted to the gear shift. *Shoot. N. Neutral.* I didn't look at the bleachers, but I imagined all the kids laughing at me. Eyes wild, I searched for the "R." Okay. Up one. I hit the gas and the engine revved again. I'd shifted to Park. *Shoot.*

"Clint, you fucking moron!" Mr. Baker shouted into his microphone. "Put the car into Reverse. How can you not find Reverse?"

"If we knew this stuff, we wouldn't be in your damn class." I pulled on the gear shift again and the car lurched into Drive. "You are such a fucking moron, Clint."

Those were my words, not Mr. Baker's. We cussed me out in unison. Anger slurred Mr. Baker's words. He whined like a high-pitched motor.

My ADHD thoughts whizzed and stalled at the same time. *If he's gonna embarrass me when I'm trying my best, screw him.* I found Drive without a problem and stomped on the gas pedal.

"Clint!"

20 …

I rounded the curve at 35.

I passed Creepy Jerry at 55. In my rearview mirror, I caught sight of him running after me.

Students on the bleachers jumped to their feet and cheered.

Mr. Baker screamed words from the tower I'd never heard of.

65 …

70…

Oh my God. I'm going 70 mph.

I fishtailed around the curve. Creepy Jerry faced me, playing 'Chicken' with a furious teen behind the wheel of a car.

Holy sh—

I shoved my foot onto the brake pedal. Tires screeched. My chest slammed into the shoulder strap. The car rocked forward and lurched back just shy of Creepy Jerry. He slapped his palms on the hood. No one told my heart the race had ended. It beat more loudly than Mr. Baker's screams or my classmates' cheers. I reached out the window and used one finger to tell Mr. Baker what I thought of him. Number one teacher.

I did not pass Driver's Ed.

When my dad ended his call with the school, he glared at me.

"Dad, he …"

Incomprehensible words slurred together at a volume on par with Mr. Baker's. I deciphered the words "irresponsible" and "idiot" and "don't deserve" and gathered the gist of the one-sided conversation—I would not be driving until I turned eighteen.

Dad stormed out of his bedroom, where we'd had our "private" talk the neighbors three blocks down heard.

Whatever. All my friends drive anyway. I craned my neck to make sure he was beyond sight and slid the top drawer of his dresser open. I folded three Marlboro Reds into a cassette case.

From the school I only received five days of In-School Suspension. I think school officials knew Mr. Baker was a terrible human that should have been fired years prior to my turn in Driver's Ed.

After school, a half dozen friends and I loitered just beyond the school grounds.

"Clint, man, everyone's talking about you and Mr. Baker." The kid flipped a lighter flame into life and cupped his hands.

I aimed the unlit cigarette pinched between my lips toward the flame.

"He had it coming," the kid added, dropping his lighter into the pocket of his quilted flannel. A forest green Dodge Intrepid rolled up to the curb. A man wearing sunglasses, a hoodie and a quilted flannel hopped out of the passenger seat. He reached for his back pocket.

My friend offered his lighter, but instead of a pack of cigarettes, the man flipped open a black billfold.

I did a double take at the Intrepid. *Oops.*

"You're all under arrest for underage smoking."

I groaned. *Can't wait for* this *conversation with my dad.*

The city charged me twenty-five hours of community service. On the last weekend, my community service representative scheduled me to work at the Minot Municipal Auditorium.

Mom clicked her blinker on and turned onto 3rd Avenue SW. She curved around to the front entrance, and my eyebrows shot up to my hairline. Police sedans and SUVs streaked with the names of cities and counties within a 100-mile radius of Minot filled nearly every single parking spot.

What the heck?

Mom's thoughts echoed my own. "Guess you won't be getting into any trouble *today.*"

I swallowed hard. The metal hooks securing the American flag to the flagpole clanged against the pole like a warning bell.

Inside, a large poster plastered to the wall read: Safety isn't a slogan. It's a way of life. A banner stretched across the entryway said: Serve with Pride.

A cop convention? You gotta be kidding me.

I paired up with a scrawny kid also assigned to community service and we spent the day emptying garbage cans, sweeping, and restocking toilet paper and paper towels. I emerged from one bathroom, and waving my hand in front of my nose. "Someone committed a nasty crime in there."

"Filthy pigs," said the kid.

We found ourselves in an empty room stockpiled with a sandwich buffet. I lifted the lid of a coffee craft and hocked a loogie into the coffee.

He laughed, picked his nose, and wiped a booger into a sandwich.

Grinning, I grabbed an apple with each hand, took a bite of both, and set them back onto the tray.

"Let's get out of here before someone notices." Plastic crinkled when I crammed chip bags into my pockets.

A tan leather purse rested on a table near the door. The gaping zipper revealed a thick stack of dough, begging, "Take me. Pick me."

With almost no hesitation, I plunged my hand into the purse.

"Dude. How much?"

"Quiet." I shoved the cash deep into my pocket and shouldered through the door of the nearest men's bathroom. We ducked into a handicap stall.

"Twenty, forty, sixty…"

He whispered, "Twelve hundred dollars."

"Shut up, dude."

"You better cut me in."

"Finder's keepers."

His eyes narrowed.

I knew a snitch when I saw one, and the kid would only have to walk about thirty steps to find the nearest cop. "Fine." I halved the money and shoved the cash into his greasy palm. I lifted my heel and slid my cut into my shoe.

The last 120 minutes crawled by.

Don't act guilty. Don't act guilty. Keep your calm.

Every time a cop walked by, I imagined twenty-dollar bills slithering out the top of my shoe from beneath my foot. Slinking through hallways, I stared at the floor and didn't see the black uniform approaching. The policeman swerved at the last second to avoid a head-on collision.

"Careful, kid."

"Sorry."

Finally, my mom pulled up to the curb. I shoved the convention center doors open. Behind me, two male cops hustled outside on my heels. Color drained from my pasty white face.

The cops burst into laughter and slid cigarettes out of their pockets. I expelled a breath and rolled my eyes at the irony of cops smoking after cops busted me for smoking.

A few weeks later, my mom calculated my earnings versus my purchases. "Did you steal your new Super Nintendo?"

"I paid for it."

"With what money?"

"Money from KFC."

"Try again."

I sighed. "I stole $600 from someone."

"Who?"

"I found a purse."

She stared at me, eyebrows up.

"What?"

"Well, come on. Let's go."

"Go where?"

"We're gonna take $600 from your bank account."

I groaned and followed her out the door. A few minutes later, scowling, I slapped $600 into her palm. Instead of taking me to the police station to make me return the money, she brought me home. We never talked about the money again.

CHAPTER THIRTEEN

Clint,

The words you spoke to me hit the nail on the head. You can really read people well. I'll pray for you. May God be with you on your journey.

Sarah, New York

SAM, 2017, ONE MONTH AFTER THE ACCIDENT

A few years into our marriage, I learned canning tomatoes is not a hobby a person "tries their hand at." Boxes and bushels and buckets of tomatoes haphazardly covered my kitchen counters and floorspace.

Four stockpots on a four-burner stove gurgled with bubbling water. *I am never going to finish.*

Trying to speed up the blanching process, I plopped more tomatoes into the pots. Water and red residue splashed and sizzled on the stovetop. The boil momentarily receded. I placed lids on each of the pots. *Okay. Good enough. Now to find my phone.*

In the living room, I slid my fingers between the couch cushions and lifted throw pillows. I opened drawers I never would have placed my phone in, looked under the couch, and scanned the shelves of the bookcase.

Sounds coming from the kitchen took a minute to register. Water rumbled. Metal lids rang and rattled. An object clanged, hit the metal stove, and landed on the floor.

I darted into the kitchen and found the scene of a mad scientist's lab gone wrong. The kitchen smelled like a pizzeria and red tomato splatter covered the stove, the wall and the floor, and my purse near the door … with my phone sticking out of it. *Fantastic.*

Water had splattered more red goop into the air because one of the pots blew its top across the room. The three other pots rattled in threat. I decided not to can tomatoes the following autumn.

With each day following the accident, I felt like the three pots threatening to blow at any given time. Even with my mom visiting from out-of-state to help, the building pressure within my heart begged for release.

After four weeks of managing details, facilitating normal, and clinging to the positive, my attitude slipped. My temper swelled with flash-flood speed, and I snapped at everyone. Clint knew where my anger stemmed from and begged me to take it out on him instead of the girls. But anger void of patience does not choose targets with clarity.

"I don't want this plate," said six-year-old Kaylynn sitting to my left. "I want the blue one."

"The color of the plate doesn't change the taste of your food. Just eat."

Halfway through the meal, Kaylynn dropped like a rag doll and fell onto my arm. The forkful of food grazing my lips slammed to the plate with a loud clatter.

"Kaylynn, sit up."

"Samantha, you really need to control your temper," my mom said, in front of my kids.

"Yeah," Clint said, "this is getting out of control."

"She's not eating her food and preventing me from eating mine. I'm hungry. It's been a long day. I just want to eat."

"Didn't you get a long break writing today?" Clint asked.

"I *worked.*"

"But it was time away from the kids, Samantha," said my mom.

They each spoke with infuriating calm.

"Yes, Mom. It was."

I stared between the two of them. *Are you two living in an alternate universe in which the last four weeks haven't happened? Truly? Neither of you see why I'm so stressed?*

The next night, my mom took me out to dinner. I suspect both she and Clint thought a night from dinner duty for the kids would "make me normal" again.

Restaurants in our town closed early and with all the bad press regarding our family and alcohol, stopping at a local bar didn't seem like the wisest choice. So, after finishing our meal and stretching conversation as far as it could go, my mom and I stepped through the front door of our house at 8:00 p.m.

I'd hoped the girls would be in bed.

Strike 1.

"Mommy!" Kelly scurried down the wooden stairs and leapt. Monkey arms and legs banded around me like I was the trunk of a Brazil nut tree. The top of her head slammed into my chin. My upper and lower jaw collided. The radiating pain of impact knocked my tear ducts loose.

Strike 2.

I closed my eyes.

She didn't mean to. Breathe. Just breathe.

Clint appeared at the top of the stairs. He misinterpreted my pained expression as impatience toward the girls.

Strike 3.

"Okay, Kelly. Run up to bed." I patted her little bottom.

"Night, Mommy."

My other daughter, Trinity, stood on an end table, waving her chubby toddler arms and shaking her diapered toddler butt. Wayward coils of blonde hair sprung out in every direction above her pink cherub cheeks and chocolate brown, anime eyes.

The day before, my mom had said, "You know, they're going to break your tables."

In the state of chaos of my family, some things slid. Like standing on the tables.

I felt my mom behind me and wanted to show her I could run a smooth household.

So, to Trinity standing on the table, I used a stern, but calm Mom voice I knew would make both my husband and my mom proud.

Because now on top of cook, clean, raise kids, work, exercise, advocate for Clint, and process trauma, I added "Pleasing Mom and Husband" to the fifty-pound salt bags on my shoulders. "Trinity, get down."

Clint heard me from the top of the stairs. "Stop *yelling* at the kids." *Strike 256.*

Breathe. Find your calm voice. "I was not yelling. I was trying not to yell."

Clint's look told me my anger was out of control.

But wait, of the two of us, which one was too drunk to find his way home while I took care of the kids all alone?

"Don't come up here. *I'll* put the kids to bed."

Then, I yelled. "Don't treat me like I'm an unfit mother. I'm doing the best I can with the situation *you* put us in."

My mom, still beside me, pursed her lips. "Samantha, I'm worried about your anger." Her tone echoed Clint's insinuation that the problem stemmed from me.

After Clint put the kids to bed, he entered the living room where I laid in fetal position on the couch, weeping.

"You've been fine for weeks and suddenly you're this upset," he said.

"Because I can be now." Details settled. Everyone who needed to know something knew it. I could let go. But apparently, not really. "I need a break."

CHAPTER FOURTEEN

Dear Clint,

We have been praying for you and your family since the beginning. So sorry for it all. We loved seeing you after the Thursday dinner. We're praying for a miracle. He does that, you know.

Love,
R&M

CLINT, 1998, JUNIOR YEAR
MINOT, NORTH DAKOTA

I wove through the school's warren of hallways bordered by maroon lockers. As I rounded the bend, Nathan Dicks spoke to a huddle of jocks with a condescending tone, his chest inflated with bravado. I strode past the group and overheard the name of a friend.

"Shut up, Dicks," I said.

His eyes sparked. "What are you going to do about it, fat ass?"

The jocks cackled like hyenas.

I slapped him across the face. The force caused him to stumble backward. "Gonna stomp a mud hole in you." I strode off, invigorated.

During third hour, lunch, I ordered my usual chili cheese dog from an a la carte stand and dropped to a lunch table seat next to Travis and his brother KC. I yanked my T-shirt down over my exposed butt crack. I didn't need some preppy jock making me a laughingstock. With a mouthful of hot dog, I said, "I'm gonna beat the crap out of Dicks."

"Jerk deserves it," said Travis.

KC bit into his sandwich. "You'll wipe the floor with him."

"Don't do it, man," said one of Dick's friends.

Dicks came in and ordered a cookie, like he did every single day.

I jumped up from the table when he walked past and slapped the cookie out of his hand. "Wanna keep making fun of my friends?" I fisted his T-shirt with both hands, lifted him off the ground and flung him into a door. He stared up at me from the floor, pale-faced and wide-eyed.

No more bravado now.

Dozens of people watched. And said nothing.

I threw myself on top of him and landed punch after punch.

"Knock it off." Hands gripped my arms and dragged me off Dicks.

The left side of his face was already black and blue. Tears soaked his cheeks. He swiped snot away with the back of his hand and clambered to his feet. Droplets of his own blood stained his torn T-shirt.

Pride surged through me. I felt heroic.

The janitor who'd pulled me off pointed a crooked finger toward the office. "Go see the principal, now. Both of you."

The fight with Dicks landed me five days of ISS. I didn't like fighting. I didn't want to fight. But I didn't know how to stop.

After school, Travis and I left the Family Video store. Travis grabbed *The Wedding Singer* DVD from my hand. "Hey, somebody get some pants on that kid."

How does Travis change his voice?

He burst into another perfect Adam Sandler impersonation. "Please get out of my Van Halen T-shirt before you jinx the band ..."

"... And they break up." we said together.

"Hey, Clint Evans, right?"

Travis and I stopped laughing halfway through a breath and stared at a kid with dyed black hair and bushy eyebrows walking toward the store. I studied his pale skin, wondering if he was strung out or just ugly.

His ratty, brown T-shirt was three sizes too big. "You're Clint Evans," he repeated. "You wanna fight?"

Travis said dryly, "Your reputation precedes you."

I shrugged. "Sure."

"Wait. Clint, what?" Travis stopped walking. "That is not a good idea."

"Where? When?" I asked the kid.

"Now? In the alley?"

I shrugged. "Okay."

We crossed into the alley and faced off between an overstuffed dumpster and a chain link fence.

"Clint," said Travis. "You don't even know this kid. Why the heck are you going to fight him?"

I have no idea.

"We don't live in a freakin' musical."

I swung a couple of times but pulled my punches and let him land the first connection.

"What? Are your fingers made of butterflies?"

The kid's furry eyebrows slashed downward, and he socked a jab into my gut with maximum effort. I felt invisible.

This is why I fight.

I fisted the kid's T-shirt in both hands, swept my leg beneath his feet, and threw him to the pavement.

The kid's voice came out in a strangled squeal.

"You're gonna kill him," said Travis.

My fist connected with the kid's nose. *Pop.* Dizzying pain radiated up from the middle knuckles on my right hand toward the inside of my elbow. *Well. Shoot.* I scrambled to my feet. "Now you can say you fought Clint Evans and got creamed. You satisfied?" I spun in the direction of Travis's house and started walking.

Travis fell in step. "Dude, are you nuts?"

I glanced over my shoulder. The kid peeled himself off the cement. I stretched and flexed my right hand, hoping I'd been tripping about the pain. Fire burned beneath my skin. *Not my imagination.* Safely out of earshot, I said, "Dude. I gotta call my mom. I think I broke my hand."

"She's gonna be pissed."

"I'll tell her I fell."

Two days later, sitting in ISS, I watched the secondhand of the clock click from one hash mark to the next. I'd already finished most of my classwork. I always worked better, accomplished more, in independent study.

Chris, a friend of Dicks hated that I'd made a fool of his friend. He arranged to fight me in the Junior Parking lot.

Only … 246 seconds until the break bell rings. 242. 241. I tipped side to side on the uneven chair legs. Picked at the crumbling purple Lakers print scrawled across my Bryant jersey. I tapped my casted right hand on the desktop. Rotated my forearm and practiced fisting my hand. The plaster only allowed my fingers to curl halfway.

Maybe if I … I pommeled the cast down on the corner of the desk.

"Mr. Evans." My female teacher stared at me over a collection of hand-written assignments.

My head jerked up.

Half a dozen students stared at me.

"Sorry. I forgot where I was for a second."

My classmates giggled, thinking I was joking.

I eyeballed the clean, yellowish-white cast. *Barely even a dent.*

The bell blared, startling the girl in the desk next to me.

I only have fifteen minutes. Hundreds of students with tortoise shells for backpacks maneuvered around a brunette gossiping in the middle of the hallway. The bulge of her muffin top hung over her too-tight jeans. Black eye makeup covered most of her eyelids. I shouldered right past her.

"Hey."

"You're in the middle of the hall, ya dumb broad." After weaving through half the student body, I shoved through the stairwell door and jogged down a flight of stairs. The door above me slammed closed and muted the chaos of class transition. My shoelaces slapped against the laminate flooring, my footsteps echoed off the cinder block walls. I slammed the push bar open and squinted against the sun.

The Junior lot, tucked around an awkward corner of the building is where students went to get away with something on school grounds. A group of high schoolers swarmed around Chris. Some of them caught sight of me.

One punk swung the lens of his digital camcorder in my direction. I spied his stupid, eager grin beneath the video camera. *Too bad I can't fight you instead.*

Chris's pretty preppy face watched me from beneath a cap of dirty blond hair.

He's stockier than Dicks. I hope this doesn't take too long. I'm gonna get in trouble if I'm not back to ISS on time. I waved my casted fist at him. "This may not be a fair fight."

"Whatever. I don't care."

I wonder who'll have the disadvantage. A ringside bell clanged in my head. *I guess we'll find out.*

We stalked toward one another, sizing, anticipating. Students created one wall of the ring, a row of rusty Tauruses, Accords, and Cutlasses, the other.

My arms bent and fingers curled. The cast snagged my attention, but my gaze remained glued to Chris's face.

Onlookers said the fight looked even for about ten seconds.

I reached for his T-shirt but couldn't coil my fingers around the cotton. *Now what?* When I glanced up, his knuckles dominated my view. In slow motion, I watched his hand collide with my face, felt bones crunch when his fist hammered my nose. Warm, wet liquid spurted from my nostrils and dripped onto my white T-shirt sleeve. My eyes flared. Awareness vanished. I swung my cast like a club at the side of his face. And felt nothing.

Chris lost his balance and stumbled backward. His body went limp. His head bounced off the rear fender of a gray Escort, and he landed, a pile of limbs, on a patch of wet pavement.

"Dude. You killed him."

I took one step forward before I froze. My heart hammered.

A girl rushed forward, knelt beside him, and pressed her fingers to his neck. "He has a pulse."

A friend of Chris's stepped in front of me and flattened both hands against my chest. "Okay, Clint. You won." He applied pressure. Several other sets of hands lightly braced my arms. "Not tryin' to fight you, man. It's over. You won."

Chris's entire body went rigid like his brain clicked "Reboot." He groaned.

I expelled a breath of relief. My brain restarted too. *ISS.* I bolted back toward the building, through the door, up the stairs into the hallway with thinning traffic, and into the closest bathroom.

I evaluated myself in the mirror. Pale crimson smears streaked my face. Fresh blood dripped from my nose. Brown-and-red splotches stained my white T-shirt sleeve and the white "24" on my jersey. I dropped my face into the sink and scrubbed my skin with my hands. I whipped off my T-shirt and jersey and shoved the soiled portions beneath the faucet. Red water, then bright pink swirled down the drain. I squeezed the fabric again. Lighter pink.

Good enough.

Cold, wet cotton slapped my bare back and waist, and I cursed. Hoisting up my sagging jeans, I bolted to the classroom.

I dropped to my seat. The metal chair leg tipped with uneven balance when I yanked the worktable toward me, rested my forearms on the surface, interlocked my fingers, and sighed.

"Clint." The teacher eyed me warily. "What happened to you?"

"I fell." My white cast was now brown and pink. The plaster at the edge, soggy and crumbly.

She frowned, unbelieving, but helpless.

The bell rang.

The teacher sighed. "All right, students. Get to work."

I smiled. *All in fifteen minutes.* I dropped my head onto my cast. *Chris, bloody, curled up on the slick pavement. When do I get to stop fighting?*

Jon, a friend of Nate and Chris, heard I was just a prick who instigated fights with both of his friends out of the blue. Knowing my third fight on campus would get me expelled, it never occurred to me I could have said 'no' when Jon invited me to the Junior lot.

After my expulsion, my parents separated again. And again my mom blamed me. Dad and I lived in a crummy apartment for a month. My self-esteem tanked. Students and teachers and my parents treated me like I was a worthless piece of garbage. And I let them, because I knew they were right.

The expulsion, however, became a two-fold blessing in disguise. It gave me safe haven from the guys picking fights with me. Also, I started to understand myself for the first time. I wish someone would have helped me realize that prior to my senior year. I learned better and accomplished more with independent study.

Meanwhile, Jon asked around about me. "No, dude. Nate totally bad-mouthed Clint's friend and then publicly humiliated Clint, called him a fat ass and had everyone laughing at Clint."

Jon apologized, and senior year we became friends. One night, Jon drove me home from a party and I heard myself say, "I'm a good guy. I'm the kind of friend you want to have around."

Jon didn't say anything right away. We drove beneath green traffic signals and the light within the car shifted. His hands remained on the steering wheel, but he rolled his palms upward. "I know, Clint. You've got nothing to prove to me. We're good, man. We're okay."

My heart eased a little.

CHAPTER FIFTEEN

Clint

May God continue to use you in mighty ways to share the gospel. I thank God for you, for your ministry, and the unique ways God's love flows through you. The agape love of Christ is something I hope you know more intimately now. May your coming days be used to share God's love with others.

Of God's Promise,

Matt Sipe

CLINT, 1991, FOURTH GRADE
SAN DIEGO

I smushed my cheek against the window, eager to see up the block. The blinds rested atop my head. I strained a little more to see. Finally, a blue bus with peeling paint rolled into sight. "He's here!" I leapt off the couch. The blinds fell with a clatter. I plowed into my mom with a bear-sized hug. "Love you, Mom."

"Oh, Clinty. I love you so much."

The blinds still swayed when I yanked the front door open. My brothers raced on my tail. Mom appeared in the doorway. "Have a good time, boys. I love you."

The driver, a volunteer from a local church, looked like Mr. Rogers down to the straight, dark hair and cardigan. Except this man, Arnold, wore glasses with thick, brown rims. Every Sunday, he picked my brothers and me up for Sunday School.

"Hello, Mr. Evanses," he said. "How are we doing this fine, sunny morning?"

"We're good, Arnold," I said, dropping on the seat adjacent to him. I bounced up and down on the seat cushion. "I memorized another Bible verse."

"You get to pick a prize. Nice work."

"Uh huh." I continued bouncing. "So, what are we gonna learn about today?"

"Ever heard the story of Jonah and the Whale?"

"Um … The whale swallowed Jonah."

"You know why?"

"Nope."

"Because God told Jonah to go one direction and Jonah ran in the opposite direction."

"Huh." I bounced all the way to church. I didn't think about this until years later, but whereas I struggled to focus in school, I retained knowledge of Scripture with ease.

In fourth or fifth grade, I received money for my birthday. My mom took me to a Christian bookstore and told me I could spend the money there. A bell dinged overhead as I opened the door. My eyes widened. I whizzed through the aisles and ran my fingers across slick covers and fluffy toys. Cardboard safari jeeps hung from the ceiling advertising Vacation Bible School. *I love Vacation Bible School.*

"Hope Set High" by Amy Grant played on the loudspeaker overhead. *Mom's cassette is practically worn out from rewinding this song soooo mannyy times.*

Then I remembered my money. "I can get anything, right, Mom?" *I'm a millionaire.* "I could buy the whole store!"

"Not quite."

Mom's blue eyes sparkled beneath her big, platinum blonde bob of hair. Her pink and purple eye shadow reached up to her eyebrows. *Mom is so pretty.* "Mom, you're pretty."

She dropped her suitcase-sized purse on the checkout counter and spoke to the female employee standing there. "What would you recommend for a high-energy boy with a super short attention span?"

The employee grinned. "How about an *Adventure Bible*?"

"Adventure" sounds cool. "Bible" sounds boring.

She led us through the aisles.

I pranced behind Mom and ran my hands along the books on the shelves.

"Clint," Mom spoke through gritted teeth, "settle down."

I plastered my arms to my sides and walked like a "normal human" for three strides. Then my feet landed together, and I became a human pogo stick.

"Here we go," said the employee.

She slipped a book thicker than a brick off the shelf.

The silver holographic cover caught my eye. "Can I see?" The cover cracked. Bold pictures filled each page in graphic novel style. My eyes popped. "This is awesome. Can I get it?"

Mom scanned the back cover. "You have just enough."

"Woo hoo." I galloped up to the register. "Can I have my money so I can pay myself, Mom? Puh-leaze?"

"Of course, Clint." She reached into her purse. "Settle down, Clinty."

Why? I handed the employee my money. She slipped my new book into a bag, and I skipped out of the store.

Because of my *Adventure Bible*, I retained more Scripture knowledge than many adults I knew. I read about Samson, King Ahaz—he was an evil dude—and the prophet Isaiah.

The next Sunday, I bound onto Arnold's bus with my Bible tucked under my arm like a football. I'd already read the whole thing. My grin stretched my face. "Arnold, look."

"What've you got there?"

"I picked out a Bible at the Family Bookstore. So, what are we learning about today?"

"Today we're talking about the four spiritual laws."

"What are those?"

"Number one is God loves you and wants to be in relationship with you. Number two—"

Darry cackled. "Arnold said 'Number 2.'"

We all laughed, including Arnold, who cleared his throat. "The second spiritual law is everyone makes, well, poopy mistakes and our poop separates us from God."

"That's only number two, Arnold," I said.

"Three and four are Jesus fixes everything. Believe Jesus will fix everything."

"That's it?"

"That's it."

"That's easy," I said.

"Well, maybe one day you can teach the class."

$$\sim$$

CLINT, PRESENT DAY

Even though I'd been "saved" forty-seven times with all the altar calls I'd participated in as a child, I didn't really know Jesus or understand who he was. Despite my best efforts to run away like Jonah, God never let me venture beyond His grasp.

Legion's perimeter around me steadily tightened, but I saw glimpses of God at work. Before I understood who God was, He granted me small moments of spiritual reprieve.

People along my journey gave me enough grace to keep going. The Royal Rangers leader, for example. Even though he often sent me to the corner for bad behavior, he never gave my parents a bad report. And on Sundays, he often had a doughnut just for me.

Whenever my dad returned from his longest overseas trip, he opened his duffel to a treasure trove of new clothes. Jerseys. Sports apparel. Nike Air Jordans. The next Monday at school, I was untouchable.

One glorious, sunny day, my dad brought me and my brother Korey aboard the *U.S.S. Jason (AR-8)*. The ship chugged out to sea, my dad showed us the mess hall, and we ate like real sailors. Korey and I used the bathroom as often as possible, because it gave us an excuse to run back and forth across the ship.

Several hours later, when the *Jason* pulled back into port, Dad patted my back. "You boys behaved well today. I'm really proud of you."

I bounced up and down. "Thanks, Dad! I love you so much."

"You're welcome, son. I love you too."

Small acts of kindness mattered. They were God whispering, "You are loved." Through these moments, God granted me glimpses of life with Him, like He'd cracked a window open of the life He prepared for me and allowed me to peer inside.

CLINT, 1998
MINOT, NORTH DAKOTA

"Order up." I slammed the bell with my fist and wiped beads of sweat off my forehead with the inside of my elbow.

Grease sizzled on the grill.

The door opened with another group of eight or so, dressed in their Sunday best and bundled beneath layers of coats, hats, and thick mittens.

A blast of December air evaporated before it reached the kitchen. A semitruck rolled past the garland-draped windows, temporarily blocking the sunlight and the view.

Thirty conversations at once created their own distinct hum.

"Clint, catch."

I spun at the sound of my co-worker's voice, instinctively holding out my hands. A box of beef patties landed on my forearms.

"Eggs are next."

I laughed, ripped into the box and deciphered the waitress's shorthand on the piece of paper dangling above the grill. I tossed six more patties on, washed my hands, and slid over to the metal counter where green onions and peppers waited to be diced.

"Clint." The waitress's head popped into view in the rectangular window.

"Yeah?" I flipped my hands, front and back, against a faded, yellow hand towel.

"One of the customers wants to speak with you."

I rolled my eyes. *Great.*

The waitress pointed to a table where four silver-haired ladies with perfect curler-curls watched me, expectantly. *I'm doing the best I can, ya' old bat.*

Behind her, a cardboard Santa stuck to the wall with scotch tape winked at me.

"Boy, you're young." The woman grabbed my palm. *What on earth, lady?* "And handsome too." Paper crinkled against my hand. Money, I realized. "This is the best burger I have eaten in a decade. Thank you for all your hard work. God bless you."

"Uh, thanks, ma'am." Still stunned, I strode back toward the kitchen.

The waitress smirked at me.

Hours later, the lunch rush died down.

"Clint, dishes." My co-worker pointed at a tower of pots and pans. I plunged my hands into the hot, soapy water.

Graduation is only two months away. You're so close to graduating. Dropouts stay at home and do nothing. The thought surprised me because it didn't feel like my own. I dried my hands and threw the towel into a basket. "I'll talk to my teachers and see what happens."

Years later, Asbury Theological Seminary taught me a fancy term—prevenient grace—which describes God loving a person before they even understand who God is. "While we were yet sinners, Christ died in our place" (Romans 5:8).

Now, when I look back, I realize God spoke to me. I experienced God's prevenient grace[3].

I learned a vast space lay between "so close" and "graduating." At midterm, I'd managed a whopping 18 percent in geology. I stepped up to my teacher's desk. She eyed me warily. I'd rolled the day's worksheets into a scroll and wrung them in my hands. "Hi. Um. I wondered if you would let me hand in any late assignments so I could bring my grade up."

"You ..."

3 Prevenient grace- "Prevenient" and "preview" come from the same Latin root. God's prevenient grace is God working in our lives for good before we know who He is or understand what is happening.

Shock erased the rest of her thought. Like her, I struggled to reconcile the obnoxious, insubordinate teen of last week with the humble boy standing in front of her.

She squinted at the box-shaped computer monitor on her desk and glanced at me. "I'm inputting those grades as we speak. And I'll be finished by tomorrow night. Whatever assignments you can hand in to me by tomorrow after school, I will give you 50 percent for."

My grin stretched up to my eyes. "Thank you. Thank you, thank you, thank you, thank you." *Graduating might actually be possible.* I spun toward the doorway, intent to escape before she changed her mind or I realized I'd heard her wrong.

"Mr. Evans."

My chin dropped. I pivoted on my heels.

She flapped a pink sheet of paper in my direction. "Do you have the assignment list, or were those the pink spitballs Terra picked out of her hair all semester?"

I swallowed a laugh. "Spitballs, ma'am." I reached for the syllabus. "Thank you."

By the end of the year, I'd brought my grade up to 68 percent.

Algebra was another matter. I'd already failed the class three times when I stood at Mr. Goodman's desk. "Will you be here early tomorrow morning?"

"Yes, sir."

"I want to try to pass Algebra. If I pass, I can graduate."

He looked up at me. The fluorescent lights bounced off his glasses' lenses. "Sure thing, Mr. Evans."

It's possible Mr. Goodman didn't want to see me the following year. Helping me meant permanently getting me out of his thinning hair, but whatever his motivations, he worked with me almost every morning for weeks. I truly struggled with math, but between Mr. Goodman's patience and my genuine effort, I finally passed the class.

I would not have a high school diploma without Larry Goodman[4].

....

4 Larry Goodman, October 28, 1947-December 7, 2017, may his family be blessed.

CHAPTER SIXTEEN

Dear Clint,
  You are good enough.

Church Youth, age 10

CLINT, 1999, POST SENIOR YEAR
MINOT, NORTH DAKOTA

I'd finally found a place I belonged. Guys named me 'Moose' because at sixteen, I could drink twenty-five-year-olds under the table. Week after week, I shined as the life of the party.

"Hurry, you idiots," I screamed. "Pass the bucket!"

The bucket. Single. For a tree fire ignited by a wayward Roman candle.

Brent, just as wasted as the rest of us, shoved a bunch of fumbling drunks into a line and organized a bucket brigade from the hose to the burning tree. One pale-faced chick in an oversized flannel passed the bucket to a kid with stringy shoulder-length hair in a Green Day tour T-shirt, who passed the bucket to me.

Water barely coated the bottom. I tossed the water at the flames. *Tsst.* My cargo jeans were soaked with water intended to douse the fire.

Starting a forest fire was our second greatest concern.

"Come on," I said. "We gotta get this out before the firetrucks get here."

Sirens wailed in the distance, their sound getting louder.

Tssst.

The line included half a dozen inebriated teens. Outdoor patio tables and every surface in the house were littered with pipes, paper, lighters, steel wool, syringes, and dozens of other types of drug paraphernalia. A 9-1-1 call meant Minot police. Minot police meant arrests.

"None," someone yelled, "of you are leaving until the fire—"

"It's out," I told Brent.

Red and blue lights flashed between neighboring homes.

"Grab your stuff and get the hell out of here!"

Two dozen boozers staggered toward the woods. Brent sprinted to the street beyond the apartment complex to greet the authorities, assure them we put the fire out, and "sorry for the trouble."

Pail still in my hand, I stumbled toward the patio table. I hooked my arm around party debris. Empty bottles, full bottles, plastic baggies filled with cheap weed and other hardware clattered into the bucket. I scanned the ground for more litter—an Easter egg hunt on LSD. Satisfied, I darted into the apartment. My eyes rounded. *Shit.* A toppled pyramid of Pabst Blue Ribbon and Keystone Light cans lay haphazardly on the square kitchen table. Dime bags, lighters and pipes littered almost every surface, including the dirty, brown carpeted floor. Smoke curled out of the chimney of a Jamaican flag-shaded bong.

Great.

Red-and-blue light pulsated through the window.

I shoved the bucket into the broom closet and whipped out a garbage bag from beneath the cheap kitchen cabinets.

No more cop car lights.

What am I doing? This isn't living.

Brent shoved his way through the front door, a huge, sloppy grin on his face. We burst into simultaneous laughter fueled by relief.

I dropped the garbage bag and pointed at the bong. "It's still warm."

"We shouldn't let it go to waste."

"No." I followed him to the threadbare couch.

Brent spun the mouthpiece to face me. I sealed my lips to the glass and inhaled.

"When you leave for Basic, Moose?" Brent said.

"Two weeks," I said, sucking the smoke into my lungs until full.

I believed the Army provided the fastest, most respectable way to get out of Minot and the downward spiral. I wanted my parents to look at me with pride, rather than disgust. When I stared at my reflection, I hated the fat sack who stared back at me. I couldn't have named the 'Hollow' then—the unsatisfied thirst.

Legion whispered sure-fire ways to solve the problem. "All you need is …"

I shoved food into the Hollow, and drugs, and alcohol, and brawling, and sex. Nothing sated or contented the hole at the center of me.

When Brent's friends came to Minot from Minneapolis and drizzled my first line of cocaine onto the table in front of me, I felt an unparalleled, euphoric ecstasy. For two blissful hours, cocaine escorted me to a nirvana beyond reckoning. When the high faded and I returned to my dreary, brown life, and the same piece of shit staring back at me in the mirror, I wept.

The Army was my last hope to whip me into shape and restore my honor.

Just before Basic, my mom called me. "Will you please come to church with us?"

I imagined my dad my dad grinning and bragging to other church members, "He goes off to Basic next week. We sure are proud of him."

I craved hearing those words like I craved a drug high, so I agreed to go. I hadn't been to church in five years and felt a little out of place. I wasn't wrong about my parents showing me off. Men shook my hand, and women hugged me with congratulations and well wishes. I expected to feel nervous or strange sitting in a church pew, but something settled inside of me, a feeling of home.

The night before I left for Basic, a friend hosted a going-away party for me. I crushed can after can of Keystone Light. My friends' praise lit me higher than almost any drug I'd ever taken.

When I opened my eyes, I stared at a hospital ceiling. White walls, white blankets. Beeping machines. Muted voices in the hall beyond the room. I raised my arm. An IV. I turned my head. My brother Korey's face stared back at me.

"Dad's pissed."

My heart lurched. *Shit.* "What happened?" *How did I screw up this time?*

"You don't remember anything?"

I shook my head. Mistake. My head stopped moving, but the room continued spinning.

"Clint, on the way home, you wrapped your car around a telephone pole."

CLINT, PRESENT DAY

Some people can use drugs and walk away. Not me. Addiction dug its claws in and imprisoned me. Within five years I went from a casual user to a full-blown carpet-surfing[5] crack addict.

Any crackhead will tell you, you'll spend your whole life "chasing that first high." That's usually their exact wording. Other users warned me. *They're exaggerating, surely.*

They weren't.

I wrapped my lips around the pipe and inhaled, anticipating the euphoria of the first cocaine high. So much disappointment—like a climax that doesn't quite reach the top. *What a nasty trick.*

I tried again. *Maybe they were wrong.*

Again. *Maybe I didn't do it right.*

Again.

Again.

Again.

Money ran out before drugs quenched the need.

Again.

Again.

Again.

Stealing to pay for eight balls became a full-time job. I walked into any place—my parents' home, friends' homes, grocery stores, department

....

5   Carpet surfing: Sniffing nasty carpet, desperate to find cocaine powder hidden in the fibers.

stores and measured valuables with two questions: *How much could I get for that at the pawn shop? Can I get away with stealing it?*

In stores, I used my whiteness to get away with things my friends couldn't. No one ever caught me. At work, I stole a grand right out of the safe and pinned it on another employee. The manager fired him—the innocent father of five.

And the grand I stole? Went up in smoke within twenty-four hours. Afterward, remorse consumed me—for sharing my crack with so many people.

In Karen Sill's testimony in *From Crack Addict to Pastor,* a book now out of print, she described using welfare checks for crack money, leaving her infant son with almost nothing for food. When cops showed up at her apartment to arrest her, they called her name through a bullhorn. She was high, paranoid, six months pregnant, and in the middle of melting her last crack rock. Desperate to avoid jail for theft, she kicked the screen out of her kitchen window and jumped down from the second floor. When she landed, her cracked glass stem made her angrier than the possibility of harming her unborn baby.

No crack addict likes who they become. Crack robs addicts blind—of money, sanity, reason, relationships, self-respect, and freedom. Most people don't understand that drug addiction imprisons the druggie.

I read about Karen jumping from a two-story window while pregnant and raging about a broken stem. *Well, of course.* I'd ditched Travis at Valley Fair, concerts, and wrestling shows. I disappeared without telling him because, beyond the high, nothing mattered. I'd stolen thousands of dollars, used people, burned through all my relational collateral. And I couldn't care less.

Urgency. Desperation. These are shadows of an addict's need. Most people need air to survive.

Imagine yourself thrown from a capsized sailboat and plunged into the sea. You fix your gaze on the sunlit outline of the sail rippling above you and claw to the surface. You're going to drown.

Your lungs burn, desperate to inhale. You reach the sail. Fatigued arms press against nylon, but the sail is suctioned to the water. You clutch fistfuls of fabric and drag your body across the sail, hand-over-hand. Your lungs are on fire. You reach the mast and boost yourself upward.

Your lips break the surface.

That breath. That first, life-reviving breath, is how addicts feel when they reach the high.

Many Christians judge addicts. "Why can't she sober up and take care of her kids?"

Pity them instead. Pray and fast for them. Thank God for the mercy He's shown you. Because you don't have to beg, borrow and steal for your oxygen. Your air is free.

My addiction transformed me into the husk of a human, void of any capacity for goodness. The world revolved around my next hit. Nothing else mattered.

Crack is a cannibal. The drug eats a person alive until the high becomes more essential for survival than food. In the throes of my addiction, I'd dissolved from 320 pounds down to 150 pounds. Bags beneath my vacant eyes formed deep trenches. My pasty, white skin paled to ashen as Satan's candy erased my existence. My outer appearance mirrored the Hollow consuming me within.

Only by the grace of God did I escape the first time. If I ever smoked another rock, my wife and kids would never see me again.

One night, I sobered around 5:00 a.m., despite my best efforts. The euphoric effects lingered with the dredges of the high and melded with the glow from the TV—the only light. I reached for the ethereal man talking to me from the box.

"What's keeping you awake this early in the morning, friend?"

"Trying to figure out how to score another 8 ball."

"Whatever it is, Jesus can help you."

"Pretty sure Jesus doesn't want to help me get high."

"He cares about you. When's the last time you told him how you felt? Maybe you feel like you're too far gone. Jesus is closer than you think."

The high dissipated. Darkness surrounded me.

The preacher's voice faded to background noise as my thoughts grew in volume.

If I died right now, no one would even know. Would anyone even cry? I'm such a stain of existence. Maybe I do need to go back to the Lord.

Not long later, my boss fired me. The managers couldn't prove I'd framed the other guy, the father. But they knew. Depressed, I slept for three days straight.

When I woke up, I guzzled a bottle of Jack to escape myself. The walls around me constricted. *I have to get out of this apartment.* Too drunk to think clearly, I failed to recognize two things. First, there's a difference between the amount of alcohol a 320-pound moose can handle and a 150-pound waif. Second, I'd drunk too much to drive, no matter how much I weighed.

I sped down 35W in Minneapolis after midnight and a billboard caught my attention. "Hope For the Addicted" with an illustration of a man who appeared as despondent as I felt. Beneath the slogan was a logo for some place called Teen Challenge.

The next morning, I woke up in a hospital after parking my car inside a shoe store.

CHAPTER SEVENTEEN

We are better for having known Clint. We are so grateful he shared a piece of his life with us.

Gordon and Melissa

CLINT, 2002
MINNEAPOLIS

Autumn light streamed through the blinds into the cramped, but clean, intake office at Teen Challenge. My mom squeezed my arm. Her touch did little to calm my nerves.

The man opposite the desk scanned my paperwork. His afro was trim, and he wore a blue, short-sleeved polo with the Teen Challenge logo across one pec. I smelled his fresh cologne.

I'd spent the weeks since the accident wallowing in depression and self-pity on my parents' couch. I'd been jonesing for a high, but my parents refused to give their twenty-one-year-old addict son their car keys. I'd raged at them, even though sober me knew they were right. Unable to drive to my dealer, I physically ached, desperate for a high. The need permeated every thought.

When was the last time I showered before work? Or got a haircut? Prior to the accident, I'd been homeless for months, drifting from couch to sketchy couch. I didn't own clothing because I had nowhere to store it. Sometimes I'd go to my parents' house after they left for work. I'd enter to the scent of my mom's hairspray, photos of me and my brothers on every end table. My mom's plate collection on the wall. Often, I'd shower and wear one of my dad's work shirts.

"Do you have toiletries?" the Teen Challenge administrator asked. "No."

He rolled through intake questions and I realized how invisible I'd become. I rocked back and forth in the chair, barely conscious of the movement. I didn't own a toothbrush. I didn't possess deodorant or extra underwear. My checking account balance was zero. Drugs had stripped me of my entire identity.

Tousled, pale blue T-shirts poked out of a cardboard box shoved up against a metal filing cabinet. *I wonder if he'd notice if I swiped one.*

"There's a Target not too far from here," the man said to my mom. "Are you able to purchase some basics for him? We're about done here."

"Sure." She stood.

A foot taller than her, I rose and banded my arms around her shoulders and held her for a really long time. "Thank you."

"You're welcome. We just want you taken care of, Clinty. We love you."

I tensed, biting back tears. *Mom, please take me with you.*

The door closed behind her.

"Mr. Evans, do you have an I.D.?"

His question dragged my attention from the door. "No." *If I had overdosed on the street, the coroner would have tagged me as a "John Doe."*

The man didn't even bat an eye. "We'll get you squared away." He smiled. "A couple last things before we show you your room."

My breath caught. *I'll have my own bed.*

"What size do you wear, Clint?"

"Men's medium or large."

The man reached over to the cardboard box and flipped collar after collar. "Here you are. A large. They feed us well here," He grinned, placing the blue T-shirt in my hands.

He led me to a closet and swung the door back. Quilts in every variation of reds, blues, yellows, greens, browns, blacks, and whites lined each shelf in neat stacks, from floor to ceiling.

He swung his arm toward the magic quilt shop. "Choose one."

My hand hovered near a tomato-red quilt with patriotic-plaid-colored squares. Navy blue yarn knotted every other intersection.

"You keep the blanket even after you graduate from the program."

I ran my hand across the material, cool to the touch. *My own quilt. I'm safe.* I fisted my hands. Opened them. I had been fighting longer than I could remember. And I didn't need to here.

The man brought me to a bin of donated clothes and let me choose several shirts, shorts, and a pair of pants. He provided me with a pillow and sheets and escorted me to a dormitory-style room.

That night, I placed my clothes and my toiletries in my dresser. I tugged my new quilt up to my chin. Just before my roommate flipped the light off, I noticed a tag sewn into the corner of the quilt.

Made with Love
Assemblies of God Church
Brainerd, MN

My roommate opened the door for me, and we entered our 'group session' room. "Man, I don't know where you're from. But you're always baggin' on me, It ain't coo'."

"Sorry." *Why do I harass people?* Thor's hammer rested on my chest. *Why?* I scrolled through the years of bullying and abuse. Years of others telling me I wasn't good enough. *To fit in. Because I felt inadequate. To put you down before you make fun of me.*

I racked my brain for a solution but couldn't find one. I sat on a folding chair in the circle with other men. Businessmen in their forties, dressed down in khakis. Teens with arms folded, glaring like the world owed 'em. A few guys in their sixties or seventies with scraggly gray hair, and missing teeth. The older ones, I learned, checked in and out of treatment frequently, when their need for three hots and a cot overpowered the addiction.

Guessing the drug of choice became a game. Alcoholics had the most meat on 'em, while pill-poppers tended to be thinner. A crack-head licks his lips and twitches the corner of his mouth, like he's still trying to taste a faded high, a trait plain as day to users and indecipherable to non-addicts. Heron (heroin) users' forearms are scarred all up and down. And meth, to a worse degree than crack, kills its own host. Meth eats away at bone density, which is why users' teeth fall out.

I made eye contact with one kid slouched in a chair straight across from me. The bottom hem of his faded, red Jordan jersey hung off the seat, and he folded his defined arms across his narrow waist. "What's yo' thing?"

"Crack."

"You ain't no crackhead. You got pretty boy fingers."

I turned my palms upward, surprised. Where had the burn marks at my fingertips gone? A strange adrenaline-like coating rushed through my entire body. I felt like two strong forces were fighting for my identity—one good, one evil.

The group leader, wearing the signature blue Teen Challenge polo and khakis, took his seat a few chairs to my right. Guys straightened in their chairs. "Hey, gentlemen. Today, we're going to talk about the methods we used to avoid life, why we're here, and what we want out of life moving forward."

Some of the men were court-ordered to be there. Some received ultimatums from wives or girlfriends. Several truly wanted to get clean for themselves.

A gangly, older man, with speech slurred by years of use, talked about regular trips to the grocery store and drinking Listerine right there in the aisle to get drunk. My roommate alluded to sexual abuse at a young age and described wrapping his mouth around his dad's motorcycle exhaust pipe, hoping to die. Others huffed lighter fluid. *The things addicts do to numb themselves would shock most people.*

The kid in the Bulls jersey straightened at his turn. "Honestly not sho' who my daddy is. My mama always had nasty dudes sniffin' around, eyein' me. I felt safer livin' on the streets, know what I'm sayin'? It don't matter what kinda drug or booze it was, long as I could stay high. When there ain't enough money, I drink hand sanitizer, straight from the bottle. I came here, ta Teen Challenge, cuz' I got busted tryin' to lift somethin' from Sears. I got'ta pick between Teen Challenge and jail time. Ta be honest, though, this place feel' a little like jail. There's somethin' 'bout this place, though, know what I'm sayin'?" The kid looked straight at me, as if asking me the question, personally.

I nodded. *I do. I just can't figure out what ...*

The boy choked up. "It's love. I ain't never felt loved before I came here." One sob burst out, followed by another.

My eyes widened. *"Something about this place" is right.*

While the boy continued to weep, a couple of men walked over and silently rubbed his back, the way a father would, which only made the boy cry harder.

The group leader's voice changed my focus. "Dear Father God, we ..."

My head jerked to the right.

The leader raised one arm upward. His eyes were tightly closed. *He's praying?* Movement tugged my gaze back to the boy. A middle-aged businessman knelt in front of him, resting his hands on his knees. *What the hell is going on here?*

Dope fiends to deacons, eh? No way in hell would I be caught crying.

More than a hundred guys funneled into fifteen-passenger vans for mandatory Wednesday night church attendance.

One dude muttered as we buckled our seat belts, "This is BS, man."

I smirked. *I'm not the only one annoyed by involuntary church attendance.*

Twenty minutes later, our van rolled into the parking lot of Mt. Olivet Assembly of God Church in Apple Valley, Minnesota. Leaders herded us up the cement steps and toward the glass-walled front entrance of the building.

Three years? Five? I couldn't remember the last time I'd darkened the doors of a church building. We filed into the sanctuary, past a heavenly display of face-sized cookies and into rows of cushioned chairs. Church members greeted us cordially and also kept a fearful distance.

I'd probably be scared too if a hundred thugs sauntered through the front door of my church. They'd be more scared if they could see our rap sheets. Theft. Gang affiliation. Battery.

Lights dimmed slightly. A male vocalist on stage counted off the drummer and, on the singer's nod, the guitar and drums jumped into a rehearsed song intro.

I made a slow panoramic scan from right to left. Everyone around me sang. Many held their arms high and swayed from side to side in worship. Some dropped their heads and, if not for the music, would have looked like they were muttering to themselves. They seemed like they'd left the room entirely and entered into another place.

Thor's hammer returned. Pain the drugs numbed for years clawed to the surface. All the rejections, the abuse, my unfulfilled craving for acceptance. I shifted in my seat, scooting away from the uncomfortable pang within. I rubbed my hands against my pockets out of habit. *Man, I need a fix.*

I barely noticed when the music faded, and the preacher launched into his message. Bits and pieces of the sermon filtered through the haze of my thoughts.

"Everyone here has something in common. Not one of us can earn God's acceptance. Our sins are too great. Each one of us stands as a criminal before the Judge. Which is why, brothers and sisters, Jesus died a criminal's death in your place. Grace isn't free, but our fines are paid in full by Jesus's death sentence on the cross. Jesus wants you to give him your hurts, your failures, your strivings, because He's the only one strong enough to carry them."

If possible, the weight on my chest increased. I wanted to release the grief, but I didn't know how.

The music started again, the same song.

My vision blurred with tears. *There is no way I am crying in front of all these people.* I jumped out of my seat, ignited with pain. Guys backed into their chairs as I scrambled past. *Bathroom. I'll splash some cold water on my face and be good as new.*

I stepped into the main aisle, knowing the bathroom was to my right. I glanced left. A couple of guys knelt at the front of the sanctuary, praying. A broad space separated them. *Me. That space is for me.*

My feet turned left. *Turn around.* Two different me's waged war against one another. *Turn around.* My knees dropped to the matted weave. Unable to pretend, unable to fight any longer, my chest convulsed and released the pain I'd punched down for years. "God, I'm sorry. I'm so sorry."

I wept away years of hurt—wept my balls off. Hands gripped my shoulders. I heard prayers over my shoulder from men who understood, who'd manhandled the pain in their lives the exact same way. As my heart emptied of all the garbage I'd stored, my spirit made room for the blessings spoken over me.

The lights turned up again. My feet were numb. My knees ached. I'd rubbed my cheeks raw. I filled my lungs and exited the sanctuary at the tail end of my group.

"Thank you for coming," a grandmother figure said. "Here, take two." She winked, placing cookies in my hand.

"Thanks." I crawled into the last van with an open door. Halfway back to Teen Challenge, I realized I'd left Thor's hammer laying at the altar.

The space at the altar had always been there for me, but for years I'd ignored God brushing past me. I'd searched for belonging. I'd seen glimpses of the truth before the world kicked the tar out of me. And all that time, I just needed to stop running. Jesus doesn't say so, but the prodigal son in Luke 15 bawled his eyes out. I know, because you can't step from your darkest place into the safest rest of the greatest love without breaking in between.

I threw the covers back. My eyes flew open. *Where? Teen Challenge.* I exhaled, hard. Sweat drenched my tangled sheets. I rolled my tongue around my mouth, searching for crack I'd tasted moments before.

Clean. You're clean.

"You were using?" my roommate's voice cut through the darkness.

"Yeah."

"Those dreams are normal. Everyone gets 'em."

I smashed the heels of my hands into my eyes. *I'm losing my mind.* Wide awake, I slid my feet into my shoes and headed to the gym.

Sunday night church attendance was optional. Most guys attended for a break from the facility. I was one of them. The pastor of Mt. Olivet met us in the atrium. "Welcome, gentlemen. We're doing baptisms tonight. You're welcome to participate."

A handful of guys around me raised and lowered hands, expressing interest.

Fresh start. Fresh promise. "I'm in," I said. Loneliness pressed against me, dampening my excitement. *God, I wish my parents could see this.*

"Okay," said the pastor, "why don't you guys come with me. We'll talk about what this means and get you ready."

We followed him down a hallway off the main entrance. His team provided a change of clothes while the pastor explained the meaning of baptism.

We changed in the bathroom and rejoined our group near the entryway. Regular church members filled through the doors and veered around our large, intimidating crew.

A high-pitched woman's voice pierced through the din. "Oh, Chuck, I do *not.*"

A man giggled. *My dad's giggle.*

My head jerked toward the declaration. I spied a head of platinum blond hair.

"Mom?"

Her voice shrill, she said, "Clint?" Her azure eyes sparkled, and her smile stretched from ear to ear. "Clint?"

My dad stood beside her, mouth agape.

My teenage brother Korey recovered first. "Hey, Clint. Fancy meeting you here."

Don't cry. I hugged my mom. Her arms felt like home. "What are you doing here?"

"Your mom decided we would check this church out tonight." My dad grinned.

I smiled right back, imagining how the conversation went.

"You called us, right?" Mom asked.

My eyebrows crinkled. "No."

"Huh. Well, maybe God knew how much I missed my Clinty."

Her cheerful note ended with a tinge of somberness. *She's missed more than seeing me. She's missed sober me. Me, me.*

The prelude music caught our leader's attention, and he ushered us into the sanctuary.

At my turn for baptism, I clambered into a large tub filled with lukewarm water and knelt.

"Clint Evans, we baptize you in the name of the Father, the Son, and the Holy Spirit." I pinched my nose. They bent me backward. *Ow.* Water covered me, rushed off me. *White T-shirt, wrong choice.*

The sanctuary erupted in applause. For me. *My family is clapping.* Someone draped a towel around my shoulders when I climbed out of the tub. Did I feel different? Cleaner. Lighter. Like God power washed the inside of me.

"Whew." Old Clint was finished. "Thank you, Jesus."

CHAPTER EIGHTEEN

CLINT, 2003
MINNEAPOLIS

I rolled my eyes upward, where red cellophane heart streamers lined the wall near the ceiling. She interrupted me again. Her voice sounded like a cartoon chipmunk on speed. In the last fifteen minutes the woman on the other end of the phone provided a detailed description of her vehicle, her three kids'—two girls and a boy—basketball and dance schedules, her most recent root canal, her ex-husband's girlfriend (who sounded incredibly attractive), her water heater, a bully at her son's school, and a co-worker who'd just had a baby, congratulations.

I worked for a cell phone company in bill collection. "Ma'am."

She rattled on about parent-teacher conferences and the cost of ballet shoes and ruined family vacation plans and someone had a birthday coming up, but I didn't quite catch if it was her daughter Olivia or her alcoholic sister, Maggie.

I pinched the bridge of my nose. Co-workers who shared a cubicle with me in the call center paused on their own calls to observe mine. "How much, Miss? I just need a number."

When cell phones first came onto the scene, unlimited call time only applied from 8:00 p.m. until 8:00 a.m. If customers went over their daytime minutes, huge per-minute fees racked up the bill.

During a special promotion period, the company instructed us, "No matter what their debt is, get the customers to tell you what they can pay. That's all they owe. But they have to tell you a number first."

Possibly, I'd freak out, too, about $1,100 of cell phone charges. Though, based on the volume of her words, this particular woman's bill made sense. *Thank God, it's Friday.*

My co-workers snickered. The guy to my right chomped on potato chips, grinning at me.

"Probably PMS …"

"Oh, nope."

"Excuse me?"

Had I spoken out loud? Doesn't matter. I capitalized on her silence. "Ma'am. I understand you're stressed. I'd love to help you. How much of your bill can you pay?"

She launched into an explanation of how she could pay more after her next paycheck.

"Ma'am. Please give me a number."

"Seventy-five dollars. I guess."

I sighed. "All right. Your new current balance is $75.00. May I transfer you to our automated payment system?"

"Wha … yes?" She shrieked. "Are you serious? Oh, thank you."

"You're welcome." All day long, I got to be Jesus for people, erasing debts they couldn't afford.

"Happy Valentine's Day!"

"Happy Valentine's Day."

Transfer.

Thud. My forehead hit the desk. *Happy Valentine's Day.*

After work, I waited for the Lake Street bus to take me to my half-way house.

It's Valentine's Day. I barely have any friends, barely any money, no girlfriend, and I'm holed up in a halfway house.

A housemate slung sideways over the recliner, paused *Halo* on his Xbox, and nodded in greeting.

"Hey." I whipped the fridge door open. Ketchup, mustard, ranch, and mayo—with the lid twisted on at an angle—clinked in the door. A Styrofoam container with mystery contents had been a resident of the fridge longer than I'd resided at the halfway house.

Six-packs of Mountain Dew, generic cola, and lime soda lined most of the shelves. For sober addicts, muscle memory remains, the satisfying nostalgia of flipping the forefinger beneath the pop top.

I grabbed a can of Mountain Dew.

Crack.

Tsssss.

After a few chugs, I dropped the can to the counter and swung the freezer door open, knowing my options would be pizza, a frozen meal, or vanilla ice cream buried in a mound of frost. While the ancient microwave spun the Salisbury steak box in a lethargic circle, my mood plummeted, and temptation amplified.

I could walk two blocks in any direction.

Freezer burn coated the edges of the green beans as I shoved them into my mouth. The entire meal disappeared before I realized I'd eaten it. I tossed the fork into the sink and the cardboard box into the garbage. "I'm gonna head up to my room."

"See you. Happy Valentine's Day."

"Yeah."

Floorboards creaked beneath my feet. I lumbered up the stairs and leaned against the door of the ten-foot by ten-foot room. Which, of course, now felt like a prison cell.

My red "Made With Love" quilt lay twisted atop the bed from my restless sleep the night before.

Beyond the window next to the bed, car tires sloughed through February slush.

Those people have lives. And cars to take them there. I have nothing. Why am I even trying?

My fingers coiled around the soda can. "Two blocks."

I can spend my savings. I get paid Monday. How many rocks could $1,300 get me? Or I could score some cheap weed or booze.

War erupted.

The angel and the demon whispering in each ear jumped inside my head and battled for control. Their weapons clashed.

Two blocks.

You'll lose everything.

No one loves you.

Your parents are so proud of you.

You don't matter.

You have a good job, a church you like, Christian friends.

You're alone on Valentine's Day. You could escape. Just one day. Just enough to make it through till tomorrow.

My gaze rested on my red quilt. *You have your own possessions again. Just one hit.*

People are praying for you. You feel alone, but you are not alone.

The metal doorknob felt slick beneath my sweaty palm. The temptation to use manifested into a physical force. *Whose brilliant idea was it to invest in a sober house on Lake Street, of all places—the most highly-trafficked drug street in the state?*

"God, I'm not gonna make it. I can't do this alone."

Legion guffawed. "Like taking candy from a baby."

Leave me alone. "I can't leave if I'm not wearing pants."

I unbuttoned my khakis. They fell to the floor, and I tossed them into the dresser. I traded my work polo for a T-shirt. *I won't get out of bed if I'm too cold.* I released the sweats I'd fisted and slammed the drawer shut.

"I can't leave if the door is barricaded."

The dresser screeched against the floor. *Guys downstairs are gonna think I'm nuts.*

I rummaged through the nightstand beneath the window. Winter air seeped in around the 100-year-old window frame. Across the street, through the twilight, I watched a crack addict limp along the sidewalk, hustlin' for his next hit.

You wouldn't have to beg, borrow, or steal. You already have the money.

I shifted my attention to the nightstand and removed my Discman and headphones. One last look at the man across the street.

Look. He's pitiful. He's hooked. You're free.

I hopped into bed and drew "Made With Love" up to my cheek. Adrenaline surged through my body like nitrous oxide. My heart hammered a million miles a minute. I kicked my legs over and over, itchy and uncomfortable in my own skin. "God, please. Help me."

KTIS, the most popular Christian radio station in the Twin Cities, blasted life-giving music into my ears, drowning out the siren song.

The Newsboys sang of God's irresistible love in their song, "Joy." Jars of Clay and Sixpence None the Richer's "With Every Breath" promised God could hear me. Mark Schultz, in "Back in His Arms Again," sang about God leading me to Himself.

Tears dripped onto my pillow. "Please, Jesus."

For hours, Christian music blared throughout my room. The words of the musicians formed a fortress around me.

"God, please don't leave me. Please. I don't want to go back to what I was."

Beads of sweat pricked my forehead. Need, the urge to use, lit every cell in my body. *Focus on the music.* I squeezed my eyes shut and murmured the lyrics.

When I opened my eyes, golden sunlight poured through the window. Tears and sweat stained my pillowcase. Fresh air expanded my lungs.

I made it.

"Thank you, Jesus." I exhaled again. "Okay." I picked up my cell phone and dialed a friend I met at Fountain of Life church. "Yeah, Jerrell. ... Think I can hang with you and your family today? ... Thanks, man. ... Yeah, I'll be ready. ... See you soon."

CHAPTER NINETEEN

Dear Clint,

In life, we encounter individuals who influence us significantly. You changed my life for the better, and I've witnessed firsthand how your presence positively impacted those around you.

Your kindness and generosity were apparent when we first met. You have a unique ability to make others feel appreciated and valued. You invest in the well-being of others.

I loved playing one-on-one basketball with you as if our life depended on it. Your skill and agility surprised me. Regardless of how intense our match was, you always expressed your appreciation for those meaningful, serendipitous moments.

Your ability to find joy in simple activities and enthusiasm for life is contagious to those around you. I miss your spirit. Even if we don't see each other again in this life, I know we'll meet on the other side, standing in God's infinite glory.

Your Brother,
Anthony Williams

CLINT, JULY 2003
WILLMAR, MINNESOTA

I dropped down next to Brent on his fluorescent-orange couch situated in front of a nylon tent amid thousands of other campsites at the Sonshine Music Festival. Rebecca St. James's "Go and Sin No More" converged with Christian punk from the nearby fringe stage.

I met *this* Brent at a church in the Twin Cities.

"Who are you texting?" I asked.

"Sam. A girl I know from Northwestern." He looked up. "You'll like her."

Like was an understatement. A few minutes later, a tall girl with doe eyes and brown hair tucked up in a sloppy bun manifested out of the crowd and greeted Brent.

He hopped up and hugged the girl whose tight, blue shirt accentuated her narrow waist and large ... personality. Brent nodded over his shoulder. "This is my friend, Clint, from The Rock. The church I told you about. Clint is my roommate for the next few days."

"Nice to meet you." Sam shook my hand.

Our crew grew to a dozen people or so. Most were more content hanging at the campsite than attending the concert. But I hadn't spent over one hundred precious dollars to sit on a couch for three days. "Anyone want to check out the stages?"

Sam jumped up. "I do."

For the next three days, Sam and I wandered through crowds and attended concerts together. She worked at CrossRoads United Methodist Church in Lakeville, Minnesota, as their youth director. Sam was super easy to talk with and was genuinely interested in my testimony. She seemed nonplussed by words like "addiction" and "rehab."

I downloaded my whole life's story, and she didn't run.

Sam wanted to see the Newsboys, a group I didn't particularly care for. So, when I stayed for the whole set—and enjoyed my time—I started asking myself questions about the girl next to me. "I'd love to take you out to dinner and a movie sometime after this."

"Like a date?" She glanced at me through her over-sized sunglasses.

"Like a date."

"I'm moving back to Chicago at the end of the summer. It can't be anything too serious."

"I'll let you pick the movie." I regretted the sentence immediately. I knew we'd end up watching some stupid girl movie like *Legally Blonde* or *Charlie's Angels*. So, I fell in love with Sam a little on the spot when she answered, *"X-Men 2."*

We continued dating throughout the summer and into fall. Five months after our first date, I invited Sam to my apartment. The engagement ring in my pocket weighed more than a defensive lineman. A friend suggested Lake Como could be the perfect, romantic spot.

She stepped into the apartment, her gaze wandered over the small space. The apartment was a one-bedroom, but I hadn't bothered moving the mattress beyond the living room—or getting a frame or boxspring for the bed. I saw my stereotypical bachelor pad through a visitors' eyes: one table, a chair, and a TV. The walls were covered with cracked and peeling paint.

I reached for my coat, draped over a chair. "Want to go for a walk around Lake Como?"

"No."

My heart dropped into my toes. "It could be fun."

"It's barely twenty degrees outside."

What do I do?

Sam sat on the mattress with her feet on the floor and her knees to her chest, staring at a brown water spot on the ceiling.

What do I do? Call an audible. I lowered myself to my knee. Sam's eyes widened. *Here goes nothing.* I opened my mouth to recite the speech I'd prepared.

"I wanna be your jar opener and your bug killer."

⌁

CLINT, PRESENT DAY

Sam didn't understand addiction, and to be honest, I didn't either. I'd been clean for more than a year and felt like I could take on the world. I had Christian friends, Christian co-workers, a steady job, a beautiful wife, a healing relationship with my parents, and money in my bank account. I took my environment for granted.

I'd followed Sam to Chicago because I was desperate not to lose her and left my entire support network in the rearview mirror. I'd traded one co-dependency for another without realizing it. We married on

March 27, 2004, in Chicago, and I took a job at an online school called Colorado Technical University in the financial aid department.

There, God taught me about good stewardship and gifted me knowledge of scholarship opportunities. Ten years later, when I graduated with my master's degree, I carried zero dollars of debt.

In Schaumburg, Illinois, I struggled to connect with preppy, clean-cut guys from our new church—all who wanted to be the next Pastor Rick Warren. My co-workers were more welcoming than church members and constantly invited me to go barhopping with them after work.

~~~~

SAM, PRESENT DAY

I don't want to write about Chicago, and I'm not sure how much to say. When we finally moved from Schaumburg, Illinois, to Lebanon, Oregon, the relocation felt like a narrow escape. Afterward, we rarely spoke of his relapses in Schaumburg and often referred to our time in the Northwest Chicago suburbs as "our dark years."

~~~~

CLINT, 2004
SHAUMBURG, ILLINOIS

I swallowed the breakfast sandwich whole and dropped the greasy paper towel onto the passenger-side floor. The garbage blended nicely with empty Monster cans and McDonald's wrappers. *Need to clean the car before Sam sees it.* I sped northwest on I-90 toward the call center in Hoffman Estates where I worked and glanced at my Saturn's rearview mirror. "Seriously?" I stole another look. "The Sears tower." I rounded a bend, and the faint outline disappeared.

I turned down Sears Parkway and faced the white stone-building. *Another day, another dollar.* Large windows reflected a blue tint in the bright sun. "Uh, yeah, so I'm gonna need that TPS report."

As I walked toward the complex, light bounced off the white gold band on my left hand. After three months of marriage the weight and the feel of the ring still surprised me.

"Hey, Snow White." Mark held out the joint pinched between two fingers in an offering.

"Mark," I nodded, "no thanks."

"A bunch of us are heading to Dave & Buster's after work. Wanna come?"

I'd love to come. And I'd lose everything. "I'll think about it." *One drink wouldn't kill me, would it?* Legion whispered.

"Dude, you're so square. Come on. Live a little."

I chortled.

"What's so funny?"

"Nothin'."

"Well. if you change your mind, let me know."

None of the guys from church *invite me out. God, Your way is so lonely. I miss having fun.*

"Mark." I eased the joint out of his hand and put it to my lips.

His jaw slackened.

The way I held the joint, the way I inhaled and held my breath, the way I talked through the hit like I'd been smoking weed for years. "I'm in."

Sam responded with enthusiasm, excited about me making friends. I flipped the switch on my conscience, determined to have a good time.

SAM, 2006, TWO YEARS INTO OUR MARRIAGE
SHAUMBURG, ILLINOIS

Finally, home.

After eight hours of lugging clothes to and from fitting rooms in the Liz Claiborne section of Marshall Field's, a Midwest high-end department store, assisting guests who expected me to work miracles, and closing down the department, I grabbed my purse from the passenger seat, along with my Clif bar wrapper. From the parking lot of our town home complex, I heard Michael Jackson declaring his relationship status with Billy Jean. "Why is it always Michael Jackson?" The situation would be hilarious, if it weren't heartbreaking.

I strode the narrow sidewalk toward our home, lit up like Soldier Field at night. A piece of chewed, white gum had been flung into the chest-high evergreen bush to the right of the front door. *So, weed tonight too.*

I cracked the door open, and Michael Jackson belted with the thunderous enthusiasm of a halftime show. I sprinted the circular floor plan of the main floor, flipping off overhead lights in the living room, stout kitchen, and bathroom. *And why does he turn on every damn light he can find before passing out?* I pounded up every other step. Hallway light. Office. I shifted the computer mouse. The monitor whizzed into life. I aimed the cursor at the blessed white "X" at the top right of the program and cut MJ off mid-word.

Exhaled.

Silence.

Thud.

My back hit the wall, and I slid to the floor. Realizations rolled over me like waves.

He relapsed.

My husband is an alcoholic.

He didn't have enough capital with my family yet. *If they knew, they would tell me to leave him. My friends would judge him.*

When I met Clint, he was on fire for the Lord, attending church every Sunday morning and Friday night. I believed God wasn't done with him yet.

Recently, his family—parents and brothers—came down from Minnesota to Chicago to visit. We barbecued on the grill in the bright summer sun. We laughed and joked and watched football. I bit my lip to avoid smiling when the Bears beat their precious Vikings. And later that weekend, I tried to tell them Clint was drinking again.

In hindsight, starting an argument with Clint about his drinking in front of his parents wasn't the best method. His mom made eye contact with me and averted her gaze, pretending she hadn't heard me.

Now, sitting alone in the office, the darkness felt darker. An all-consuming, night wrapped around me, cutting me off from hope. I wept so bitterly that my stomach convulsed. I wrapped my arms around my knees, in a futile attempt to hold myself together. *I can't believe this is happening. Jesus? Should I leave him?*

Sam, you do what I've called you to do, and I will take care of Clint. You do what I've called you to do, and I will take care of Clint.

Faith strengthened my arms as I pushed myself off the floor. After what might have been five minutes or thirty, I stood. I flipped off the master bedroom light. The lamp on Clint's nightstand spotlighted his form, passed out face down on the bed. *At least passed out drunk Clint is better than belligerent drunk Clint.* I'd learned that lesson quickly.

I grabbed towels from the bathroom and raised Clint's hip enough to slide the towels underneath him.

I'm not quite ready to give up yet.

Clint remained sober more often than not. On his sober days, he frequently vocalized two different thoughts. One, I needed to live into God's call for my life and pursue youth ministry. And two, he wanted to get sober, and doing so meant he needed space from his current environment.

I'd experienced a growing conviction that Marshall Field's wasn't where God wanted me. Complacency bordered disobedience. If I was willing to follow God, I should be willing to follow Him anywhere.

In the kitchen, I opened the cabinet with mixing bowls and found an empty bottle of Jack. *I need to start cooking more, apparently.*

The next day I started applying for youth ministry jobs all across the states.

THE THIRD WORST NIGHT
2004, TWO MONTHS INTO OUR MARRIAGE

I'm so glad Clint's finally spending time with co-workers.

I gathered clothes to create a full load and spotted a pair of Clint's cargo shorts shoved beneath the bed. I tugged them out and mechanically slipped my hand into each pocket, expecting to find change or a pen. In his right cargo pocket, my hand connected with a plastic sandwich bag.

A leftover food wrapper in your pocket, Clint? Gross. I tugged on the bag. *Not food.* The contents looked like oregano seasoning. I held the baggie up to eye level. *Weed. My first time holding a bag of weed.*

My heart dropped into my toes. *He's been lying to me.* I withdrew my cell phone from my pocket and dialed his number. While the phone rang, anger surged. I practiced my rant. *How could you do this to me? Come home this instant. We have to talk about this.*

No answer.

At 3:30 a.m., our apartment door banged open, startling me from sleep. The chain lock bounced against the door. The ceiling fixture burst into life. I squinted against what felt like a UFO beam of light.

Clint dropped onto the mattress and closed his eyes. Each knuckle was flayed open and bloody.

"Where have you been?"

"I don't know."

"How did you get home?"

"I dunno."

"How did your knuckles get bloody?"

His mouth sagged onto his bloody fist.

"Clint?"

My mouth popped open. My eyebrows furrowed. *Did he just pass out?*

I woke up the next morning surprised to realize my clothes were wet. *So are the sheets. Am I sweating?* I rolled over. Clint's mouth was agape. I yanked at blankets and sheets, tracing the source of the moisture, and shuddered.

I'd woken up in a puddle of my husband's piss.

THE SECOND WORST NIGHT, SEPTEMBER 2005
EIGHTEEN MONTHS INTO OUR MARRIAGE

I returned home from the late shift at Marshall Field's at Woodfield Mall. Light streamed from every window. Michael Jackson shouted for the entire neighborhood to beat it. *What on earth?*

I eased the door open, dropped my purse onto the nearby couch, and slid out of my low heels. "Clint?" I eased around each corner, confused, flipping off lights. "Clint? Where are you?"

I jogged up the stairs and ducked my head into the master bedroom. "Are you drunk?" I turned off the music coming from the computer and stormed into the bedroom. "Clint, wake up." I shoved his shoulder. "Wake uuuup!"

"Whaaa? Whaa?" He sat up, bleary-eyed and disoriented.

I intended to wake up my husband and shout at him, nag him. I jostled Bruce Banner instead. Cell for cell, alcohol consumed Clint's entire personality. I don't remember the first words of the argument, but volume and gestures on both sides escalated with furious speed.

He roared in frustration, tight-fisted and flexing. Veins surfaced, snaking up each arm and protruding from his neck and collarbone.

I planted both hands on his chest and shoved him in frustration. "How could you?" He stumbled backward. His bare back scraped against the bedframe. In a mirror I saw three long abrasions on his back. My eyes widened. *You caused those marks, and you're sober.*

The Hulk wrapped both his hands around my neck and choke-slammed me onto the bed. He growled. His fingers tightened.

"Clin... Clin... I can't... breathe."

I dug my fingernails into his forearms.

He jumped backward.

And I bolted. Down the stairs.

Clint roared. A high-pitched, hollow thud sounded, like he'd dropped a ream of paper.

Before the flame on his temper ebbed, he'd punched five holes into walls throughout our house. His fist decimated our glass top stove. His final word of our argument was me, cowered in the corner of the bathroom with a shattered Jack bottle at my bare feet.

Within a span of minutes, we caused irreparable damage to our townhome. And our relationship.

Married less than two years and recent homeowners, pride and convenience tethered me to a marriage I should have walked from. The next morning before work, I packed a duffel bag of clothes, toiletries, and a few miscellaneous items. The master bedroom was above the kitchen. If he was getting food from the fridge, he'd see the bag drop. I listened at the top of the stairs but couldn't determine which room he was in. The master bedroom's sliding glass door rumbled open, and I stepped onto the balcony. *Please don't see it.* I released the handles and dropped the bag onto the patio below.

I descended, giving myself a pep talk. Stairs creaked. *You're in a good mood. You're chipper.*

On TV, sports announcers updated viewers of the latest NFL predictions. As the leather couch came into view, I saw Clint's eyes glued to the screen.

"Bye, Clint." I strode out the front door, rounded the corner to grab the duffel, and stuffed the go-bag into my trunk. I drove to work, like the day was as normal as any other.

Thoughts of our marriage conjured the smell of his alcohol-saturated urine.

$$\textit{twenty}$$

THE WORST NIGHT
NINETEEN MONTHS INTO OUR MARRIAGE

The Hulk resurfaced a couple weeks later, and the argument escalated. I grabbed my flip phone.

Clint wrestled my cell from my grasp. "Don't call the police. Please, we don't need the police."

Lie. "Okay, I won't call the police."

"Promise?"

"Promise."

Rather than arguing with him, I ran past the holes in the walls I'd patched, sanded and painted myself, and grabbed our cordless landline from the office. I bolted out the sliding glass door in the kitchen and knocked the screen off its track. I sprinted to my car, climbed inside, and locked the door.

My first time dialing 9-1-1.

"9-1-1. What's your emergency?"

Fuzzy silence interrupted the female voice on the other end.

Please hear me. "Hi, my name is Samantha Evans." I spouted off my address. "My husband is drunk and belligerent. I'm waiting in my car."

"We'll send someone over there right away."

The line crackled with static.

Clint appeared at the driver's side window. Frantically, he tried opening my door. He pounded on the window with both fists. "Please don't call the police. Talk to me."

Am I overreacting?

A squad car pulled into the parking lot a few minutes later. Two officers bent him over the back of the squad car to cuff him.

"Get off me, you filthy pigs" Clint spewed obscenities.

I dropped my head onto the steering wheel. *I'm arresting my husband.*

After securing Clint in the back of their vehicle, the officers asked for my statement.

I emerged from the car. *I'm not wearing a bra. Or shoes. Or socks.*

In court, I dropped the charges. The judge titled his glasses down on his nose and looked me in the eye. "Well, I hope we don't see you here again, Mrs. Evans."

Yours is not like the cases he sees every single day, God seemed to say.

"You won't, sir."

His every word dripped with skepticism. "I hope not."

Me too.

I strode out of the courtroom questioning Wisdom. "You better be right," I said to God. "Because I have no idea what I'm doing."

A feeling took root deep within me that God wasn't finished with either of us yet.

Sam's Journal Entry
Friday, June 23, 2006

God doesn't do safe.

A church from Oregon called to tell me they'd narrowed down their choices between me and one other candidate for the youth ministry position I'd applied for. *Please choose the other person.* I sat on the bed that night, praying and reading Luke 9. "Clint, do you think I put my hand to the plow and then look back?"

"Sam, you're a good warrior. Keep fighting." Then he fell asleep.

CLINT, PRESENT DAY
RECALLING A MOMENT FROM 2006 IN SCHAUMBURG, ILLINOIS

Do you know why alcoholics are the worst regarding drinking and driving? As an alcoholic, I felt immense shame. My ability to hold my liquor became one of my few boasting rights. *I don't need your help. I'm fine.*

We planned for me to stay in Chicago until the townhome sold while Sam moved ahead to Oregon.

One night, about three weeks before Sam's move to Oregon, I partied with friends and climbed behind the wheel of my Red '99 Ranger XL. *I can handle my alcohol. I'll be fine.* False pride replaced the gaping wound where my self-esteem should have been.

As I drove home, Wisdom shouted at me to pull over. I didn't argue, just parked in a grocery store parking lot and laid across the bench to sleep it off.

A loud rap on the door jolted me awake. I opened my eyes. A white beam of light pointed at my face caused me to squeeze my eyelids shut immediately. But not before I registered the swirling red-and-blue lights lighting up the cab of my truck. *Oh, no.*

"Sir, I need you to wake up and show me your driver's license and proof of insurance."

This isn't good. I pushed myself up and my knee hit the keys dangling from the ignition. *Oh, no.* I rolled the manual window down, passed the paper he asked for, and rested my hands on the wheel. *Alotta good trying to sleep it off did me. I'm gonna get nailed anyway.*

Because I hadn't been driving the vehicle, and, in fact, tried to make a wiser choice, my lawyer talked the DWI charge down to a reckless endangerment.

God knew.

God knew eleven years later, the difference between a DWI and a reckless endangerment charge would matter.

I spent the night in jail. A few mornings later, I stirred before the rest of the world. I rolled my head toward the alarm clock beside the bed. *4:30 a.m.* I felt Sam shifting beside me.

Her silence scared me more than her volcanic rage. *Scream at me already. Get it over with.*

She threw the covers off and stumbled toward the bathroom. When she returned, I said, "Say something."

"There's nothing left to say."

Bad sign.

"Tell you what, though. This better not follow us to Oregon." She switched her lamp on, chasing shadows to the corner of the room.

"You have no idea how badly I want to leave this behind," I said.

She tightened her lips. Her eyes sparked with unspoken fury, and I could only imagine the words she bit back.

"God's been warning me for awhile," I said. "With Robinson last week and …"

"Who's Robinson?"

"The Vikings player."

"Right. Obviously. Gargh. You use nothing but pronouns when you describe people I actually know, but when you talk about NFL players, you refer to them by name. It's mind-boggling. I never ever know who you're talking about."

I sighed. "Three days ago, Koren Robinson, a Viking's wide receiver got arrested with a DWI charge, as well as fleeing police—which is a felony. He blew a .11. When I saw the story on Sports Center, I sensed God saying, 'That could be you. You're gonna get caught.' God didn't want me to get arrested. Alerting the officer broke his heart, but He was fed up, and I wasn't listening. He was done."

"So, God spoke to you?"

"Yeah."

"Huh."

Part Three

the people living in darkness
have seen a great light;
on those living in the land of the shadow of death
a light has dawned.

Matthew 4:16 NIV

CHAPTER TWENTY

Diary of a Faster, Day 3

January 3, 2019

Dear God,

Continue to work on the heart of my friend and husband. Obliterate the shame seeded in him as a child.

You are a piece of garbage.

You are worthless.

No one wants you.

You are unlovable.

These are the lies he begs to be silenced. Clear his heart of these wrong perceptions and grant him the grace to see himself the way others do. In Your mercy, reveal to him what you see when You look at him. Jesus, You are the only one with the power to slay these misconceptions in his heart.

This man is a bridegroom of circumcision to me. He is a fighter. And he chose a fighter for a wife. He is a man worth fighting for.

Use Your sword. Be sharp and quick. Let his remaining heartbeats on this earth know intimately Your joy and freedom. Move him out of his own way and Yours. May You be a force to be reckoned with through Him.

SAM, 2007
LEBANON, OREGON

"I gave up everything for you!" I launched a pillow across the living room. "I took a new job. For you. I moved across the country. For you. I left my family. For you. Because you said you needed a new start. You needed to get out of your environment to get sober. Well, guess what? You brought your environment with you. If you keep getting drunk, I could lose my job over this. Do you understand?"

"Sam, I'm sorry."

I shook my head, hot with rage. "You need to leave."

"Leave where?"

"I don't know. Leave me. Go live with your parents. I don't know. I don't care. I'm done." I was no longer screaming, which terrified me. "God, I am really done."

"I have nowhere to go."

"Not my problem."

I grabbed my purse and slammed the door behind me. I drove to the parking lot of the church where I worked. Twilight colored the sky. I dialed my friend Carolyn.

She answered on the third ring.

"I want a divorce. And hi." Words tumbled like the tears plopping— onto the steering wheel. "Our lives are speeding in two different directions. I can't do this anymore."

"Sam, I'm going to call my parents and have them pray for you."

"No …" Embarrassment and shame colored my weak protest. *Now everyone will know I was stupid enough to marry an addict. I should have listened to my gut.*

The week before our wedding, I'd purchased a six-pack of Mike's Hard Berry. I came home from work one day and three of them were missing.

"Did you drink those?" I'd asked him.

"I'm not gonna get drunk off of three Mike's."

But you don't even like Mike's. Which means you're drinking just to drink.

Call off the wedding, a voice inside me screamed.

My parents have invested thousands into the ceremony.

People are flying in from all over the country.

I don't want to be that bride.

Everyone is getting married. If I call this off, I'll be the odd woman out.

People will look at me and think, "What's wrong with her?" I'll look at me and wonder what's wrong with me. "Why doesn't anyone want me?"

In that moment, with rain splattering the windshield, I regretted marrying Clint.

My friend's words hit home, "When you're ready to leave him, you'll know."

I'm ready. I'll quit this job, take my stuff, and move back home. Clint can have Oregon. He can keep the whole freaking West Coast.

Being married to an addict was lonely, and I was tired of calculating who I could trust with which pieces of truth. "All right, Care. You can tell your parents." After the phone call ended, I lolled my head back and listened to rain patter on the fiberglass, watching the designs streaking down the window.

Hours later, I returned "home." The duplex was so much smaller than our townhome, a storage unit with small pathways to get from one area of our stuff to another.

I am living across the country from everyone I know in a closet-sized duplex, tethered to a human I want nothing to do with. At least he closed the bedroom door.

I ducked into the second bedroom, where a full-sized mattress, boxspring, and headboard—all separated—leaned upright against the wall. A dresser butted up to the bed, and on the other side of the dresser stood a tall stack of Rubbermaid totes. I slid a comforter and pillow off a stack of precariously balanced boxes and lay on the couch.

God, give me a portrait of comfort. An image materialized of me, weeping in the bedroom with my head on Jesus's lap. Jesus cradled me, rocked me, consoled me.

"Thank you, J ..."

Like the flash of a camera, the picture changed. Jesus wept in the bedroom, alone, and needed me to console Him. *Oh, no. Nope. I want the other image, thank you very much.*

I knew the image was a command to console Clint in the bedroom. "I just want to sleep." But I couldn't erase the image of Jesus sobbing. *Don't even have control of my own thoughts, apparently.*

"Fine." *I'll go into the bedroom, but I'm not sharing covers. I'm not talking to him or touching him. I can't even look at him. So, this is as much obedience as you're gonna get.* I threw off the covers and stomped into the bedroom, dragging my own blanket behind me.

"What are you doing?" Clint asked.

"I'm going to sleep. Leave me alone."

I lay so close to the edge of the bed, my hips practically hung off. *I don't wanna have anything to do with him, Jesus. I'm done with him. I'm done with this marriage.* I faced the wall, unwilling to look at Clint, and closed my eyes.

When I opened them, murky sunlight streamed through the vinyl blinds. I glanced over my shoulder and found the other side of the bed empty.

How long can I hide here?

Not long, my bladder replied.

A few minutes later, I strode toward the fridge in search of breakfast. Clint sat at the kitchen table.

"At least I knew you wouldn't call the cops on me again," Clint said. "Since everyone in town would've found out, including members of our church."

I whirled on him, eyes ablaze. "I'm not a narc. I didn't know who to call, because the one I would have asked for advice from? Support? Protection? Was the one assaulting me. I didn't know what to do."

As if a valve released Clint's bitterness and resentment, his entire demeanor shifted. For a length of time, he said nothing. Then, "I'm really sorry I wasn't there for you, Sam."

"Thank you." I sighed. "I can't go back there. I don't have enough strength to face Chicago again. If you drink again, I'm out."

"I know. I need help."

More silence.

"Why did you come into the bedroom last night?" he asked.

"I didn't want to. God nagged me."

He tapped his fingers on the table. "I prayed for our marriage last night, asked God to show me a sign that our marriage would survive."

"What sign did you ask for?"

"That you would come back into the bedroom."

CHAPTER TWENTY-ONE

Clint,

Thank you for being a good friend and helping me through that difficult time in my life. You and Sam are wonderful people with big hearts, and I am so happy to have met you. I bet you are a wonderful father. I'm glad you two were able to start a family.

I miss you guys.

Love,

Aaron

CLINT, 2007
LEBANON, OREGON

My city-girl wife gazed into the vast dark of Lebanon, Oregon's countryside. The high beams showed nothing but fields for miles.

We parked in the farm-length driveway of the pastor's home. A young adult small group gathered on mismatched chairs collected from different areas of the house. Sam's friend from work had invited us. The people seemed nice enough. Welcoming, warm, gentle. The study vaguely reminded me of groups I'd participated in at Teen Challenge, minus the addiction-recovery piece.

At the end of the night, the leader asked, "Does anyone have any prayer requests?" My knee bounced up and down uncontrollably. My heart thundered at a million miles a minute. Sharing at Teen Challenge, where everyone else was an addict was one thing. Sharing with a group of strangers in a house I'd never stepped foot in before? Terrifying. But what I felt like I was supposed to do next with my life would be even harder. I forced the words out. "I do."

Everyone turned to me, appropriate since I'd spoken, but my body heated like a pressurized volcano. At any moment, I'd instantly combust into a porous glob of sweat. I dropped my head and spoke toward the carpet. "I feel like I'm supposed to go to college." My hands swished together like I was trying to start a fire in the middle of the nice pastor's living room. *What if I fail out again? What if a bunch of punk eighteen-year-olds make fun of me for being so old?* "I'm terrified. The first try at school didn't go so well."

The whole group bowed their heads and prayed for me by name, like I'd been their friend for years rather than a visitor they'd known for an hour. Peace crashed over me, washed through me.

The next week I called an online school—to apply for a job—because I'd already talked myself out of returning to school. The admission rep was a jerk, and I found few well-paying jobs in financial aid. I applied to be an Oregon State Financial Aid adviser. Despite my impressive resume, OSU hired someone with zero experience and a bachelor's degree.

Doors slammed in every direction. I was like Bruce Nolan in the movie, *Bruce Almighty*, praying for a sign, yet blind to God's answer.

I settled for a job at T-Mobile that paid less than my previous job. The hourlong commute required me to wake up at 3:30 a.m. *This isn't what I'm supposed to be doing.* A couple weeks in, I slid behind the wheel of my Ranger, discouraged about the long drive home. Over the radio, Superchick sang about making the most of each day.

My cousin, Leigh, who'd grown up in Minot, moved out to Oregon months before Sam and me. During the time of my great debate, School or No School, we received an invitation to Leigh's Master's graduation.

After the ceremony, I wrapped my younger cousin in an embrace. "Congratulations, Leigh." *It's so weird to have so much family in Oregon.*

"Thanks for coming." Leigh's face radiated in the joy of her accomplishment.

"I've been thinking about going to college, but I'm scared out of my mind."

"Oh, Clint. You'd be great. You're not the same person you were back then."

"I'm not even sure what I would major in."

"Start with your generals and figure out the rest of the classes as you go."

Sam pursed her lips. She didn't need to say, "I told you so." But the encouragement felt different coming from Leigh. She knew how great a failure I'd been. She didn't have to tell me I'd be great the same way my wife did. *If Leigh thinks I can do it, maybe I can.*

A few weeks later, I stood on the corner of Vine and Park waiting for a shuttle to transport me to Linn Benton Community College in Albany, Oregon. "Back to school, back to school to prove to dad I'm not a fool," I sang. And I laughed at myself. *I am a grown man about to take the bus to school.*

Every day, the same girl, eight years younger, I guessed, waited at the same stop. "Hi," I said one morning.

Her glare manifested frost across the summer grass. My eyebrows retreated. *Sorry to be so offensive.*

I didn't try to talk to her again. Each day, she stood stiff, like she had a pole shoved up her … spine. She went out of her way not to speak to me or even look at me.

Ignoring her was easy enough. I stood at the corner and sipped my tar-like coffee, waiting for the shuttle to roll to a stop at the curb.

Several months later, at the stop, she turned to me and said, "Hi."

Eyebrows raised, I returned the greeting. When the shuttle arrived, I motioned for her to get on first, as I did each morning. The oversized van rocked us from side to side.

"What are you majoring in?" she asked.

"Psychology. Why are you talking to me all of a sudden?"

She blushed. "I just figured any grown man who drinks out of a Mickey Mouse mug can't be all bad."

Really? Is my appearance intimidating?

I stepped back for half a second to see myself from her eyes. Tall. Shaved head. Tatted forearms. I slurped out of my Mickey Mouse mug.

"I shave my head because I'm balding. The tat spells out 'Prodigal Son,' which is my story. I wandered away from God and found my way home again."

"Oh."

The shuttle hit a bump, and we bounced on the seats. "Things are different than they seemed?"

One day, a guy her age with prickly, white hair eyed her like a snack. She shifted uncomfortably. I moved next to her. The guy zipped his gaze in another direction. Guess I wasn't his type.

When I told Sam about meeting Laura, she said, "Well, of course. You look like a felon."

"I don't like what you're telling me."

"So, lift less and grow your hair out."

She burst into laughter.

"Ha. Ha. McGuffin looks way scarier than me," I said.

"McGuffin can dead lift 500 pounds."

"More than 500, actually."

She rolled her eyes. "Clint. You play football and weightlift. You don't feel strong because you measure yourself against the 5 percent of this world who can lift five hundred pounds."

"I just don't want to end up with my dad's little chicken legs."

"Well," she snickered, "mission accomplished."

CHAPTER TWENTY-TWO

Clint.

I have never met a more gentle giant in my life. Your composure and collected reasoning skills make you a great asset to the Kingdom. You can be a force unparalleled, yet in most cases you take the meager and meek road instead. I value greatly your friendship and appreciate your sense of humor and camaraderie. I feel great things are ahead for you and you are just the man for the job. I love you man keep up the good fight.

Dana

CLINT, 2008
LEBANON, OREGON

Water droplets glittered on tall grasses stretching up the steep embankment at the edge of the plowed cornfield. I squinted against the sunshine blinking through a canvas of bare trees. The booming voice I resented all my life came in handy. I shouted across the makeshift football field. "Chance, dude, where's your other shoe?"

"I dunno." Chance jabbed his thumb into the air over his shoulder. "Somewhere between the twenty and the end zone."

"Never gonna see your shoe again," Guillermo said, a boy from Chance's team.

Chance shrugged, the period at the end of the conversation. Brilliant white teeth grinned from a face caked in mud. "Let's play."

"All right. You heard the man. Line up."

Teens wearing red, white and blue Warrior jerseys and others in green U of O Duck tees trudged toward me. Their feet slurped with each step.

In Lebanon, Oregon, the Civil War lasted all year long. Kevin dried his muddy hands across the front of his Oregon State Beavers T-shirt. "The line of scrimmage is three feet that way."

Cold fall air blew across my bare scalp. The mild twang of cow dung lingered in the air. And I was in heaven.

Kevin whined. "And why do you get to be all-time QB?"

"He's living out his childhood fantasies," said Gabe, who wasn't wrong.

As a boy, I was rarely allowed to be loud without restraint. Leashed energy pulsed through me, craving an outlet. I also loved all things football. So, when farmer David approached Sam and me with the concept of mud football, the child within me jolted into a very undignified happy dance. *Tell me more.*

Sam was the youth director of Our Saviour's Lutheran Church. One Saturday each autumn, David McCready hosted Mud Football. He'd hosed down a patch of dirt and ran limestone powder lines to measure off a perimeter, end zones and hash marks.

"Dude, quit complainin'." I crouched down. "Hut, hike."

The ball sailed. CJ caught it. Neil tackled him.

My friend AR yelled, "Two-hand touch, man. Unnecessary roughness."

I laughed. "There's no such thing."

Feet tromped. Speedy track stars trudged to get open. Football in slow motion.

Thirty minutes later we were all sucking air. My sweatpants, caked in mud, felt as stiff as starched denim. The fabric hit my shins with each step. The boys and me—and Taylor, the one brave girl in the crew—climbed up toward the barn where huge vats of steaming chili waited.

"No way." David's wife Lona aimed the hose at my center mass. "You're not comin' anywhere near my food lookin' like mud zombies." Without warning, she squeezed the trigger.

I sputtered and laughed beneath the spray. Spreading my arms out wide, I tried to catch my breath from the shock of the cold water.

One-by-one she hosed each of us down, enjoying her job a little too much.

The hazing was easy enough to forgive, because when each of us was clean-ish and dry-ish, we lined up outside for chili, hot dogs, and cookies.

After prayer, I held out my empty Styrofoam cup for a ladle of cinnamon-scented apple cider. The heat from the cup felt glorious against my red fingers. Steam curled upward.

"It's hot, Clint," Lona said.

I sipped and jerked the cup away from my lips.

"Still hot, Clint." Lona smiled.

Kids stood around a fire in a metal barrel. Some sat at a picnic table to eat, others in clusters on mismatched chairs.

Heaven.

Sam remained clean except for one Chance-sized hand streak of mud on her left cheek. "Hey, guys, listen up."

Only a handful of people turned, so she walked up near two kids paying no attention and whispered, "If you can hear the sound of my voice clap one time."

They clapped.

"If you can hear the sound of my voice, clap two times."

More kids clapped. After three claps, everyone was paying attention.

"Some of you know this Christmas we're performing a pageant called *The Best Christmas Pageant Ever*. Some of you are characters in the pageant. In the story, the six no-good Herdman children graffiti and burn down Fred Shoemaker's toolshed."

"Poor Fred Shoemaker," I said.

AR pointed at them. "You should be nicer to Mr. Shoemaker."

Everyone laughed.

"Where are my no-good Herdmans?" Sam asked.

Six kids raised their hands.

Sam revealed the cans of spray paint she'd been holding behind her back. The kids' eyes widened. "Here is your paint." She pointed to four upright pieces of four-foot by eight-foot plywood nailed together to create a box in an adjoining field. "And you can thank Farmer Dave for the tool shed you're about to burn down.

"Don't start tagging until we get the video camera set up. We're gonna show the footage during the play, and we only have one shed to burn down."

CLINT, PRESENT DAY

I'm pretty sure Sam became my hero that day.

With Sam's example, I learned ministry was as simple as being present for the people in front of me. Some of the kids came from sturdy families. Many of them came from broken homes. Most of the kids—mostly boys—did not attend our church. A couple of their dads were in jail.

Sam and I attended tons of football games beneath the Friday night lights, where the whole town seemed to gather, because half of the youth group played on the football team. We all fit together somehow and became a family. At times my heart overflowed with fulfilled purpose.

When Christmas came and we performed *The Best Christmas Pageant Ever*, I sweat inside a church member's actual firefighter gear. Seven or eight children hung off my arms, legs and abdomen, and I lumbered from the back of the sanctuary toward the stage. The oversized helmet muted the kids' elated squeals. *How are this me and Old Clint the same people?*

The pageant showed the transformation of the no-good Herdmans, more importantly, the play revealed the necessary transformation of church members' attitudes toward the Herdmans. The story's message was simple: Everyone has a place in God's kingdom. Everyone is worthy of God's love.

As I stepped into my own ministry roles, I felt fiercely protective of the Herdmans in my life. After all, I was a Herdman myself.

Everyone who knew me before and after recognized the change Except for me. God changed my heart toward Him and others, but I couldn't release the shame-riddled version of myself I saw in the mirror. "Everyone is worthy of God's love," we taught the kids. But I couldn't believe the words myself.

Legion still stalked me. I could feel his narrowed gaze, calculating. I'd been sober for three years and he was cunning enough not to dangle the taste of alcohol in front of me. But sometimes when no one was nearby, I could hear him whisper, "You're a phony. And one day they're all going to know it. Stop pretending you're like them. We both know the truth."

CHAPTER TWENTY-THREE

Dear Clint,

I am very proud of you and impressed by you. I know it was a long road, and not always easy, but you stuck to it. What a great example of perseverance. God is going to use you in powerful ways. You've had a really positive impact on my life. Thanks for everything.

Oregon Youth

CLINT, 2009
LEBANON, OREGON

Most custodians aren't hired with the promise or expectation of job advancement.

I'm not most people.

As I attended school, I also worked at our church as the custodian and volunteered with the youth group. Sometimes, when I was cleaning, I'd see a kid in our parking lot shooting hoops and venture outside to join him. The youth group grew from less than ten to forty.

They're coming here? To us? To me?

At one point, Sam met with the senior high kids at a coffee shop, and I wrangled the seventh and eighth graders. Tons of boys with tons of energy. I'd abandoned the youth room for the large, carpeted gym. "Gentlemen, and ladies, we're playing Blob tag. Levi, you're it. Go."

My teaching method was simple: Run the kids so ragged that sitting to listen to a Bible story sounded appealing.

"Line up on the wall." After a body-odor-scented flurry most of them slammed their backs against the painted cinder blocks. One boy galloped in a circle. *The 'me' of my past, and I knew exactly how to deal with it.* "AJ, What's gotten into you? Six laps around the church, go."

AJ bolted through the steel doors.

Two boys talked while I spoke. "Anthony, Nick. Thirty push-ups."

"Alright, everyone, have a seat." My voice boomed off the walls of the gym without anyone shushing me. *God, did you actually give me this voice for a reason?* "Tonight, I'm gonna teach you about a really important guy in the Bible who only got one verse. One sentence.

"Everyone open your Bibles to Judges. Judges is the seventh book of the Bible. If you see Samuel, Kings, or Chronicles, you've gone too far. Raise your hand when you get there…all right. Turn to Judges 3.

"Judges 3:31 says, 'After Ehud came Shamgar son of Anath, who struck down six hundred Philistines with an ox goad. He too saved Israel.'

"All right, so the Israelites cycled through times of obedience to God. They'd serve Him for awhile and then get bored or distracted and start doing their own thing. Then they'd get attacked and cry to God for help. And God raised up judges, basically temporary leaders to help free the people.

"So, God calls this guy named Shamgar. He says, 'Hey, Shamgar, I want you to go over there and kill those Philistines attacking my people. What have you got?'

"Shamgar looks around him. Nothing. Then he looks down in his hands at his ox goad, which is a big, pointy stick. 'I, uh, I have this stick.'

"'That'll do,' says God. 'Go get 'em.'

"So, Shamgar killed 600 men with a big, pointy stick." I held out my arm and pointed an imaginary stick at each of them. "We all only get one verse. And God is calling us to use the tools right in front of us for the tasks at hand. What's your tool? What's your talent? We all only get one sentence. What is yours gonna say?"

In between mission trips and weekend retreats, the youth group laughed and spent time together. I don't know if they remember any Bible lessons I taught them, but I hope to hell they remember I loved them. My kids, my sheep. Before God placed a seven-pound, helpless, little girl in my lap, I'd never felt so fiercely protective of anyone in my life.

Sam came up with the craziest ideas for games—toilet paper mummies and egg tosses through hula hoops. One year, at a retreat, the kids made a sandwich out of Graham crackers, Oreos, chocolate syrup and who knows what else. They called it a "Skid Mark Sandwich," and expected Sam and I to eat. So, we did. After one Girls Only lock-in, Sam came home with new highlights in her hair. She let a teenager dye her hair. And Adrienne did a fantastic job.

I remember never feeling like we were making a difference. The boys were so wild. *Is what I'm saying getting through? Does what I'm doing matter?*

Sam and I constantly measured ourselves by our mistakes. Too often, we focused on the disappointments and failures. Following a heartbreaking church split, Sam lost her job. While we figured out our next steps, we volunteered at the youth group in town led by a friend where a lot of our kids had migrated.

One day, I was out playing basketball with the guys. The net backed up to an eight-foot-high wooden fence with a residential backyard on the opposite side.

Midway through a game someone yelled, "Hey. Traveling."

"I only took two steps."

I laughed. "Dude, you know what you did. Hand it over."

"Quiet down you brats." A string of cuss words followed.

I caught the ball, mid-dribble. *Did I hear a crow or a woman?* The boys seemed nonplused. "Why is she screaming?"

Austin waved flippantly. "Eh. She always yells at us …"

No, she doesn't.

" … says we're being too loud."

"You're being too loud?" The ball dropped to the ground and bounced a few times before Kordell shoved a heel out to stop it. *I hate bullies. Even if they're 115 years old and shriveled, with one foot in the grave.*

"Clint?" Kordell said.

"Clint," Austin said, "what are you doing?"

No one screams at my boys. They're good *kids.* I'd already reached the end of the parking lot driveway and veered right onto South 7th street. I marched up her front steps and pounded on her front door. *Loud? I'll show you loud. Wait until you meet Clint Freakin' Evans.*

Fifteen minutes later I returned to the parking lot, to the boys, to the basketball game. The old crow never bothered them again.

CLINT, 2019
SLEEPY EYE, MINNESOTA

In Oregon, God showed me His field ripe for the harvest. So many people struggled through life on their own strength, oblivious of God's love.

I played in a semi-pro football league—a bunch of athletic guys in their twenties and thirties who loved the game. I met a ton of people throughout the Willamette Valley and lead multiple teammates to Christ. I'd catch them off guard with revealing comments about using drugs, and they couldn't reconcile their image of a drug addict with the person standing in front of them. Far from pushy or preachy, I simply answered questions about my life and didn't shy away from God's role in my story.

One night, I shot hoops with a kid in the church parking lot and he started asking questions about Jesus. Surrendering to God's plan was a ball on the rim, tipping into the basket. When I invited him to pray with me, he spooked.

"Uh, I've gotta get home," he said, and he bolted—hopped on his bike and pedaled like Big Foot was chasing him.

I never witnessed anyone come so close and retreat. I mourn what might have been. I'll never know if he tipped the ball in.

One kid in the youth group gave me hell every week. For several years, we tried everything to help him, but his behavior and biting words affected the entire group dynamic.

Finally, we had a hard conversation with his mom. "We love him. We really appreciate you bringing him, but it's obvious he doesn't want to be here. We're open to suggestions, but maybe if he doesn't want to be here, he shouldn't be forced to come." He left for a long time. When he returned, it was because he missed the youth group.

Seven years after we left Oregon, I received a message from that kid that made me bawl like a child.

> Thank you for believing in me, for pushing me to be better, for never giving up on me.

While we were still in Oregon, one of our teens got into legal trouble. While I was in class, Sam attended the court hearing. The judge declared if no one volunteered to temporarily house this boy, he'd return to the juvenile detention center for the months leading up to the trial.

After three beats of silence, Sam stood. "My husband and I can take him."

Later, I received a text:

> Well, surprise, honey. It's a boy.

When I asked her why, she shrugged. "Mostly, he reminded me of you. There are so many moments from your past when I wish someone had stood up for you."

CHAPTER TWENTY-FOUR

Dear Clint,

Hey you, how are you? I landed another thirty days for unpaid fines in a different county, but I want to tell you good news. I prayed and asked God to show me a sign to tell me where to go. Then your letter came. So, I wrote our brother Bill asking to be reaccepted at Teen Challenge. I'm headed back to complete the program.

The plans I set for myself weren't good enough to keep me out of trouble. I now have my heart totally set on doing the Lord's work. I want to bring people to our Father through Jesus so they can receive love and understanding and all the things the Lord has to offer. I know the Lord wants me to be a missionary and I trust He will pave the way for me as He does for all His children.

The letter you sent made a big impact. Thank you so much for caring. I pray all is going well there in Minnesota. Are you adjusting well to pastoral life? I'll be at county till the 26th of this month, the day after Christmas, but I feel so at peace for doing the right thing, and I can't wait to go back to Teen Challenge and be surrounded by my brothers in Christ.

Merry Christmas to you and your family,

Joshua

CLINT, 2009
LEBANON, OREGON

I enjoyed classes at the community college more than I'd thought I would. Two years later, I received a blue cap and gown in the mail. I fingered the gold tassel, which signified a GPA greater than 3.8, certain they'd mailed the thing by mistake.

"When is the ceremony," Sam asked.

I turned my palm up, in question. "I'm not going."

Sam's twinkling features iced over. "Graduation is a big deal."

"It's just an associate's degree and there will be thousands of people there, and I'll have to sit there for hours and …"

The rest of the conversation doesn't matter. I lost.

I am happy to report, however, I won the battle about what I wore to graduation. The day of the ceremony, I emerged from the bedroom in a Vikings T-shirt and royal blue basketball shorts. On the couch, I slid white sneakers over black tube socks that stretched up to my shins.

"You cannot attend your graduation in gym shorts."

I loved Sam's horrified expression. "Watch me."

"You have to dress up."

"Why? The gown covers the clothes."

"This is your graduation."

"Do you want me to go or not?"

I'll confess, I felt a bit smug driving to the ceremony.

After attending Linn Benton, I enrolled at Oregon State University. Instantly, I missed the laid-back vibe. At Linn Benton, older people attended classes to pass time, guys who hated school acquired welding certifications, professors went by their first names, and many people pursued a second or third career. I fit in with a melting pot of misfits.

Still, Oregon State University taught me one of the most important lessons God needed me to see. During a Psychology class, my atheist professor mentioned offhandedly he'd once been a pastor. My pencil stilled. *How can you shepherd God's people without knowing God? No wonder people are walking away from the church. They can't find Jesus there.*

After class, I approached his podium and greeted him. "Your lesson today inspired me to become a pastor."

His jaw slackened.

Later, I sat at the kitchen table while Sam wiped the gas stove after dinner. Evening sun spilled over my shoulder and onto the orange-and-brown kitchen carpet of the 1920s house we rented.

Sam had been in youth ministry for eight years. She'd seen the way self-centered, egotistical, jealous "Christians" chewed up pastors' families and spit them out. "Congregation members care more about new carpet than newcomers," she'd said once. "I don't want that call."

This won't go well. "Hey, Sam, I think God is calling me to pastoral ministry."

Her palm stopped. Her facial expression echoed my professor's. "I think you're wrong. Go back and try again."

She was half-kidding. We both knew if God called me to pastoral ministry, then obedience was inevitable.

"I specifically asked you before we got married if you had any intentions of becoming a pastor. You told me no."

"I didn't have any intentions of becoming a pastor until today."

She muttered, "One point, God."

The coastal range created a sloped, periwinkle boarder between the yellow farmland and the azure sky. Now daylight, I scanned the ditches on either side of Fayetteville Drive, but spotted nothing except stiff, thirsty grass.

A few minutes later, my car bounced into the semi-circle parking lot. *Who needs shocks?* I strode through the front doors of the Willamette Campus of the Adult and Teen Challenge. A stocky, former officer emerged from the office.

"Kyle, hey." A grin stretched the corners of my mouth. "Dude. You're never gonna believe this. I hit an owl on the way home last night."

"Seriously?"

"The thing flew right into my windshield. I—"

A distance shout came from the dorm room down the hall. "Leave my stuff alone!"

Kyle and I shook our heads.

"I've got this one." I jogged down the fluorescent lit hallway, past the offices, to the dorms at the opposite end.

"Break it up." I shoved the door open with two hands.

Two guys postured. Their dormmates hesitated, debating if stepping in was worth an elbow to the gut.

I shoved my body between four coiled fists, faced Paul, the bigger of the two, and forced space between the two snarling men. "Break it up." My flat palms applied firm pressure to Paul's chest. "Jake," I said to the guy behind me, "go talk to Kyle."

Jake crinkled his nose. "Smells like a damn urinal in here."

Worn sneakers stomped across the linoleum floor. The door latch clicked.

Jake's not wrong about the smell. "You guys have all seen fights before. Go get ready for dinner. And if you ran out of deodorant, tell Kyle."

After a rattle of nine baritone voices, squeaking shoes, and the creaking door, the room cleared.

"Paul." I looked him in the eye. "Dude, what are you doing? You could break Jake in half."

I felt Paul sigh. I released my hold and backed off.

"He kicked a bunch of my stuff when he climbed down the ladder and called me an f'ing slob."

I glanced toward the bunk Jake and Paul shared. Shoes, shirts, jeans, streaked boxers, magazines, soda cans, and candy wrappers lay strewn around the bottom of the bunk like a bedroom bomb exploded.

"Did Jake kick your stuff," I said, "or was he trying to get down from the bunk with nowhere to step?"

Paul dropped his gaze.

"I don't think Jake's the first one to ever call you a slob. Come on, Paul. You know this mess isn't acceptable." I paused, searching for the right words. "Get your stuff cleaned up and get to dinner. If you cause any more trouble tonight, I'm gonna have to write you up ... and I don't want to." I spotted an open letter on Paul's bed. My heart sank. "Your mom wrote back?"

His shoulders sank. "Yeah."

"I did a lot of damage to my family. They came around. Maybe yours will too." I cleared my throat. Initiating gushy stuff with guys didn't come easy. "Wanna pray about it?" *Please say no.*

Paul dropped onto his bed and picked up the letter. "I guess. Yeah."

I sat beside him and placed my hand on the edge of his knee. "Dear God, thank you for bringing Paul to Teen Challenge and giving him the strength to get clean. Thank you for all the things he's learning and the ways he's grown since he came. We pray, Father, You will soften his mom's heart. Help her to heal from hurt, and help her to forgive. Lord, we know You are turning Paul into a new creation. We trust You're not done with him yet, not done restoring the brokenness in his life yet. So, we're gonna trust You with his mom, that she's gonna give Paul another chance to see his baby girl again. We love You and praise You for who You are and the work You've already done. Amen."

"Amen." Paul sniffed.

I opened my eyes. Small, wet circles spotted the letter in his hands.

"You hungry?" I asked.

"Yes, sir."

"Well, finish cleaning up this mess and meet me down there. I'll save you a seat. Food fixes anything."

"Yes, sir."

Kyle waited in the hallway. "Did a fistfight seriously break out because of a pair of skid-marked boxers on the floor?"

"Paul's improved since he's been here." Kyle's eyes bugged out, and I smiled. "He's only been sober for three weeks." I stopped outside the dining hall. "Picked four fights his first two days here. Getting sober sucks. Getting sober with a bunch of guys harping on you all the time and zero privacy? I'm surprised we don't have more fights."

Space restrictions turned the dorms into an ongoing cage match. Testosterone-charged addicts, angry with themselves, angry at the world, on fire for the need of a high, were all shoved into the same living quarters.

Kyle and I drifted toward the dining hall. "So, you think I should give him more grace?"

"Paul needs patience. If I thought he needed a hammer, I would've brought it."

Kyle chuckled. "Don't doubt it." He was quiet for a second. "How's Sam?"

My heart jolted. "I don't think I ever told you. She had a second miscarriage while she was writing the book about the first. And a few weeks ago, her sister called, apologetically—poor thing—to tell Sam she was pregnant."

"Clint, man, I'm sorry."

"I'm okay. Honestly, I wasn't ready. Full-time school, working here, volunteering at the church. We have a lot going on. I'd rather wait until I graduate to have kids. I trust God will work through this in His way, His time."

"And Sam?"

"Wants to be a mom. Right now. She's pouring herself into writing. She's trying to trust God, but she also keeps trying to tell God the best way to write His story."

"Doesn't work that way."

"She knows."

"I got six requests for deodorant."

"You're welcome."

CHAPTER TWENTY-FIVE

2010

Clint,

Thank you for all you do for me around here. You do a lot and it's not for the money. We haven't talked much, but I wanted you to know I appreciate what you do. People think you're hard on us, but I know it's because you care about us and what happens to us. I spent the last 11 years of my life homeless in California. Not too many people gave a crap about me or what happened to me. I can tell you really care. Thank you for praying for me and my family. It's made a difference. Thank you from the bottom of my heart. God has a special place in heaven for you.

Eddie

CLINT, FEBRUARY 26, 2011
WILLAMETTE VALLEY TEEN CHALLENGE, LEBANON, OREGON

I eased into the parking lot of the Willamette Valley Adult and Teen Challenge Center. "I don't know if I'll ever get used to another person in the back seat. She's so quiet."

Sam laughed. "She's your daughter. She won't be quiet forever."

Before Kaylynn's birth, I took simple things for granted—like walking into a building. I raised the hatchback on the minivan and wrestled the gigantic stroller out of the car. I pressed on two red tabs and shook the contraption. Nothing happened. *Stupid thing.*

"Hold her." Sam handed me the car seat with our five-day-old bundle of pink frills nestled within, and opened the stroller. Abracadabra.

We passed through the double doors of the gathering space. Table-cloths covered each table. A large screen on a small stage displayed the Teen Challenge logo. Speakers on tripods flanked the podium and strings of lights draped from one end of the room to the other.

The monster truck-sized stroller didn't fit between the circular tables, but I tried anyway, clanging the stroller against metal chairs. After displacing half the dinner guests, Sam, Kaylynn, and I subtly took our seats.

Burly, uncouth former addicts with hearts of gold "ooed" and "ahhed" and begged to hold my little girl.

My eyes connected with Paul. His smile dropped.

Teen Challenge guys filled the empty seats reserved for Paul's family. His mom and daughter hadn't come. And I'd just paraded my beautiful baby girl into Paul's graduation ceremony. *I'm so sorry.* A swift, sharp pain pricked my heart.

Pastor Ron, a white-haired man with exaggerated facial features that reminded me of Rodney Dangerfield, approached the podium. "Welcome, everyone. Bow your heads with me?"

An older woman scurried through the door, a young girl's hand clasped within hers. "Sorry." The woman tried to catch her breath.

Paul jumped to his feet.

The girl squealed. "Daddy!"

Paul darted toward the woman and the girl, enclosing both in a wide embrace.

The festive lights swathed across the ceiling illuminated the tears smeared all over Paul's cheeks.

"I love you, Paul," his mother said. "I'm proud of you, boy."

Paul sobbed. Each face I saw—Pastor Ron and his doll of a wife Jeannie, Kyle, Sam, even Jake—teared up with the palpable emotion.

Just another Friday at Teen Challenge.

Substance abuse builds a wall, shutting out emotion. Sobriety demolishes the wall, so years of suppressed emotions hit like a wrecking ball.

The excitement subsided. Men at Paul's table vacated seats closest to Paul to make room for his family.

Pastor Ron prayed and milliseconds after "amen," forks clattered against plates. The room erupted into a murmur of dozens of conversations. After dinner, after worship, graduates shared their stories of how God worked in their lives.

Paul's beefy hands grasped crinkled and sweat-soaked loose leaf. "This 'new creation' stuff is no joke."

Laughter rippled through the room.

"Heh." His exhale into the microphone, amplified through the speakers, sounded like a rocket launching. "I prostituted my soul. I stole to survive, stole to get high. People had zero expectations from me. I was so strung out I couldn't tell heaven from hell.

"Courts gave me a choice between more prison time or mandatory treatment. I figured, 'Well, Teen Challenge can't be as bad as prison.' Boy was I wrong."

The crowd burst into laughter.

"I went from having a cell to myself to sharing one room with twelve guys who felt like the showers were too far away to bother. I came in swinging and almost got kicked out of the program for starting fights. I fought myself too.

"I fought change. Changing meant admitting I'd wasted *years*. I fought sobriety. Being sober meant facing emotions I'd numbed with a needle for years.

"I fought authority. I lost track of times staff wrote me up for an untucked shirt—look Clint," Paul grabbed his polo, "tucked in, or for tardiness. I scrubbed a lot of toilets and dirty dishes for Jesus. Now I'm grateful they believed in me enough to demand the best from me. My whole life, people told me I was a piece of garbage, and I believed them. Every time the high wore off, their 'truths' crept back in.

"My biggest face off at Teen Challenge was against God. God spent months wrestling the lies away from me. He pinned me on my back and shouted, 'I love you, Paul. Just like this. You don't have to earn it.'"

Paul sniffled into the microphone. "God's voice sounded a lot like Clint's, and Kyle's, and Pastor Ron's. Thank you for teaching me how to write a resume. Thanks for practicing job interviews with me at nauseam. I'm not quite ready to thank you for the write-ups but thank you for showing me how much God believes in me. Because of the Teen Challenge staff, I'm sitting at the same table with my daughter for the first time in three years."

His tone indicated the end of his speech. Everyone in the room jumped to their feet and applauded with fury. Not a dry eye in the house.

CHAPTER TWENTY-SIX

Clint,

You live life large. You are not apathetic—you laugh and love and seek adventure. This challenges me to live in the moment better. Thank you.

Care

CLINT, MAY 2011
LEBANON, OREGON

Spring rain washed away winter silt when I received a letter in the mail from Oregon State University. "Hey, Sam, what is 'Magnum Come Laddy?' It sounds like an '80s, cop-themed porno."

She tore her eyes away from her computer screen and glared at me over her shoulder. "What the heck are you talking about?"

"Magnum Come Laddy."

"Magna Cum Laude." Her mouth popped open. "You're graduating Magna Cum Laude?"

I looked down at the already-crinkled paper. "Uh, yeah?"

"Clint, it means you're graduating with a GPA higher than 3.7."

"Three point eight."

"I graduated college with a three point two. You're graduating at the top of your class, with honors."

I flipped the torn envelope over. *Clint Evans. My address.* Now positive the letter had been addressed to me, the implications made even less sense. *Magna Cum Laude.*

"I'm proud of you, sweetheart."

Two months later, we hopped out of the minivan beneath a bright, blue dome of sky. Sam rounded toward the hatchback, cradling Kaylynn's car seat. Her glorious smile flat-lined. She pressed the magic button that transformed the jumble of plastic into a stroller. "You're not going to get the stroller open by shaking it."

"It was worth a shot."

Kaylynn wore bright orange footsie pajamas that spelled "Beavers" in black down one side. "We match, Little One, don't we?" Kaylynn cooed and wrapped her whole hand around my forefinger. "Yes, we do. Yes, we do."

Sam rolled her eyes.

Continuing in my baby voice, I said, "At least they're Oregon State shorts this time."

Kaylynn babbled up at me. Her hazel eyes, partially hidden by a floppy, pink hat that matched mine.

Sam tucked my 2XL Oregon State T-shirt around Kaylynn.

"Nice baby blanket."

Between the T-shirt and the floppy, pink bonnet, Kaylynn's chubby face was the only visible part of her. Drool seeped from the corners of her mouth and soaked my T-shirt—and I didn't care. *She can puke all over me and I don't care. That's true love right there.*

Sam and Kaylynn strolled toward the packed bleachers. *God, please don't let me take them for granted. Help me not screw this up.* Sam hadn't argued about my gym shorts and cut-off shirt this time, which honestly took most of the fun out of it.

I scurried toward a cluster of guys wearing the same costume. *Wish I wore even less under this stupid dress.* I sweltered in the sun with thousands of other graduates forming the processional to our seats.

I rolled and unrolled the thick program into a damp, sweaty scroll. Every once in awhile, I'd open the booklet where "Magna Cum Laude" was bolded. I dragged my finger down the list. "Clinton Marvy Evans." *My name is still there.*

Time blurred. Long lines, uncomfortable chairs. I pitied the professors botching graduates' names. My row stood.

"Clinton Marvy Evans." I strode across the stage and accepted my diploma for my bachelor's degree. The significance of my accomplishment vanished with a single thought: I just waited two hours for six syllables.

This doesn't feel possible. The crack addict stealing food and the alcoholic blitzed out of his mind still occupied a dark, shameful piece of my identity. *I'm living this blessing, and it doesn't feel real.* I opened the booklet again, pressed my finger over my name.

What are you doing here, God? What are you doing with me? Deuteronomy 31:8 immediately came to mind. "The LORD himself goes before you and will be with you; he will never leave you nor forsake you. Do not be afraid; do not be discouraged."

LORD, if this screwup can overcome and succeed in unimaginable ways, by your hand, then anyone can. Help this ceremony go quickly so I can down a cold Mountain Dew and some Red Vines.

Addiction stalked me, always, but in those days Legion's grasp was weak. My life was so full of light I no longer needed to drink to avoid the shadows. Sam and I had miscarried twice just as I started my first semester at OSU. Sam transformed her darkness into a book titled *Love Letters to Miscarriage Moms.* She continually looked over her shoulder while she typed, waiting for temptation to overtake me. I might have fallen, relapsed.

Yet, the group who prayed for me at the beginning of the journey, walked alongside me the entire way. Without their friendship I might have quit. Throughout those four years, we'd hiked together, played basketball, worshiped, prayed, and held bonfires together. I felt loved and accepted by a group of Christian men, just as I was, for the first time in my life.

I thought back to my time in Minneapolis and friendship with Jerrell, the one I'd called the morning after my Valentine's Day battle. Jerrell had taken my spiritual success upon himself. I sat at church with his family, and I ate dinner at his home. All the while, God-like grace was so foreign to me, I couldn't accept it.

But I think Jerrell and Jacki's you-don't-have-to-earn-it love paved the way for me to receive the same grace from others.

CHAPTER TWENTY-SEVEN

Clint,

Thanks for your leadership on this trip and all the personal sacrifices. Your affection for them inspired a large group of people. The youth will always hold the people of this town in their hearts.

Greg

CLINT, MAY 2011
OREGON

Our Teen Challenge minivan chugged upward through the Cascade Range toward Bend, Oregon. Sky-high pines forced the car around sharp corners at a steep incline. The trees' massive height blocked out any hope of cellphone reception. The engine, as ancient as the trees, groaned in frustration.

"Want me to get out and push, Kyle? Or maybe shove my feet through the floor and run the car up the mountain?"

"Couldn't hurt."

"I think I actually see light coming through the floor."

We laughed and then fell into silence. Pastoral ministry? The thought resurfaced with increasing frequency. *God, what do you want from me?* I chuckled.

"What's so funny?"

"You shoulda seen Sam's face when I told her God wanted me to be a pastor. Her eyes almost popped out onto the stove."

Kyle glanced in the side mirror and checked his speed.

Through the passenger mirror, I noted a blue Explorer riding our rusty bumper. "I keep asking God what to do next, which way He wants me to go and I—" I startled at the vibrating in my back pocket.

Kyle whipped his head to the right and back to the road. "You're getting reception?"

"Yeah. Uh." Sam's name flashed on the screen. "Hey, Sweetheart."

"Hey. So, you know how we talked about wanting to go back to Minnesota?"

"Yeah?"

"Well, Care just called. She was eavesdropping on a conversation between two pastors and told me about a youth pastor opening in Pequot Lakes, Minnesota. We'd only be a few hours from your parents."

"How far from yours?"

"Closer than a four-hour plane ride plus a two-hour drive."

Kaylynn will actually know her grandparents. "Is this what you want?"

"I think so."

"Ok, have Carolyn give them my number." Silence responded. I checked the screen, guessing the call dropped. Four bars, 30 percent power. "Sam?"

"She already did."

"What?"

"Care already gave them your number."

The call dropped. Kyle eased the minivan onto a pull-off and allowed an Explorer to surge past. "What did Sam have to say?"

I snapped the phone closed. "I think God just phoned in with an answer to prayer."

✳

SAM, JUNE 2011
LEBANON, OREGON

Twelve guys who didn't want Clint, Kaylynn, and I to move stood beside me. Algae residue coated the white garage door. I yanked the black metal handle upward. "This house was furnished when we moved in, so half our furniture is already in the garage." End tables, a dining room table, chairs and desks littered the one-car, detached garage.

I pointed to a velour couch imprinted with sepia-toned flowers and an armchair upholstered in maize-colored, carpet-like fabric. Both items were shoved against the far wall. "Those stay," I said.

"Aw, come on." Nick snorted. "They're classic."

"So was the mint condition, Mike Ditka rookie card I found shoved in the back of a bedroom closet, but that also belongs to Mike, the guy we rented from."

Mike, the church member who rented the two-bedroom house to us had moved his ninety-five-year-old mother out of his childhood home and into a nursing care facility. Until the day we moved, I still found random items like his mother's clothing, stacks of Styrofoam containers. and a sandwich baggie filled with toothpaste tube caps. I used the toaster with the fabric-coated cord until the day the hunk of metal burst into a puff of flame and smoke.

Bobby clapped his hands and rubbed them together, a huge grin visible beneath his frayed baseball cap. "Let's get to work."

Less than an hour later, our friends ran out of boxes to load. Inside the house, I threw random items into laundry baskets, pillowcases, and random bins that vanished before I finished filling them.

"Outta the way." Clint burst in, carrying eight Little Ceasar pizza boxes. The smell of marinara and melted cheese followed Clint into the bare living room. Like cartoon characters, our friends followed the aroma.

AJ, a six-foot, two-inch teen from our youth group, pressed his glasses higher on his nose. "I'm starving."

Clint dropped the boxes on the dining room table staying with the house. "You're always hungry."

After lunch in which AJ devoured an entire pizza by himself, the guys hitched our Dodge Caravan to the back of the truck.

The whirring of the vacuum stopped, and Bobby hoisted the appliance over his shoulder. His nimble footsteps receded down the wooden front porch steps. I tossed my purse over my shoulder and lifted the car seat. Kaylynn's blue eyes and damp smile gave her a Gerber baby appearance.

Clint sidled up to me, and I shifted the car seat weight into his hands. Sunlight filtered through disturbed dust. I scanned the room, saying a silent farewell.

"Um," Nick pointed to the minivan, "don't open those doors until you get to Minnesota."

"We packed it to the gills," Kyle said.

With jokes about Clint's bad driving, hugs and well-wishes, we said goodbye to our friends.

In Portland, Clint parked in the first available space he saw. *That's gonna be a problem later.* We met up for a bittersweet farewell with our family—two aunts, an uncle and a cousin. The photo pops up faithfully every year in a memories album on Facebook—Clint in a tank top, balancing chubby Kaylynn on one of his forearms.

Clint's poor parking choice resulted in a thirty-three-point turn and the help of a stranger. I tightened my lips and swallowed my nasty response.

The drive smoothed out on I-84. Snow-covered Mt. Hood pointed toward heaven. The Columbia River shimmered to our left and after no time we passed Multnomah Falls. I tilted my chin up to see the top. *Remarkable.* I wiggled Kaylynn's tiny baby toes. "We'll bring you back here someday."

The gorge shot upward on both sides of the river. The sun bared down on the windshield. "Oh, no." Clint braked hard.

Cars in both lanes slowed to a dead stop. Sirens wailed behind us and both lanes of traffic shifted awkwardly toward the right shoulder. A fire truck careened past, soon followed by an ambulance and multiple police vehicles.

"Dear God, let everyone be okay."

After forty-five minutes, there'd been zero movement. Impatience won out and I cracked the door open.

"Where are you going?"

"To see what happened and see if they're close to clearing the road."

"Why? We're here either way."

"I'll have answers."

Other drivers exited their vehicles too. A twenty-five-yard expanse of the guard rail lay completely flattened. Deep holes in the dirt remained where guardrail posts been torn out of the ground. A dead sparrow lay beside the crinkled metal.

"This could have been us." *We were close.*

The front end of a trailer poked out from a shallow ditch. Four tires pointed skyward. The impact smushed the white metal into a flattened rectangular box.

So, the trailer took out the guard rail. Where's the truck that pulled it? I brought my hand to my mouth.

Not just any truck—a semi—a gas tanker—flipped at a ninety degree angle so the tires and the underbelly of the truck faced onlookers. The truck blocked the right shoulder and both lanes like a wall of crumpled steel.

After speaking with several people, I returned to our air-conditioned U-Haul. and updated Clint. "Authorities won't let anyone past. At an exit a mile west of here, they're rerouting drivers off the interstate."

His gaze roamed to the various vehicles boxing us in.

"Can we turn off the truck to save gas?" I asked.

"Not with Kaylynn."

"We'd take her out of her car seat, out of the truck."

"And what? Go picnic near the gas tanker that could explode at any minute?"

"That's what that was."

"What *what* was?"

The trailer in the weeds I assumed was a flatbed was actually a gas trailer. "Never mind. At least we filled up recently."

Clint pursed his lips. "At least."

I put my hand on the door handle. "I'm going to go tell other drivers what's going on."

"Sam, just stay here."

I ignored him. What if some of these cars were low on gas? One by two, coupes and sedans performed multiple-point turns and drove the wrong way on the shoulder toward the detour

After three hours, only us and semis remained. Clint hopped out of the truck and found me gabbing away with truckers in the middle of the highway. "We can't wait here forever, the gas needle is getting lower."

"Can't turn the truck off?" one trucker asked.

"Our five-month-old is in there."

The trucker studied our truck and trailer. "You know, I bet we could turn you around. Back the car off. Unhitch the trailer. Turn the truck and the trailer separately."

My face lit with hope. "Really?"

"Should be pretty easy with all of us."

Ten minutes later, we thanked our new friends and turned onto the detour. Branches scraped the truck on the narrow mountain pass.

Clint sighed. "You realize, we wouldn't have been able to turn around if those other cars hadn't moved, right? You helped."

"They would have figured it out."

"I'll never understand your ability to talk to strangers." The front, right tire dipped off the pavement, and I eased back toward the center. "This road is super narrow."

Just then we read a yellow diamond: Road Narrows Ahead.

We burst into laughter. I scrubbed my face with my hands.

"This feels like a scene in one of your cheesy Hallmark movies," he said.

I smirked. "Don't start."

I took over driving at some point in Washington. Clint barely spoke of his time in Kennewick, Washington, and I assumed he'd have pleasant memories of the place he once lived. When I drove past the Tri-Cities sign I said, "Is there any place you'd like to visit while we're in Kennewick?"

Clint perked up and noted our surroundings. His eyes widened. "No. Go. Go."

I saw signs for Kellogg, Idaho, and begged to stop and buy a box of Frosted Flakes. "I've never stepped foot in Idaho before."

"We'll never get to Minnesota with all the stops you want to make."

"It'd be funny."

"No."

He fell asleep around midnight, just before we reached Idaho's panhandle. My mouth quirked up with mischief, and I eased the truck over on the side of the road. I inched the truck door open, careful to only allow my left foot to touch the asphalt. I snapped a quick photo and jumped back into the car.

Then I snapped a picture of Clint and Kaylynn. He'd propped his pillow up by her car seat, rather than the window, so the two of them slept soundly with faces inches apart. I signaled to non-existent traffic getting back on the road and said to sleeping Clint. "Now I can say I've stepped foot in Idaho—but not feet. Just foot. We'll call it a compromise."

Clint woke up and took over driving on the western end of Montana, the multi-lane highway dwindled down to a dirt road. Oops. This was before GPS, in the era of printable MapQuest directions. I pulled out the two-foot by three-foot road atlas. "Let's figure out what turn we missed."

Turned out we hadn't missed a turn. We were driving in a road construction zone with zero evidence of construction equipment. Oh, sweet Montana. Eventually, the paved road simply reappeared. I shrugged. "Because why not?" Next, we passed a car with flames and black smoke shooting out from the windows. Fire had gutted the entire interior and crawled all over the hood.

Clint slowed, but we didn't see anyone to help.

On the eastern side of Montana, Clint and I rented a cheap motel straight out of the 1970s with shaggy green carpet and wax paper cone cups, rather than coffee mugs. I stared at the paisley bed spread and wondered if it would be safer to sleep atop the comforter or beneath it. We were so happy to leave the next morning, we accidentally left my favorite outfit of Kaylynn's behind.

As we entered North Dakoka, we passed flooded farm fields. Clint's jaw dropped. "The water came way out here?" The breadth of the Mouse River flood damage shocked us.

The stress of the drive mounted. By the time we reached his grandma's home in northwest North Dakota, we were using the word divorce. Turned out, we just needed to get out of the truck.

CLINT, JULY 2011
MINOT, NORTH DAKOTA

Travis laughed through the phone. "Dude, you should hear people when I tell them you're in ministry. They ask if we're talking about the same Clint Evans. Can't wait to see you guys."

I'd spent a lot of time on the phone with Travis after the June 20 Mouse River flood, and Sam and I saw news footage. Four thousand homes under water, some completely submerged. Aerial footage showed a motorboat chugging over railroad tracks and water to the top of the 4th St NW sign. But nothing prepared me for the drastic difference between my memories of Minot and the city before me.

A month after the flood, two-story mounds of debris lined the boulevards for miles. Water seeped from the trash piles into the streets and spilled into the gutters. Bridges made of pallets stretched from the street to the sidewalk. Various businesses created dunes of dirt that reached higher than the roofs of their buildings. *Maybe I can bring a mission trip team back here.* I smiled at my inner desire to aid the place I'd spent so much energy hating.

My jaw remained slackened from one end of Minot to the other en route to my Aunt Lisa's house.

She held Kaylynn for 90 percent of the visit.

"When's it my turn?" my uncle Dale whined.

Lisa bounced Kaylynn on her legs. "Ba ba ba ba ba."

It amazed me how adult vocabulary disintegrated around babies.

Lisa ignored everyone else in the room. "Aren't you just the sweetest thing? So, here's the plan. We're gonna move Joe out to the garage, and you can have his old room."

"Does Joe get a say?" My cousin Joe glanced at his watch. "Shoot. Gotta go. Mom, turn on the TV."

Joe's brother Steve grabbed the remote and pointed it at the TV. A few minutes later, Steve nodded at the television. "There he is."

Sam gawked at the weather report. "That's Joe? Where's the news station? In your basement?"

"Close," said Steve. "Less than a mile from here."

The camera cut to another news reporter and Joe walked through the front door.

I grinned. "Nicely done."

CHAPTER TWENTY-EIGHT

March 24, 2013

Dear Friends in Christ,

Three years ago, Grace United Methodist Church in Pequot Lakes desperately sought a youth director. Thanks to the connectional system in the United Methodist Church, we heard about a man in Oregon interested in the position—Clint Evans.

The Spirit's leading sent us a true blessing. He has energized our youth program in every way. Teens responded to his energy, enthusiasm, and his very deep love for the Lord.

His genuine concern and caring for the adults in the congregation has also made a big difference in our church family. The gifts and graces Clint possesses make him an excellent candidate for ordained ministry. This year he enrolled full-time in Asbury Theological Seminary. Please prayerfully consider this servant of God, Clint Evans.

Blessings to you,
Peggy Johnson

CLINT, OCTOBER 2011
PEQUOT LAKES, MINNESOTA

Two weeks. *Two weeks* after Sam eased Kaylynn into baby cereal, Sam emerged from the bathroom holding a pregnancy test. All the color had drained from her face.

At youth group a few Wednesdays later, my ADHD brain blurted, "The first two people to memorize all the books of the Bible can come with Sam and me to learn the sex of the baby." Later, I decided Sam should know, since the plan involved her bare belly.

Levi and Maddie came to the appointment with us. They "oo'ed" and "ahh'ed" at the ultrasound screen. Sam and I shared a smile over their heads.

Five months later, the night Sam went into labor with Kelly, Sam sang "Trading My Sorrows" on a repeating loop for the fifty-minute car ride. She paused long enough to shout things such as "Stop singing with me" and "I do this drive in thirty-five minutes. Get me to the hospital, grandma!" By the time I parked at the ER, Sam was seven cm dilated.

When she pushed, blood vessels across Sam's cheeks and forehead broke, causing a rash-like appearance. *She looks like a super-hero bench-pressing a Buick.* I told her so. She glared at me.

A nurse entered Sam's delivery room and suggested I move our vehicle. Stupid me. I left it running in the carport when I hurried Sam into the ER. When I returned to the room, nurses were urging Sam not to push.

Dr. Dovre entered, rolled across the floor on a stool, and had slid his hands into gloves sometime between the door and the bed.

Kelly crowned, and I saw a tuft of hair. "Our baby has a fro."

With one last push, a small human escaped from my wife's body— the weirdest, coolest, thing I've ever seen. Kelly emerged gray, bloody ... and silent.

Dr. Dovre held her in one palm and rubbed her chest with the other. A quiet squeal passed through her lips. "There she is." He laid Kelly on Sam's chest and a nurse wrapped a blanket around my newborn. Dr. Dovre handed me a pair of scissors and showed me where to cut the umbilical cord.

This is so cool.

"Well, last in of five, first to deliver," the doctor said.

"So, Sam won," I said. "Yes, it was a race, and my wife won."

Sam rolled her eyes.

"Oh, you guys need to take a picture of this." Dr. Dovre held a knot in the umbilical cord. "If this cord had tightened, Kelly could have died."

God protected my little girl.

With Minot, North Dakota, still being rebuilt after the flood, our church joined service teams from around the country. Assigned to Roosevelt Park, we rinsed silted river rock from a veteran's memorial and painted thousands of metal park benches. Maybe dozens.

Sam brought both girls on the trip. Kel was only two weeks old, and they stayed with my grandma.

Three months after Kelly's birth, our growing family returned to Minot for Travis and Savannah's wedding. At the reception, Travis' brother KC said, "Clint, we're hitting up the bars."

"No thanks."

KC taunted me with vivid emasculating imagery.

I can't believe those comments used to bait me.

"No, dude." I turned and shouted, "Sam, come over here." My wife abandoned her conversation and strode over. "KC, ask Sam when I drank last."

"September 16, 2007," Sam said without hesitation.

"Oh, man. Sorry," said KC. "You're not coming with."

Sam and I had taken swing dance classes together so we spent the night talking with friends and dancing like fools. The crowd thinned and the people who remained grew sloppier. The Ghost of Drinking Past yanked me back by the collar and said, "You used to be him."

We drove home to Pequot Lakes, and Sam squeezed my hand. "You're still five years sober.'"

"Had you scared for a minute there, though, didn't they?"

"My fists were poised to face off with KC in the parking lot."

"There's no way, Sam," I chanced a quick glance at our babies in the rearview mirror. "I have too much to lose."

"Good, because I can't do Chicago again. Especially with the girls. If you relapse again, Clint, I'm done."

The thing about the countdown to a life-changing event is you don't realize you're counting down until the event happens. Then, in retrospect, utterly mundane moments hold new meaning.

In 2014, the week after Trinity's birth, Sam brought all three girls to our youth group Halloween party. The fellowship hall erupted in pure, beautiful chaos.

I spotted one of the newer kids—Tre's—holding my newborn daughter. "Look." I exclaimed. "It's Tre's and Trinity. Threes."

Sam rolled her eyes at me. I heard "terrible joke" from various parts of the room. I laughed but internally struggled to roll off the comments. What I considered my greatest flaws, God used as tools to reach others. But his message that I mattered just couldn't seem to sink in.

You're such an idiot, Clint. If God's chosen you, He must be at the bottom of His barrel. I hadn't heard from Legion in awhile and his input caught me off guard.

As the father of three daughters under four, I never returned home after work to a serene household—a steaming casserole cooling on the stove, clean children sitting patiently at the table with hands folded, ready to pray. My wife beaming, and pleasant, tenderly kissing my cheek with a warm, "Welcome home."

Monday, October 27, 2014, five days after the Halloween Party, was no exception. I opened the door to our home. A naked, grinning two-year-old streaked past the dining room toward her bedroom. Our newborn, who'd skipped the quiet, infant cry stage and launched straight into pterodactyl screeching, wailed from the other room.

Sam sighed with resignation, velcroing a poopy diaper into a tight cannonball. "I never fit 'changing dirty diapers' into my picture of 'fighting for the gospel.'" Only eleven days post-partum with our youngest daughter, Sam rose from the floor with careful movements. "Kelly escaped again. Can you nab her? I need to feed Trinity." She gathered her sagging ponytail and disappeared into our room.

I jogged down the hallway toward the naked toddler. "Come here, you little magician. We need to get you in a diaper." Kelly squealed. I followed the sound to the bedroom she shared with Kaylynn and stopped in my tracks. Dolls, blocks, and books were strewn across the floor like land mines. "Did you girls leave any toys in the closet?"

They both giggled. I lassoed a squirming Kelly and roped her into a diaper. "All right girls, we need to start cleaning up or your mom will lose her mind."

My back pocket buzzed. Tre's sent me a message through instant messenger.

> Hey, Clint. What are you up to?

I didn't think Tre's wanted to hear all the details of my excitement-filled life, so I replied:

> Helping my wife with the kids and dinner. Can we talk at 8?

> Yeah, thanks.

> Did you not go to football practice tonight?

No reply.

After dinner, bathtime, and bedtime, a stack of dishes in the sink formed the shape of Mt. Hood, and soap suds slicked the floor of the bathroom. Depleted of all energy, I discarded three dirty diapers and dropped onto the couch beside Sam. I slid my phone from my pocket and stared at the screen.

"Tre's still hasn't replied?"

"No." I messaged Tre's.

> "You still want to talk?"

"It's no big deal. I'll see him Wednesday." I set my phone on the end table.

The next morning, my phone rang just after 8:00 a.m. *Who's number is this?* "Hello?"

"Clint, hey, I'm glad you answered. This is Chip," said the high school principal. "Something happened last night."

Chills coursed through my body. I hopped up and started pacing.

Sam emerged from the bedroom with bedhead hair and twisted pajama pants, asking a silent question. I held up my pointer finger. She noted my demeanor and stiffened.

"What is it? Chip?"

After a torturous silence, he said, "Tre's Llyod committed suicide last night." Chip kept speaking, even though my brain stopped comprehending. "I have a bunch of kids in the office here, friends of his. They're asking for you."

Me? I stared at Sam, and beyond her. We lived walking distance from the school. "I'll be there in five minutes." I grabbed my nearest pair of shoes and slid my feet into them. "Tre's committed suicide last night." Saying the words aloud didn't make it feel any more real.

"His death is not your fault."

I appreciated her intuitiveness and her ability to skip past platitudes, but I didn't believe her. I shoved my other shoe on. "I told him I was too busy for him."

"You said you were busy in the moment and offered to talk to him a couple hours later. He didn't give any indication of crisis."

I replayed the messages in my head. "I feel like I could have stopped it somehow."

Reverently, she whispered, "God didn't stop it either."

I shook my head. "I'll call you later."

I slammed the car door harder than I meant to. To my left, capital letters spelled "PEQUOT LAKES HIGH SCHOOL" on the side of the building above "Home of the Patriots." I stormed through the entryway doors and wrapped around to the front office. The glass wall gave me a clear view of a room filled with over two dozen teens sitting in white, plastic chairs lined along the perimeter of the room.

Chip, sitting among the teens, noticed me with a double take and popped up. "Thank you so much for coming." He shook my hand. "We're getting more chairs."

More? I didn't recognize all the kids in the room, but I knew most of them.

"Army trained us for death." Chip spoke so only I would hear. "Even suicide. But words on a PowerPoint didn't prepare me for this."

School staff entered, arms racked with folding chairs. More students filed in around them.

My eyes burned. *He messaged me last night.* I longed to confess those words, but the guilt of failing Tre's clawed at me. I patted Chip's back. "Well, I've got this part."

"Thanks, Clint."

To the left, skaters, who tried to break the stereotype, fell right into it with baggy khakis, black T-shirts, and either piercings or spacers in their ears. Football players in blue home jerseys lined the right wall. Under different circumstances, the obvious cliques might have been funny. Instead, I saw friends sitting near friends and the obvious missing link who fit in with both the preppy jocks and the marginalized.

Most of the kids leaned forward in their chairs, grasping their heads. Some leaned back with arms hugging their middles, others stared straight ahead, faces impassive. There were girls scattered throughout the mix. Black mascara and eye liner streaked down puffy, red faces.

I sat and covered my eyes. "Tre's." My voice cracked on his name. My stomach convulsed and sob escaped my chest.

Teens who'd held in their emotion cried until they gasped for breath. With a shuddered breath, my gaze roamed from teen to teen. A cluster of guys stared at me. Their eyes were red, but not from crying. *Oh, you are blitzed out of your minds.*

"Clint, thanks for coming for us."

I lifted my eyebrows in a knowing grin at the high-as-a-kite teenager. *I know you're high.* He grinned right back. *I know you know.* We both sobered, well, me more than him. "It's my honor." I folded my hands. "Thank you for the invitation. Let's pray." I lowered my head. "Dear God, thank You for defeating death. Thank you for rescuing Tre's, rescuing all of us. Give us peace. Be with Tre's's friends and family. May they feel Your presence in their deepest grief. And tell Tre's we say hi."

Four days later, Sam and I entered the packed sanctuary of Gloria Dei Lutheran. Pastor Frank was a friend, and I did not envy his position of delivering the day's message.

"I've never seen so many letterman jackets at a funeral." Sam's tears dropped atop Trinity's bald head. "They're just kids. They should be texting friends and graffitiing property." I looked at her. "Well, you know what I mean. They shouldn't have to deal with a classmate's funeral. A second classmate." Tre's was the second suicide within six months. "At least 'Chat and Chow' is paying off."

"How so?" I asked.

Sam shrugged. "Funerals are terrifying but look how many kids in here have already been in this church, have already met Pastor Frank. Heard his jokes and his prayers. They got to meet him when he was wearing jeans and a polo before ever seeing him in his alb."[6]

Gloria Dei was the church nearest the school and once a week community churches worked together to provide free—off-campus lunch for kids called "Chat and Chow" that included a prayer and a short devotion. Flyers posted around the school read: "Stuff Your Face For Jesus." Every time I saw a flyer I grinned, proud of my wit, and my part in creating the program. Chat and Chow drew dozens of unchurched kids, many of whom I noticed sitting in the sanctuary.

Sam was right. Frank wasn't some lofty stranger in a robe. If nothing else came out of Chat and Chow, the work would be worth it for this moment. "Let me hold Trinity." Without waiting for Sam's response, I stole Trinity from her arms.

"Oh, okay."

"Come here, little one." *Tre's and Trinity. Threes.* Tears streamed down my cheeks. *I guess the Trinity is holding you now, Tre's.* I held Trinity against my aching heart like a security blanket.

....

6   Alb- a typically white or off-white robe often worn by clergy in more traditional denominations

Five months later, Sam and I sat at a Mexican restaurant in St. Cloud, Minnesota, across the table from District Superintendent Phil Strom, who offered me a job in southern Minnesota. "Sleepy Eye, Minnesota."

"Never heard of it," I said.

"Famous for a shout out in *Little House on the Prairie,* and it's where Charles Schultz's real-life friend Linus lived."

"Huh," Sam and I said.

At the end of the meeting, Sam blurted, "Clint and I keep talking about the Matthew passage: "the gospel is forceful advancing, and forceful men take hold.""

Phil grinned. "Maybe don't lead with that one."

In five years of ministry, I'd dressed as an aviator for VBS, dressed as a woman for a fund-raising effort—which freaked eighteen-month-old Kelly out—worn red head paint, all in the name of loving others the way I believed Jesus would. We'd played silly games like "Balloon Deer Antlers" and "Baby Relay Races." Amidst retreats, lock-ins, concerts, and spectating extracurricular events, I hoped I'd taught the kids about Christ's love.

I accepted the pastoral call in Sleepy Eye and Fairfax, Minnesota, knowing I'd made an impact. More important was the impact Grace UMC and Pequot Lakes left on me.

What I do matters.

CHAPTER TWENTY-NINE

Dear Clint,

    I loved lasagna night with our families.

Scott

CLINT, MARCH 2016
FAIRFAX, MINNESOTA

The faded RC Cola sign rocked back and forth on its squeaky hinges above an otherwise unmarked door. I shoved my bare hands into the pockets of my thick coat to shield them from the thirty-six-degree morning.

Fairfax, Minnesota, population 1,000 is a blink-and-you'll-miss-it type town. And it's one of my favorite places on earth.

A small bell announced my presence at the Smokey Hollow Cafe. A chorus of "Hey, Pastor Clint" erupted from eleven "retired" church members seated around square Formica tables. One owned his own business, two drove a bus, one taught piano, and one often filled in as an interim pastor.

"What, no girls?" Joyce asked, her disappointment evident.

I waved my arm toward Jeff. "Pastor Jeff and I are visiting Millie today."

"Millie would've loved to see the girls," said Chuck, Joyce's husband. "They're cuter than you."

"No argument there. They wanted to come." There was no use explaining how my little munchkins sometimes made working difficult.

Millie's living room, stacked with newspapers and baubles was an avalanche waiting to happen. Imagining Kelly's squirminess or Trinity's chubby, two-year-old hands reaching for a knick-knack in Millie's home actually caused me to shudder. I nodded at the table. "You'll see them this Friday when we carry the cross."

"Promise?"

"Promise."

Christians who lived in Fairfax gathered at Fairfax UMC every Good Friday to carry a large, wooden cross to St. Andrew's Catholic Church across town. I couldn't wait to see the procession.

"We're supposed to get into the sixties on Friday," said Delores, another church member. "Maybe some of the snow will melt."

"What can I get for you, Pastor Clint?" The waitress held her pen at the ready.

I knew better than to ask for a menu. There weren't any. "Black coffee and cheesy eggs." And I wouldn't be surprised when I received a plateful of eggs with a single slice of American cheese melted on top. I wasn't there for the food or the decor, but rather the people around the table. The members of Fairfax provided the only atmosphere I needed: A joyful and loving one.

More than once, I'd looked from person to person and thought, "these people should be pastoring me." I'd never met a church who acted so much like Jesus. They simply make room for everyone at the table.

Jeff sipped from his coffee mug, and the steam fogged his glasses lenses, hiding the small blue eyes behind them. He laughed at Frank's comment and threw his white head of hair back in laughter. The grin took up his whole face.

Transitioning into pastoral ministry would have been impossible without the retired UMC pastor's support. His wife Char shoved a subtle elbow into Jeff's ribs.

He turned his smile on me. "Well, it's probably time."

Chuck passed me a package of folded wax paper. "Those caramels are for your girls. Don't you go eatin' them all."

"Yes, sir."

Ten minutes later, Jeff and I strode up to Millie's front door. I pressed my thumb into the cracked, white circle and listened for the chime. I eased the front door open. "Millie? Jeff and I are here."

"Come in." Millie greeted us from her burgundy recliner.

Family photos in mismatched frames covered most of the pink walls. Meticulously stacked newspaper piles rested on the multiple end tables. A low-wattage lamp near the recliner cast an orange glow across Millie's face and a crocheted afgan of blacks and reds enveloped her withering frame.

"Did I ever tell you gentlemen about my grandson?" Millie smiled. "He called me at Christmastime. He's engaged now."

Jeff's voice carried so much enthusiasm he might have heard the story for the first time rather than every week of the new year. "That's great."

"Would you like a cookie?" Millie pointed to a package of generic cookies atop an old box TV now being used as a table.

I recognized the yellow package from the groceries we'd packed for shut-ins the previous week.

"I sure am going to miss the cross this Friday. Everyone bundled up, singing hymns. Catholics, Baptists, Presbyterians. The Lutherans always say they know when the Methodists arrive because of our singing."

"You won't miss my singing, promise," I said. *God, give me better words.*

"You're more a part of holy week than you realize, Millie. Remember the story of the widow's mite?"

"She gave two pennies, everything she had."

"And Jesus was proud of her. That story took place between Palm Sunday and Good Friday."

"See that, Millie," Jeff said, "you're right on schedule."

"These are way tastier than pennies." I displayed two cookies in a cheers fashion and popped them into my mouth. Millie's eyes lit with pleasure. "Can we take communion together, Millie?"

"Oh, that's always my favorite part of your visit."

"Mine too." I withdrew my communion kit from my pocket—travel size grape juice and wafers. "Pastor Jeff, would you do the honor?"

"Of course. The Bible tells us that where two or more are gathered, God will be among them. On the night in which He was betrayed …"

Jeff recited the Bible passage from memory, and there in the quiet living room with no audience, the three of us felt God's presence fill the room. I didn't want to leave.

After several moments of silence, I said, "Well, Happy Easter, Millie."

"He is Risen."

"He is risen, indeed," both Jeff and I said in unison.

I opened the front door, and bitter winter air blasted my face. You haven't experienced true winter until you breathe air so cold you choke on it.

"The package was already open. She fed us those same cookies last week."

Jeff cackled. "A bit stale?"

"More than a bit." I shifted the car into Drive. "But she felt important today."

"You did a good thing."

Boundaries training accounts for a large portion of ministry education.

1. Don't be friends with parishioners.
2. Don't be alone with the opposite sex.
3. Don't be alone with children.

If seminary were a boot camp, these three mantras would be shouted by each student, all day, every day—with a harsh 2:00 a.m. wake up call, while doing push-ups, or crawling beneath razor wire. Every seminary private would graduate from Basic Training with those three admonishments drilled into their skulls.

Why? Because the fastest ways to destroy a pastor's ministry or a church's reputation are breaking one of those rules. After years of ministry, I realized, while those rules apply to small town pastors, there's much more gray in regard to "don't be friends with parishioners" because the other option would be "have no friends," and both statements are equally detrimental.

That's why Jeff mattered so much. He'd spent decades in pastoral ministry, so the rules felt different with him. When I moved to Sleepy Eye, Minnesota, he became my closest friend.

November 2, 2016, Jeff crawled into a van with me and six other clergy half his age to peacefully, prayerfully, and lawfully protest the pipeline through sacred Indian grounds at Standing Rock. Jeff inspired me with his fearless battle for the underdog. *I hope I can be half the man he is when I'm his age.*

I never worried about a time without him present.

CHAPTER THIRTY

Hey Bro,

Finally got your video to load on my computer. Very nice—you have the tools, the heart, the faith, and the vision to excel in each field. I can't tell you how happy I am to claim you as a brother and to be part of these two churches where you are bringing new life, hope and vitality. I am very proud to claim you as my pastor and the pastor of church the I care deeply about.

Grace and peace, bro,

Jeff

CLINT, OCTOBER 2016
SLEEPY EYE, MINNESOTA

Members of Faith UMC in Sleepy Eye taught me the term "salad" mustn't be unimaginatively limited to fruits and vegetables. A pinch of imagination blends any manner of surprising ingredients. I honored them by eating. Best job in the world. I often heard: "Pastor Clint, here, have seconds." Or "Pastor Clint, would you like to bring some home?"

On Wednesday nights, our church hosted a kids program called JAM—Jesus and Me. I greeted participants and led a short devotion and prayer.

I introduced an activity to the kids called "coffee can questions" that provided students the opportunity to ask a questions anonymously. Hand-written questions I withdrew from the can ranged from "what is your favorite … " to how do you know God exists?"

Impressed by my witty slogan, "stuff your face for Jesus," I reused the phrase every time a church event involved food. I used the saying for every church event.

Once a month, our congregation hosted a community meal called Dinner on Us. The feast provided opportunities for low-income families to save money, mothers to take a night off from cooking, and strangers to become friends.

Members of Faith opened the doors to Sam and me, made space for us to serve in our areas of giftedness, and welcomed us as friends. Their invitations butted against the seminary education ingrained in me. *Don't befriend church members. Blurred lines.* Regret filled the void where intimate friendships might have been. Alex. Jaime. Scott. Erin. Loneliness and isolation remained ever-present like ice at the edges of a windshield.

But my professors would be proud. I stayed strong, followed the rules.

In October 2016, I found Sam with our daughter's pumpkin painting in her mouth and painter's tape in her hands. Several more pieces of artwork—hand-print spiders and construction paper pumpkins on a fence—littered the ground at her feet.

"Sam, I've been sober for nine years. You can buy the ingredients for a mudslide if you want. I'll be fine."

She stilled. "No thanks. I'm good."

"No, really. I hate that you can't buy alcohol because of me, and I know you love mud slides, so if you want to treat yourself, you can."

Sam tore off a piece of tape and stuck Kelly's pumpkin to the wall. "You kissed me at my graduation party and reeled back from the taste of Mike's on my lips. Sometimes I blame that kiss for your relapse in Chicago a few months later. I don't think alcohol in the house is the best idea."

The angel on my shoulder grabbed the hood of my sweatshirt and tugged. I swatted him away. "I've come a long way since then."

Three conversations later, Sam strode into the local liquor store and came home with vodka, chocolate liquor, and rum. She blended two mudslides over the course of three weeks, and I congratulated myself for coping so well.

But the vodka bottle didn't fit in our cupboard, so it rested atop the fridge. Every time I walked into the kitchen, the bottle mocked me. And I continued lying to myself. *I'm fine. Everything's fine. I'm doing fine.*

Eventually, I asked Sam to move it to the garage. I should have dumped it, but Legion had already moved in. *That'd be a waste of money.* And, *what if you need it sometime and it's not there?*

For months, I avoided the garage, and sometimes I forgot about the bottle. But the fishbowl effect of living in Sleepy Eye grew worse.

The parsonage rested on the church property. The sidewalk leading to the church passed just below our master bedroom window. Sam often joked on Sunday mornings that anyone who looked up on their way into church could watch her getting ready. Once, hormones heated up between Sam, but Sam stopped cold. "Isn't there a church meeting starting in fifteen minutes?"

"Yeah." I reached for the button on her jeans. "But I don't have to be there."

"Yes, but Clint. Church members will be walking into the meeting."

My libido wilted like I'd cannonballed into a polar plunge. *Cock blocked by my church. Fantastic.*

One time, Sam pulled Kaylynn into our house to reprimand her during outdoor Vacation Bible School games. Sam looked up and saw three boys shielding their eyes from the sun, noses pressed against the glass of our home.

Members and delivery drivers rang our doorbell at 6:00 a.m. asking for keys, and my wife was forced to answer the door no matter what state of chaos our house of three littles was in. Other times, people rang the doorbell for keys after we'd put the kids to bed.

One morning the doorbell rang before seven. Trinity had just puked all over Sam's pajamas. Sam knew she had crazy bedhead hair and the second she opened the door she represented the whole church. So, she greeted the person at the door with a generous smile, passed over the keys, and called me the second the door was shut. "These people have such a lack of regard and respect for the pastor's family. It's unbelievable."

Police officers who rang our doorbell at 1:30 a.m. to 3:30 a.m. were different. They always apologized for the hour, and I was honored they contacted me when a patient at the hospital needed a pastoral visit or last rights. Those were emergencies. The other weren't.

Everywhere I went, my position preceded me. Close clergy friends lived anywhere between fifteen and forty-five minutes away, but easy-going conversation always pivoted toward ministry discussions during my "time off." The football field became my sanctuary—a sacred place where I could be myself. My favorite football practices took place the night after council meetings. But each practice required a one- to two-hour drive and the distance wore me down.

Pressure mounted, and all the while the vodka bottle called, "Don't forget me, Clint. I'm not too far away."

On Friday, January 20th, 2017, Sam drove four hours to Wisconsin Dells for a writer's retreat. I played an episode of *Bo on the Go*, a brilliant show that invited viewers to join Bo on her adventures—running when she ran and jumping when she jumped.

"Shee how high I jumped, Daddy?" Kelly said. "Did you shee it?"

"I did. I did shee it. Good job."

Kaylynn fisted her four-year-old hands in determination. "I bet I can jump higher than you."

"Good job, Kaylynn," I said.

"Juh."

"That's right, Trinity. You juh." Her tiny two-year-old feet didn't even leave the ground.

My phone vibrated across the end table. Char's name appeared on the screen. *I hope she's not sick. Is she slated to play the organ this Sunday?*

"Hey, Char. What can I do for you?"

Multiple sentences toppled out of her mouth at the same time. I pieced together "Jeff," "9-1-1," and "sons" before I cut her off. "Whoa, Char. Deep breath. Can you slow down a little so I can understand you better?"

She spewed air into the receiver. "Jeff slipped on our icy front steps, fell back, and hit his head on the concrete. He's still breathing, but I can't wake him up. EMT's are on the way. I have to call my sons. Oh, God. I don't know what to do. I—"

"Char." I stood in our sunroom, on the opposite end of the house from the girls but hadn't remembered walking in there. *Not Jeff, Please not Jeff.* I stared into the possibility of a world without him. *God, he's a lifeline to my sanity.* "One thing at a time. Let's pray and then I'll be there as soon as I can."

"Don't you have the girls this weekend for Sam's writing thing? Oh, Clint. Don't ask her to come back for this. She works so hard for those girls. Moms need their time away."

I huffed. *Char and her knack for details.* "I'll figure it out. In the meantime, tell me who you want me to call for you. Let me pray with you, and then you can call your sons."

She sighed heavily into the phone. "Okay."

"Dear God, protect Jeff. Please don't take him home yet. Give Char and her family and me a peace beyond our wildest dreams tonight. Guide us with your wisdom. Amen."

"Amen."

I darted back to the living room, thankful the *Bo on the Go* episode ended while I'd been on the phone. I scooped Trinity up. "All right girls, time for bed."

"Aww, Dad. One more?" Kel set her big, brown eyes on me. Another night I would've caved. "Not tonight, pun'kin. Each of you choose one book tonight for story time."

After the circus of jammies and teeth and gathering the necessary blankets and stuffies for story time, I sat on the wooden desk chair in Kaylynn's room and cracked open the first board book. After *The Very Hungry Caterpillar* gorged through his week, the girls giggled through the *Biggest Thing in the Ocean*, and Little Pookie danced with fabulous shoes on his fabulous feet, I tucked each girl beneath the covers and kissed them goodnight.

"Good night, sweet girls. It's time to take your rest. Lay your sweet head upon the Savior's chest. We all love you, yeah, but Jesus loves you best, so we say good night, good night, good night.

"I love you princesses, more than words can say. I love you more each and every day. You're the best thing that's ever happened to me, so I say good night, good night, good night."

I came up with the second verse myself and the girls dubbed it "the daddy verse." I left their bedroom doors open a crack and sluffed down the stairs to the living room. My phone screen showed no missed calls or texts. I dropped the phone on the couch, picked it up, studied the screen again, and dropped the phone back onto the couch.

Reaching for the remote, I turned on the TV. Too distracted to watch any particular show, I just scrolled through the channels. I couldn't say how long I left my finger on the down button before my phone rang again. Char. I turned the TV off.

"Redwood is airlifting Jeff to North Memorial. He's in a coma. The doctors didn't look hopeful, and Clint, I signed a DNR. It's what Jeff would have wanted." As she spoke, I sobbed. "I know, Clint. I'm sorry."

"Why are you sorry? He's your husband."

"I know how much you love him."

Our call ended. The floor lamp beside me provided the only light in the house.

Legion's foot soldiers stormed into the living room and chanted, "Vod-ka. Vod-ka. Vod-ka." Voices I believed long since dead stirred with a vengeance. Battalion leaders shouted bolder, more targeted lies. *After all, you're nothing. You're a poser, a fake.*

"Leave me alone."

A text chimed. Sam.

> Made it to the Dells safely.

I hit "Call."

She picked up almost immediately. "Hey, everything all right?"

No. I'm so depressed, scared, and lonely all I can think about is the vodka in the garage. "Me and the girls are fine, but Sam, Jeff fell tonight and hit his head. He's in a coma."

Silence.

After several beats, she said, "Do you need me to come home?"

I sighed. *Yes.* "The hospital is flying him by helicopter to the Twin Cities."

"Well, maybe the girls could have some grandpa / grandma time tomorrow while you go visit him." My parents lived in Minneapolis. "Let me know if they're not available. Is there anything else?"

I'm thinking about drinking. I corrected myself. *I'm about to drink.* After all, what had I accomplished since arriving in southern Minnesota? Legion told me, "Nothing." And I believed him.

"Nothing," I said.

The call ended. The voices, polite enough to quiet down during my phone call, took up their chanting again. "Vod-ka. Vod-ka. Vod-ka. Vod-ka!"

Be quiet. Please, just stop. I pressed the heels of my hands into my ears and rocked back and forth. *Please make it stop.*

Years of practice taught me how to silence them. I rose from the couch and flipped on the light in the dining room on my way to the kitchen. With a sigh, I removed a glass from the 1970's cupboards. Large ice cubes clinked against the glass. I poured Diet Mountain Dew over the rocks.

Legion's commander took pity on me. "You've got this. You're strong enough for just one drink. No problem. Just enough to take the edge off, to feel normal again." Legion waterboarded the still small voice reminding me of the price. *Ten years of sobriety. Family. Ministry. Home. Ordination.* The battalion leader applied pressure to the back of my sputtering conscience's neck, suffocating the goodness. "Sam won't notice a centimeter or so."

Legion's words assaulted me like a battering ram. His insults sounded so crisp he might have been in the room with me. "What good are you? No one loves you. Sam runs away every chance she gets. If people at church knew the real you, they'd run too. Your children deserve better than a worthless piece of scum for a father."

The chorus of voices screamed, "Vod-ka. Vod-ka. Vod-ka."

I gripped the door handle of the garage and twisted. The voices hushed. Blissful, peaceful silence.

Resting on a shelf unit right inside the garage, I didn't even need to step through the doorway to reach the bottle.

The metal cap tinged as it wobbled on the counter. I poured the liquid into my soda. Just a little. Then a little more. *Looks like water.* My voice blended with Legion's. "No one will ever know."

I brought the glass to my lips and let the nostalgic burn slide down my throat.

"Amazing Grace, how sweet the sound…"

Char, Jeff's sons, a close friend of Jeff's, Char's friend, and myself huddled around Jeff's hospital bed, crying through the familiar hymn.

I cupped both of Jeff's cool hands in mine. The bright 'Do Not Resuscitate' bracelet scraped my wrist. Pale white on a good day, Jeff's complexion appeared translucent beneath the intrusive oxygen tube. *Jeff, please don't leave me. I want to tell you what I've done. I need your help.*

Char placed her hand on my shoulder. "Pastor Clint, will you pray for us?"

"Of course." I cleared my throat. "Dear God, thank you so much for Jeff. Thank you for all the ways he served You by serving others. We praise you for the words Jeff will soon hear, 'Well done, good and faithful servant.' Be merciful to him, and to us in his final moments. Give us all wisdom and strength."

The doctor had kept Jeff on life support until his son arrived from Denver. Now it was time.

"How does this work?" Char asked.

"I unhook and turn off the life support, and we let Jeff set the pace. It could be minutes, or weeks. There are no rules for what happens next."

Nurses in blue scrubs appeared and scurried to the doctor's side. One nurse peeled away the medical tape adhering the oxygen tube to

Jeff's mouth. The other removed the IV from his arm. Only the heart rate gauge remained attached to his chest, so nurses would be notified the moment his heart stopped beating.

The doctor exhaled and pressed several buttons on the life support apparatus. The machine whirred and slowed to silence.

The nurse adjusted the volume on the heart rate monitor.

My body shattered into sobs. *Jeff, please wake up.*

Five days later, the doctor reentered the room and switched off the heart rate monitor too.

Part Four

You will surely forget your trouble,
recalling it only as waters gone by.
Life will be brighter than noonday,
and darkness will become like morning.
You will be secure, because there is hope;
you will look about you and take your rest in safety.
You will lie down, with no one to make you afraid,
and many will court your favor.

Job 11:16-19 NIV

CHAPTER THIRTY-ONE

Dear Clint,
    I loved doing JAM things with you and your family and praying for the Sleepy Eye Public Schools together.

                                   Church Youth, age eight

CLINT, FEBRUARY 2017
FAIRFAX, MINNESOTA

The Fairfax choir's voice reverberated against the walls of the sanctuary for "Down in the River to Pray" in a harmony angels would envy.

I dallied toward the pulpit and glanced to my left, at Jeff's spot. Strangers sat there instead. *Jeff would love that.* Men and women occupied every spot available in the diamond-shaped sanctuary. People crammed into doorways and lined the walls in rows of two to three.

"Jeff would wonder why none of us have anything better to do on a Tuesday. He would also be happy you're here in this place. Not to say goodbye to him, but to allow God to say hello to you. As we enter into God's presence on Earth, and talk about Jeff's in-person presence with God, let's pray. I need to pray." I turned my head to sigh away from the microphone.

I don't remember my message, but when I finished speaking many people, including Sam, said it was my best sermon ever. I'd not drunk again, but regret for the relapse gnawed at me. Shame discolors and distorts reality. High praise for the sermon filtered through "you don't know what I've done" and translated to "I'm such a piece of garbage for duping such gentle believers."

Sam had returned from the writer's retreat with eight cans of Mike's still in the box. "You're sure you're okay with this?" she'd asked.

"Sam, I'm fine."

I needed to stop. I wanted to stop. I wasn't ready to quit. I didn't drink every night. I was scared Sam would figure it out. I'd not forgotten her oath to leave me if I ever relapsed, and I believed she would.

Legion slithered back to his camp for a time. Even the commander of 5,000 demons feared my wife. At night I decompressed with ESPN's take on who would win the Eagles-Patriots matchup for Super Bowl LI. Super imposed images of Tom Brady helmet-to-helmet with Carson Wentz flashed on the screen. *They should have more statistics for linemen.*

CLINT, MARCH 2017

Church ministries gained momentum. A vision team of ten birthed the idea of "Community Connections Week," a week of service projects around town.

Amidst all of this, I snuck in a few quickie drinks, but, like diving into an aluminum-laminated chip bag for just one, salty chip, my taste for liquor increased.

I studied Sam's patterns. Each night after laying the girls down to sleep, Sam holed up in the sunroom just off the kitchen to write. Unwittingly, Sam guarded my escape.

One night in early April, I said, "Hey, Sam, would you like to get out of the house to write tonight?" *You're such a piece of garbage, Clint.*

Her eyes widened with surprise and delight. "Um, sure."

"You deserve time away, sweetheart." *And you deserve so much better than what I'm doing to you right now.*

Legion return. "You get what you want, and husband points to boot."

The headlights of her Trailblazer flashed into the dining room and then veered away. I headed straight for the garage.

Several days later, Sam confronted me in the living room. "Clint, have you been drinking? The level on the vodka looks low."

"No." I furrowed my brow. "What? It must have evaporated some."
Her eyes narrowed, but she took my word for it and left the room.

"Whew. Close call," Legion and I said.

A couple weeks later, she popped her head into the living room again. The icy glare in her eyes squelched any hope of lying my way through the conversation. "You are drinking again, Clint. Do you think I'm an idiot? Five of my Mike's are missing, and I've been watching the vodka bottle. You want to give me the scientific explanation for how there's *more* vodka rather than less? You can admit you filled the bottle with water after drinking or you can try to convince me Jesus has been hanging out in our garage."

"Alright, I've been drinking."

"You told me you were fine. You told me I could buy alcohol."

"I wanted you to buy alcohol."

"What?"

"I wanted you to buy alcohol for yourself." I lied. "That was back in October. It's April. I didn't expect you to buy the damn economy size, and I certainly didn't expect the liquor to still be in the house seven months later. And then you come back from the Dells with even more." I threw my arms into the air. "I'm an alcoholic."

Our words gained volume with every volley. "You said you were fine."

"I lied."

"I knew it. Evaporation," she said in a mocking tone. "I wanted to believe you weren't drinking again. We've come so far since then. Tell Fred. Tell Nick. Please tell someone."

"If I tell one of them, I'll lose my job, my income, my ministry. We'll lose our house, Sam. We live in a parsonage."

"What about AA?"

"Some of our church members attend AA."

"AA in New Ulm."

"Same thing."

"You need help."

"Fine."

"Do you understand how much we have to lose if you don't get help?"

More than she knew, but she pointed the stakes out anyway.

"Clint, you're nuts if you think I'll let the girls experience you drinking. Get help, or I will leave with the girls. Figure out who you can talk to. You need help." She shook her fists. "Get help."

"Fine. Okay. Fine."

Her nostrils flared. She stormed out of the room. I heard the garage door open, the metal scraping glass as she unscrewed the cap and the unmistakable *glug glug glug* of liquid vacating the bottle.

Thank God. I took a deep breath. *I can do this now. I'll be fine. Especially if I only have one occasionally, like on weekends. After football.*

I lived two layers of life at once. Sam's sister, Jorie, and their family came to visit. Jorie and her husband raved about my accomplishments. My secret relapse tainted each beautiful memory with a bitter taste.

On May 8, I performed a baptism in Fairfax. I allowed the baby's whole hand to wrap around my index finger, and I whispered to her, "When we could do nothing to earn God's love, God died for us." I shared the good news about Jesus's unrelenting love with everyone around me, but wouldn't let mercy reach my own heart. My inability to love myself destroyed my ability to recognize others loved me.

CLINT, JULY 2017
SLEEPY EYE, MINNESOTA

During Faith UMC's Community Connection Week, church members gathered every morning for a week. "You've been prayed for by your friends at Faith UMC," scrawled in kids' handwriting, was seen by each person who walked, ran, or biked the three-mile trail around Sleepy Eye Lake. Church members passed out encouragement notes to business owners, shut-ins, and people walking along Main Street.

One woman read her card. "'Live your life to the fullest every time.'" She smiled. "Well, I would say I do. I am 102 years old."

Church members reconvened in smaller groups on school grounds to pray over every school in town.

Everywhere I looked, our church made a positive impact. And the shame I harbored grew heavier.

Men hauled grills to the front of our building and overloaded the front lawn with tables. We encouraged church members to leave open seats at each table for newcomers and welcomed anyone to join us. Conversation never lulled. Cross-generational team members shared stories about working, sweating, laughing, getting soaked in a thunderstorm, singing, playing, praying, eating, serving, and talking.

God moving. God working. Our congregation making a difference in the community. But each day, every moment, the same script played in my head. *You're a fake. You're such an imposter. They would never love you if they knew the real you.*

†

CLINT, AUGUST 2017
FAIRFAX, MINNESOTA

The wind flapped against my sermon notes, and I squinted at the white paper. *If I can't focus on my words, how will anyone else?*

Each summer, my churches hosted a combined service at Peichel's Hill, a bluff above the Minnesota River with a panoramic vista.

I glanced at the congregation to gauge their interest. Every single person stared, unblinking, above my head. For a split second, I considered Jesus's second coming, and I could say with all sincerity, "He's standing right behind me, isn't He?"

I craned my neck to follow their gaze. Not Jesus, but close. A flock of low-flying white egrets swooped down in a single file line and sailed with wings outstretched unhurriedly across our path. My fisted sermon notes crunched against my hip. I stared at God's creation in awe. After they passed, I said, "Well, how's a man supposed to compete with that?" While the congregation laughed, I yanked my notes taut and attempted to regain my rhythm. After the sermon, we shared communion.

True fellowship, true spiritual growth happened in those days. Yet, all the while, Legion whispered to me, mocked me, cheered for me.

Within two years of pastoring Fairfax and Sleepy Eye, I'd fostered such vulnerability that congregation members knew they could ask me anything. During confirmation, one leader asked, "So you don't drink? Ever?" *Except that.*

A friend once nicknamed me "Snow Monkey" for my ultra-white complexion, and for the first time in my life, I blessed God for my pale skin because there was no color to drain from my face. "No. I don't." I lied. Even if I were ready to come clean, I couldn't think of a more inappropriate confessional than confirmation. "I can't drink. I don't have an off switch."

"But you do." Legion whispered in my ear. "You've been drinking in moderation for months. All this time and you haven't even gotten drunk. No one even knows. We're so proud of you."

Addicts only confess when they want change and need help. The worst statements anyone can make to addict include "I don't think you were out of control," "I don't think your problem is that bad," and "You can have just one." Those words grant the addict permission to return for seconds. And thirds.

Those statements were some of Legion's favorites.

CHAPTER THIRTY-TWO

Sam's Journal Entry
November 2017

I'm losing myself. The enormity of what lies before me is an oppressive weight on my chest. I want to escape 'me.' But I can't. I get why people drink and cut and commit suicide. I'm not suicidal, but ending the pain seems blissful.

Jesus. Do you hear me? These struggles are dragging me into the dirt. I'm five feet under and losing the fight. Maybe I'm a phoenix too.

SAM, NOVEMBER 2017, SIX WEEKS AFTER THE ACCIDENT
SLEEPY EYE, MINNESOTA

Two weeks after my meltdown, I balanced my phone between my shoulder and ear and threw random items into a suitcase. *I haven't worn this sweatshirt in three years, but I'll probably wear it while I'm gone. It's November, but you never know when you might need a swimsuit.*

"Samantha, I don't think you should go. You should stay home with Clint."

My mom's words poked a hole in my euphoria balloon.

"*You* told me I needed a break." I stared at the dresser mirror, feeling like no one saw me.

"But I don't think this is the right time."

My voice carried undertones of panic. "Then when, Mom? Next week is Thanksgiving. When do I get to take care of myself?"

"Well, Samantha, there were years when I didn't get breaks."

205

"Yeah, but Dad took us for two days at a time every week."

"That was the court's decision."

She missed the point.

The repercussions of Clint's choice continued piling on months after the accident. Grief ambushed me in ways I never could have imagined. People gossiped about our family. We required Clint's boss's permission to attend our daughters' Christmas pageant. Pending legal charges prevented Clint from obtaining a passport. If the felony charge stuck, he'd never be allowed to leave the country. The bishop and the district superintendent relied on me for updates regarding legal matters. My reports determined Clint's possible reinstatement or termination.

The fallout unreservedly drained me. *Mrs. Evans, there's been an accident.*

Mrs. Evans, we found something on the CAT scan.

I've been drinking for seven months.

Sam, I'm taking you off pulpit supply.

Can you believe what he did?

Sam, my kids are being made fun of because Clint is their pastor.

Sam, we're gonna need to buy a new car.

Sam, we need to cancel our Wesley Pilgrimage to England … I get it. This would have been my first chance to use a passport too.

Six hours. My life dive-bombed in six hours. I lost my future, church, reputation, trust in Clint, time, focus, and finances—all within six hours.

I ended the call with my mom like my phone was on fire.

No one gets to tell me how to cope with this or say they understand.

My phone rang again.

"Sam, I don't think you should go." Clint's mom.

I pinched the snowpants hanging in my closet in consideration for the suitcase. "Clint and I talked about this together. We planned this."

"That was before his doctor's appointments dates changed. You need to drop everything you're doing for yourself and focus on your husband."

My brain short-circuited on possibly the worst advice I have ever received in my life. Stalled. Several seconds of zero brain function.

Rebooting....

Rebooting...

I clarified for the hell of it. "So, you think I should stop exercise—"

"Yep. Exercising. Writing. All of it. Stay home and administer to your husband's needs. That's what I would do. That's what I did, when the boys were little."

"Hmm." For a flash, I felt inadequate. *Maybe I should stay home and ... And what, spoon-feed Clint? Stick a thermometer under his togue every two hours? Dude just got home from the gym.*

Anger, disquiet, doesn't just need an outlet, it creates one if caged too long.

I'm not binge eating or picking up a smoking habit. I'm not divorcing Clint, which is still on the table. I'm not cheating on him. I'm not going on a spending spree. I am asking for three days, three days, of silence to hear God's voice instead of...

My mom

Clint's mom

Clint

My kids

Clint's boss

Clint's boss's boss, a.k.a. the bishop

Church members

Friends

Strangers at the store

Strangers at restaurants

The police

The judge

Lawyers

Doctors

Nurses

Journalists

"Dawn, I'm going."

"Samantha, he needs someone at those appointments with him."

"Then you and Chuck can go."

How does everyone suddenly have a huge blind spot in regard to how all of this started? Where are my *advocates?* I learned something critical that night. People with unhealthy boundaries don't understand people with healthy boundaries.

If we'd found the cancer by natural means, then *cancer* would have been the obstacle. I would have become his cancer treatment champion. But I was emotionally emaciated. I strived so hard in those days and weeks and months to keep it all together. I had no more kindness left in me, no more rational thought, no more capability of handling one more thing.

I still resented Clint. His decisions drastically affected my life. He cheated on me with alcohol. I understand alcoholism better than most people. I understand it wasn't a choice, but an inescapable siren call. Yet, if he'd sought help, if he had come clean before the accident, the fallout would have been so much smaller.

And we wouldn't have found the cancer.

That's messed up, right? He came home from every football practice proud of new bruises. He attributed all his physical pain to football. The girls constantly brought germs home, so we attributed sniffling and coughing to the newest trending sickness at school.

If indicators were there, we missed them. So, his great betrayal to me gifted us more time with Clint.

Oblivious to what I would find in the suitcase when I unpacked it, I hauled my luggage downstairs.

Clint emerged from the kitchen and met me in the dining room. "So, you're still going then?"

Had he asked his mom to call me? His tone suggested, 'yes.'

"If I don't do this," I started. *Our marriage will fail.*

Clint, Clint, Clint. How's Clint? How is Clint doing?

Why can no one see what a hollow husk I am?

I tossed the suitcase into the SUV.

Clint pressed his hand against the doorjamb. "Please don't go. I need you."

There's nothing left in me to give. "I need my oxygen mask."

I rolled out of the driveway and headed north. Guilt gnawed at me. *You need this.* Dusk gave way to twilight. I traded cornfields for the outer edges of the Twin Cities. I blasted my favorite songs on repeat and sang at the top of my lungs without judgement. Guilt faded to the edges like the dredges of a migraine.

The Brainerd Lakes visitor center appeared on my left. I glimpsed the shadowed figure of Paul Bunyan waving at me as I passed by.

God, give me my favorite view?

There is one spot on 371 just north of Baxter with Gull Lake to the west, Round Lake to the east, and only enough land between them for the highway. A five-second window of breath-taking majesty after miles through a corridor of evergreens.

The view opened like a locket protecting a priceless photograph. The full, white moon spotlighted the ink-and-silver waves on each side.

I inhaled, for the first time in weeks and eased my foot off the gas. The sensation of homecoming filled the broken cracks. Less than thirty minutes later, I turned into the driveway of my friend's lake home, located on a dead-end road.

This is what breathing feels like.

My phone rang. Clint's mom. I rolled my eyes and greeted her. "I just arrived in Pequot Lakes, an almost four-hour drive."

"I know, Samantha, but you need to turn around and go home. Clint needs you."

Clint always needs me. When do I get to need him? "Dawn. I'm not coming home." I hung up on her.

Laurie opened the front door before I climbed to the top step. "Welcome." She took my suitcase. "I have food laid out for you. Are you hungry? Can I make you a sandwich?"

"Yes, to the sandwich."

"So." She chuckled. "Tell me what's going on."

Laurie was a retired counselor, and I imagined her opening each session with the same phrase.

Two hours later, Laurie and I sat on her couch. We talked, while I intermittently typed. I paused to inhale a quiet house and no one in need of me. I inhaled the permission to be my whole self without anyone demanding.

My phone rang.

"Clint is everything okay?"

"No, I still don't have answers from Mayo. I don't know how to do this without you."

Laurie's gaze gave me strength.

"Clint, This is ridiculous. You asked what I needed. I said, 'a break.' We planned this trip together. I organized babysitters and meals. You see how fried I am. You need to respect my boundaries."

"Are we okay?"

"No." The whisper sounded like a plea. "I'm turning off my phone now." I tossed my powered-off phone aside. My lips mushed against my palms. "Am I doing the right thing?"

"Sam." Laurie tugged on my arm. "Look at me."

I faced her.

"You're not running in spite of your family. You are taking a break for your family. You are one of the wisest people your age I've ever met, and you know this cancer battle is a marathon. Three days will pass in a blink for Clint. For you? I wish all my former patients stepped back and paused when facing trauma. These three days will be pivotal because they'll enable you finish the race."

"I left my husband while he has cancer."

"The cancer will be there when you get back."

"I don't have the energy for him to be mad at me."

"He'll get over it." She shook my arm. "I am so proud of you."

"My friend Joanie and I decided we wanted a turn in jail."

"Oh, yeah?"

"Someone else makes your meals. You get quiet time, and no one knows your real name is Mommy. Did I tell you about the bishop?"

"No."

"He stared straight at me and said, 'So, are you gonna leave him?'"

"What'd you say?"

"'Well, I'm here for now. That's the best I can do.' Then he prayed over us."

That first night disjointed fragments of thoughts surfaced like that. Tiny clips of life buried beneath the noise of everything else.

I wrote forty, single-spaced pages in three days. Almost 20,000 words.

The next night I met two friends at Bites in Pine River. A gray, stone fireplace takes up most of the dimly lit dining area. The food is exquisite.

"I thought about divorcing him," I admitted.

"No one would blame you," Lynn said. "But I don't see it."

"Laurie said the same thing." I picked up my water glass. "Care to expand on that?"

"Plenty of people divorce for valid reasons. But you play out scenarios to the end. You're compassionate and forgiving. And in addition to everything else, you're a fighter. You're strong and you won't give up just because it's hard. If anything, you'll fight harder."

I thought she was right. That terrified me. I didn't have the energy for a fight in me.

CHAPTER THIRTY-THREE

Hey Clint,

Our line was a dope example of five different men from different lives coming together as a unit with the same goal. Thanks for teaching me it's possible to be a loving person and still play this sport like a monster. Rage and anger don't have to be the only motivation to play well.

M'Angelo Harris
Sabercats #57

CLINT, NOVEMBER 4, 2017
401 CHICAGO AVE, MINNEAPOLIS, MN 55415

I withdrew my cleats from my duffel and mentally transported from a stuffy locker room in the dead of winter to a sunny, late spring afternoon. My white jersey changed to pale blue. I removed my helmet. Air swept across my saturated bandana and felt like paradise.

Harris, our left tackle, squirted Gatorade into his mouth after a grueling first half. "Hey, Clint." He shifted his weight on the bench. "I know the Renegades were your team, but you're a Sabercat now."

I sat beside him and rested my arms on my legs, breathing heavily.

"That player workin' you, bro?" Harris punched me in the arm. "Or you goin' easy on 'im? You playin' nice?"

I lowered my water bottle away from my mouth. The plastic made a suction sound. "Hey, man. I'm a pastor. Nice is my nature."

"Naw, man. You better baptize his ass."

The whole bench erupted in laughter. Myself included.

I shook my head and spit my water out. "MH, you one sexy beast."

"Where I come from, we don't take that. I will from you, though. Love you, bro."

A few minutes later, Coach Yogi shouted, "Oreo line, you're up." Our nickname for the offensive line, for which I, the whitest guy on the team, played center.

I tossed my water bottle to the ground. Harris and I sprinted toward the fifty-yard line shoulder to shoulder, well, my head to his shoulder.

"Baptize 'em, preach," said Harris. "Don't you be goin' soft on those guys."

"Yeah, yeah. You just remember what everyone's favorite part of the Oreo is."

Harris laughed and crouched on the line.

After a few downs, a member of the Renegade Defensive line whined. "Ref didn't you see Evans? 67. Unnecessary roughness, ref."

Pong, our right guard, muttered next to me, "Thought we were play-ing football." We squatted into position. His shoulder brushed mine.

Another Renegade complained. "Sixty-seven, the center, holding. You blind?"

To my left, Harris chuckled. "That's what I'm talkin' about."

During the next play, over the QB's cadence, Harris barked, "Rebuked dat boy, bro."

I snickered and hiked the ball.

Three years had passed since then. I laced up my second cleat in the fluorescent lighting of the locker room and wondered how many guys I'd played with, and on how many teams. I left the locker room with the other Warhawks.

"We sound like prissy tap dancers," said Rueb, the team's left guard and one of our captains.

As the locker room tunnel gave way to the field, the clacking of our cleats echoing on the cement walls faded into the background of our thoughts. Grown men fell into reverent silence. U.S. Bank, home of the Minnesota Vikings, was so new most NFL players hadn't seen it yet. I scrolled through the Vikings 2017 roster and imagined each of them walking through this hall. *How am I here? Is this real?*

Time stood still. *This is my real life.*

"Dude," said James Tyler. The team called him "James Tyler" for short. "Pretty sure this is what walkin' into heaven is gonna feel like."

Couldn't have said it better. We filed in behind Coach Jackson along the sideline. My gaze veered around the stadium and upward, to the top of the dome. Two hundred seventy feet. *Nine hundred seventy-five million dollars. Are we allowed to step onto the field? Well, you're here to play a game, Clint. Not sure how you expect to win without stepping out there.*

I tried it, half expecting someone to blow a whistle and kick me off the astro turf. In my best Billy Madison impersonation, I said, "Oooh, that's nice." Suddenly, I wished Travis was in the stands rather than eight hours West in Minot, North Dakota.

I glanced at the sea of purple stadium seats. Sam brought her mom and sisters to Matt's for Juicy Lucy's. I didn't expect to see them, but I looked anyway. A man waving caught my eye. *Do I know him? Is he waving at me?* I squinted. *J.J? Here?* He pivoted toward the stadium entry and waved to someone walking down the stairs. *Jeff?*

"All right ladies," Coach Jackson called. "Sprints."

I yanked my helmet over my bandana and clicked my chinstrap into place. The runners in our crew formed the front of two lines of white jerseys. After dashes, lunges, and hip circles, we spread out to stretch. I stopped on the braid of the Viking's logo at the fifty-yard line. *You're not going to smear the paint.*

Rueb shouted, "Toe touches. Left."

This is surreal. I reached for my foot and inhaled, clearing my head. Muscle memory and routine replaced my scattered thoughts until only the game existed. On the other end of the field, the reigning-champion Wildcats counted off jumping jacks.

Before the coin flip, I glanced into the stands where I'd seen J.J. and Jeff. They'd been joined by Sam, her family, my parents and brother Darry, and Levi—who'd been present for Kelly's ultrasound. Spectators filled most of one side of the stadium.

My gaze connected with Sam's—veiled anger and hurt. Fire and Ice. She'd kept me at a distance since the accident, minus occasional, stress-relieving conjugal visits. Now, the space between us shrunk. And I couldn't look away. *The only one who hates me more than you is me.*

Legion strut up beside me in full uniform. "If the people in the stands knew the real you, they wouldn't be here."

I dropped my head with shame and recoiled from the story Legion had told me for months. Years. Decades. *No, demon. That's not true, because everyone here knows exactly what I did, who I am. And they came anyway.* And there were more people who wished they could make it. *Because they love me anyway?* I stared at nothing in particular. *Even Sam, who's furious with me, showed up to support me. They love me? Why?*

With false sympathy, Legion said, "They don't love you."

I'd confessed to my team after the accident, at that next practice. "I messed up. I'm such a hypocrite. I'm so sorry."

They stared and blinked.

"That it?" James Tyler asked.

"If anything, man, it makes us love you more," said Adamson, our quarterback. "You're not some high and lofty, judgmental Christian. You have struggles. It makes me want to listen to what you have to say. Now, can we knock off all this emotional B.S. before we find ourselves wearing women's panties?"

Done. Finished.

They responded more like God would than anyone else had.

"Evans."

"Don't fall for it. Don't be a chump," Legion said.

Shut up, demon.

The undeniable truth stared me in the face but wasn't computing. *My friends love me.*

"Evans. You with us?" Coach Jackson's voice plunged into the confusion I'd found myself in.

Oh. Football. Football makes sense. "Yeah, I'm here."

"Welcome back. I get it. It's a lot to take in," he said, referring to the stadium.

You have no idea.

"Practice snaps. Evans is starting center. Adamson, QB. Rueb, LG. James Tyler, RG.

Eleven years. I looked at the white jerseys on the field with me. *My brothers.*

Legion grumbled.

That demon is going to follow me to my grave. God, please free me from my demon of shame. I caught the ball Adamson tossed to me. "Hey, Adamson. I love you, man."

"Shut up and snap, Evans. Love you too."

I rubbed my fingertips against the ball's laces. Adamson yelled a cadence. I pitched the ball through my legs and into his hands.

"Perfect." He flicked the ball off his fingertips, and it spiraled toward me. "Again."

CHAPTER THIRTY-FOUR

Sam's Journal Entry
December 2017

No one, no one, gets to tell me how to do this. Everyone is panicking over Clint's cancer. Pity comes easier by focusing on the cancer instead of the drunk driving. Meanwhile, I'm absolutely shattered.

Sharing news of the accident and the cancer fell to me. I repeated the details of what I knew a gazillion times. I repeated hopeful outcomes and the positive details, desperately clinging to them myself.

But grief is an opponent who plays with no holds barred.

SAM, NOVEMBER 2017
SLEEPY EYE, MINNESOTA

Forty-five days after the accident and the initial discovery of the abnormal mass near his ribs, we still waited for answers. After the girls' ninety-minute bedtime routine, I lay on the couch in the sunroom. I tucked my bare feet beneath Clint's red quilt and engrossed myself in a novel with predictable outcomes.

The door from the kitchen creaked open and Clint popped his head in. "The hospital called. It's cancer."

My whole body stilled. *One more thing to deal with.*

"I'm going to go call my family now." He closed the door and left me in silence.

He must be so scared, feel so alone. I shook my head, unable to comprehend "cancer." *I should call my family too. But then I'd have to talk. I don't have enough energy to talk anymore.* I waited half a second for tears to come, but I didn't even possess the stamina to cry. A large void existed where strength once had. So, I dropped my gaze back to my novel with a predictable happy ending.

One week into December, details of Clint's illness continued evolving. The first hospital labeled it a melanoma, rather than sarcoma, two cancers treated in vastly different ways. And then the Mayo Clinic in Minnesota, spent *weeks* diagnosing the cancer correctly, refusing to settle for uncertainty. The December 7 CT scan showed cancer growth since October 1.

Eavesdropping on Clint was as easy as standing within a two-block radius. So even though he paced between the dining room and kitchen, and I folded laundry on a separate floor of the house, overhearing his side of the phone conversation required no strain.

"What do you mean you're booked out a month?" *Mayo-Mankato,* I surmised. "I can't wait a month … They're scared to take me since they misdiagnosed the cancer. … Fine. … Bye." After a length of silence, not knowing I could hear him, he said, "Sometimes I feel like God wants me to die."

I closed my eyes against the welling tears. Footsteps tromped up the steps and Clint appeared in our doorway. "Mayo-Mankato is booked."

"I heard." I tightened my lips into a thin line. *You've been so brave.*

He shoved a plastic hanger through the top of one of his hoodies. "What doesn't kill you makes you stronger."

I paused with one hand on a hanger and the other on a black hoodie. "That's not funny."

We stared at each other for a second and burst into a fit of laughter.

"I think I want people to wear leis at my funeral," he said.

His out-of-the-blue statement caught me off guard. "Why is that?"

"Because then people could say they got lei'd at a pastor's funeral."

I guffawed and dragged the collar of my shirt up to my eyes, hiding my face. "People," I said, still laughing, "would judge us if they could hear this conversation."

"People are judging us, and they *can't* hear this conversation. Let them, Sam. Judgment is small-minded people trying to shove big concepts into their tiny brains. Take it as a compliment. You challenge them, your ideas are larger than their worldview."

He slammed a few dress shirts, crooked on their hangers, into his closet. "I think I want a tat right here." He scratched at his right ribs. "A claw scratching. Satan tearing at me, trying to take me out. Whether I live or die, he ain't winning." Clint motioned to his upper back. "And a phoenix here, rising from the ashes. God killing old Clint and resurrecting something new."

The laptop strap dug into my shoulder. I swiped my car keys off the dining room table. They jingled in my hand.

"Where are you going?"

I met Clint's expectant stare. Nausea churned. "To write. I have twelve of twenty devotions finished for *Adventure Devos*."

"You've been leaving a lot to write."

"Yep. Writing gobbles up every spare second."

"You're using writing to avoid me."

"That too." I shrugged, too exhausted to sugarcoat my feelings. "There's no reason we both need to stay home with Trinity."

The tragic cancer diagnosis became a more pressing priority than the fallout of his drunk driving accident for everyone, including Clint. Yet, the betrayal I felt didn't simply disappear. I couldn't even look at Clint. The church conference suspended Clint, disguising his absence as medical leave, so suddenly he spent every day, all day, at home. My best temporary remedy for our marriage was to leave the house often.

"I don't feel like you're supporting me, Sam. You're always leaving. I don't... I don't feel like I can talk to you anymore."

Seething, I stiffened. *You can't talk to me. You broke our marriage.* "You broke my trust. I'm allowed to be angry."

"How long are you going to hold that against me?"

"I'm not being mean to you to punish you, for heaven's sake. Or spite you. You hurt me. I told you when you relapsed in 2007, if you drank again, I'd be done. Our marriage would be done." *My heart is done.*

"Then go. Either forgive me and support me or move on."

"No, we have to deal with the legal stuff, and chemo, and whether or not you'll go back to work. Then you and I can decide whether divorce is our best option. I don't know if what you broke can be fixed and I need time—I deserve time—to figure it out. My response is not your choice. You made your choice. Now I get to make mine."

"I need to know if you're gonna be in my corner on this."

All marriages experience stress. Marriage to an addict creates entirely separate stressors. Following a relapse, love comes with caution.

I felt skeletal. *There is nothing left of me for you to take. I am your stump in Shel Silverstein's* Giving Tree. "I'm too exhausted, too frail, too far extended, to make any rational choices, and certainly any important ones." I took a breath and fought against the burn of anxiety, anger, and despair that took up permanent residence in my chest. "If a friend hurt me as thoroughly as you did, I would have stopped speaking to her. But you're my *husband*. Do you not understand?"

Our families overlap, our friendships, our children, our ministries, our finances… everything is tangled. I feel trapped.

"I understand better than anyone. It's unbearable, actually, so I try not to think about how much pain I've caused. Because, when I do, I believe the world would be better off without me."

Oxygen vanished from my lungs.

"Sam, what do I have to do to make it right?"

Barely above a whisper, I said, "You can't do anything to glue us back together."

"Do you even love me?"

"How can you ask me that?" But I already knew the answer. Clint craved hearing he was good enough, but he never believed I meant what I said. At his core, he knew he was unlovable, so "I love you" never made sense.

He'd spent more than a decade investing in the people around him, conveying the love and grace of God at every opportunity. But whenever I said, "You are making such a huge, positive impact on the people around you," he'd disagree. Because what good can come from someone so unlovable? *God, please destroy those lies.*

"Are you," Clint asked, "going to drive me to my first chemo appointment?"

"Are your parents or brother able to help?"

"They work."

I guffawed. In the midst of all the hardships we faced, Clint still managed such a stereotypical male response. *And what the heck do you think I do all day long?* "Sure. Kaylynn's six. She can watch five-year-old Kelly and three-year-old Trinity for ten hours alone, no problem."

"Well, you could find a babysitter." *Oh, can I? Can you?* I hesitated to call babysitters if we had an alternative because I suspected we would need more help in the future. I tried to reserve our favor capital. Also, Clint's diagnosis terrified the girls, so if both of us were gone, they'd be worried.

"Doesn't your cousin Joe (the weatherman cousin) live in Rochester now? Maybe you could stay overnight with him."

"I haven't talked to Joe in years."

"Clint, I can't do everything."

"I want my wife to be there."

Insert knife. Twist. "Then find a babysitter to watch the kids."

"Why can't you?"

"Because I'm *working.* You're not. I'm exhausted. You have no idea how much I've done behind the scenes. I need someone else to help us."

I felt like Clint couldn't see the traffic jam of consequences his decision to drink and drive created. I actually started a recurring line in my journal: "The newest thing I need to forgive Clint for."

"You really don't want to bring me to chemo, do you?" he asked.

"You're the strongest man I know. And right now," tears formed in my eyes, "I need to believe you'll be fine. It's just chemo, just cancer, and cancer's got nothing on you. Because I don't have enough strength to cry about cancer too."

"Oh, Sam."

"I'll go with you. If you find a babysitter, I'll go with."

I strode into the living room, to Trinity, who sat on the couch point-ing at Superman and the Flash on the cover of a DC comic book. "Bat-an. Bat-an." Every character was Batman. I kissed Trinity goodbye and strode out the front door. At the library, I stared at my laptop screen and camped my finger on "delete" for the hundredth time. "I'm kid-ding myself if I think I can write right now."

Clint and I had built a good marriage, but it'd never been great. We clashed in many areas. I never felt like he was someone I could lean into. My hesitant trust stemmed from his relapses within the first couple years of our marriage.

Most days, Clint came home from work, stood in the doorway to the living room, and greeted me with, "I've had such a crappy day." After what felt like fifteen or twenty minutes, sometimes he'd look at me and say, "So, how was your day?"

Trinity puked in her crib, I spent the whole day washing laundry, scrubbing floors, doing dishes, making meals, changing poopy diapers and listening to wailing children. I hardly ever felt I had space to pile more onto his shoulders. "My day was fine."

A few days after our conversation about his first chemo treatment, Clint drove to his first chemo treatment alone. Late that afternoon, I received a text from him.

2:26 p.m.

I'm so lit on Benadryl right now. You'd be laughing.

LOL. Take a video.

2:32 p.m.

The doctor casually asked if I'd been exposed to toxic chemicals. I told him, "No. I'm a pastor. Only toxic people."

5:19 p.m.

I'm with Joe and Lindsey. I'm doing okay, just tired. We'll see how things go over the next couple hours.

6:58 p.m.

I'm going to stay overnight at Joe's.
Too dizzy.

Thank you for being wise. The girls and I
will miss you tonight.

8:44 p.m.

Yeah, I'm really sick now. Glad I
stayed in Rochester.

Me too. I'm so sorry you're sick.

On Facebook, he posted:

Chemo went well, just a bit tired right now. Thankful for Joe
Goldade and his wonderful bride Lindsey for their wonderful
hospitality. Thank you everyone for your prayers and support.

He also changed his "About Me" to read: "The enemy thought he
broke me, but Jesus be like, 'Nah.'"

8:48 p.m.

It's no joke. Hoping I feel better
tomorrow.

9:55 p.m.

Puking my guts out. So thankful
I'm here.

The last text, accidentally sent four times, shocked me. I imagined
him sitting next to the toilet, fumbling with his phone. Clint and I
both underestimated how sick the first chemo would make him.

Joe and Lindsay drove Clint and his car home the next morning.
They stopped twice along the way so Clint could puke on the side of
the road. When the cars pulled up to our home and Clint emerged,
he plastered a fake smile on his face and greeted our excited daughters
with energy. The nap he took lasted eighteen hours.

When he woke up, he lumbered downstairs. Red splotches covered his arms and the thin skin beneath his eyes—a side effect from "The Red Devil" treatment. Stretch marks across his collar bone turned pink and his whole body looked sunburned.

I jumped up from the living room couch where the girls and I were reading the newest Dolly Parton Library book and swallowed a gasp. *The burn is coming from the inside out.*

"Last night was rough," he said. "I've never felt so sick in my entire life."

"I'm sorry, Clint."

"God got me through it though. Held my hand every time I threw up. I'm gonna beat this thing."

I hope you're right.

"Fred called to ask how I was holding up. Asked me if I felt up to preaching on January 14."

"That's great news."

"He said there would be a church meeting beforehand though. Where people get to tell me how angry they are with me." Clint dipped his fist with fake enthusiasm. "He worded it better."

Clint would not appreciate my thoughts on the matter.

Clint sighed. "I wish all the accident garbage could be over so I could focus on the cancer."

Traffic jam of consequences.

"I deserve it though. I'm such a piece of shit."

My heart jolted. *Wrong conclusion. There's a space between "I made a mistake" and "I'm a piece of shit."*

I sighed. "Your congregations love you, Clint. They'll forgive you. They need a chance to work through the shock and disappointment."

A couple of weeks later, I wrote in my journal:

December 29, 2017

I'm watching Clint walk through his crucible and I believe what God raises up will be unshakable. The accident killed, the chemo is killing off, old Clint. God is getting Clint out of Clint's way. What God did with Himself with His resurrection, He does for each of us.

CHAPTER THIRTY-FIVE

Morning Clint,

I didn't get a chance to last night, and I'm sorry for not connecting sooner. My head has been in a fog. The words are still hard to articulate. But what I want to say is how much we care about you. I'm scared for you and your health. I wish you only the best and I always pray for you. I want you to get this thing nipped. I can only imagine how tough last night was, to hear what everyone said. Thank you for your strength and patience and for being there. Dealing with this stress on top of your medical condition, I can only feel for you and your family. But today is a new day, a day the Lord has made so let us rejoice and be glad in it. This is another hard road ahead of us together, but I know we can do it if we take it slow and listen to God and pray. If God is for us, who can be against us, right? :)

Love,

Your brother in Christ

CLINT, THURSDAY, JANUARY 4, 2018
SLEEPY EYE, MINNESOTA

The church basement exhibited all the characteristics a 100-year-old church basement should. A drop ceiling, small, rectangular windows, maize-colored tiles, and air tinged with the scent of must. Muted halogen lights shone above the heads of thirty church members sitting in a circle of folding chairs. Some of the faces around the circle held pity, some stared with contempt.

A divided council voted to reinstate me. My actions split the room into allies and enemies. The district superintendent Fred, who'd visited me in jail, organized the meeting to give church members opportunities to share grievances.

I felt like he'd tied me to the railroad tracks.

Legion, seated in the circle, gazed at the men and women in attendance whose ages ranged from early twenties to mid-eighties. "These people hate you. Now they know the truth. You're a worthless piece of shit, a fake. You don't deserve to be here."

Fred stood. The circumstance dampened his gregarious nature, but he opened the meeting with a generous smile. "Thank you all for coming. Bow your heads with me for a word of prayer?" Church members leaned forward and bowed their heads. Metal creaked with shifting weight. "Dear God, we thank you for all those gathered here. We know You are bigger than all of our mistakes, our hurts, our questions. Let Your presence be with us tonight. Guide this church, your people, in fruitful conversation. Amen."

Everyone murmured, "Amen."

Shame pressed my head down with palpable weight. Joe, a man my age, whose dad was a United Methodist pastor, attempted to smile encouragingly, but I couldn't meet his gaze.

My heart pounded like I'd taken a hit of crack. My palms sweated. I cleared my throat. "The first thing I need to say to each and every one of you is I am so, so, sorry. Words cannot express how badly I feel. I am doing everything possible to get help and make this right, which is why we're here." Fred had coached me on this introduction. "I'd like to open the floor with the question." *But I'd rather open the floor to swallow me.* "What are your thoughts, feelings, and concerns about the events of the last few months?"

"Pastor Clint." Gina's use of my title made me cringe. "Your actions really hurt me, but I know you're hurting too. I forgive you."

I tilted my head upward and met her eye. "Thank you." The weight of my shame slammed my head down again.

One elderly man said, "Alcoholism is a weakness. I've lost all respect for you. I will never respect you again, and I do not support your return to the pulpit."

Legion threw his head back and cackled. He laughed so hard he grabbed his sides to brace his aching stomach.

Surprise, surprise. This man had never liked me. Every month at council, he complained about the service time. And he wasn't even *on* the council.

At one meeting, I lost my temper. "You obviously care more about your country club church than new, young families attending, because an 8:00 a.m. service start prevents them from coming."

The venom in his words didn't surprise me, nor the hardness of his heart. I won't lie. His words hurt—as he intended, but his hatred confused me. *How is your love so blank?* Despite everything I faced, I pitied him.

A young mom said, "You lied to me. You said you don't drink. You can't drink. You lied to me."

I gestured with empty hands. "You're right." It didn't matter that as a church member, she would have been one of the last to know, behind my boss, my wife, my accountability partners, other pastors and the confidential Staff Relations team. I hadn't told anyone. *Church members will never see it that way.* "You're right."

"I'll never forgive you."

"Nor do you deserve forgiveness," Legion added.

Again, the absence of Jesus in her admission broke my heart. I recognized the hatred. And I wouldn't forgive myself, either.

"I wish we'd known you were struggling so we could have prayed for you," said my wife's feisty close friend. "But I'm the last person who's going to judge you. I've been there. I know the pull of addiction. You're always teaching us about grace and extending grace to us. Now we have a chance to show you God's grace as well. As far as I'm concerned, Pastor Clint, the slate between you and me is clean."

My eyes stung with tears. "Thank you, Erin."

"I'm really mad at you," said another woman, a teacher. "I would have been fired immediately if I received a DWI."

"I agree with you. I should have been fired, and I think it's really important for me to publicly own up to my mistakes."

As I sat there and endured the meeting, I sensed God asking, "Am I not bigger than this?"

I am the scum of the earth.

After three days, the two-hour meeting ended, and despite my best efforts, the worn linoleum did not part and swallow me whole.

SAM, THURSDAY, JANUARY 4, 2018
SLEEPY EYE, MINNESOTA

The church doors opened. Murmurs. Feet crunching along the salted sidewalk. The girls' bedtime routine complete, the house fell into a reverent stillness. I tiptoed down the steps and leaned against the doorway of the living room, exhausted. My eyes fell on Clint, sitting in his spot on the couch—not reclined back, cackling at a Will Ferrell comedy as I expected to find him.

He hunched forward, elbows propped up on his knees, head in hands. Light from the floor lamp beside him cast a yellow glow over his left shoulder, leaving the rest of him in shadow. I remembered this posture from ten years prior—a vivid memory from the day we lost our first baby. I hadn't recognized him then, either.

"The meeting?" I asked.

He didn't respond, not even a chuckle.

Should I give him space or does he want company? Indecision kept my feet planted.

When he spoke, his voice sounded scratchy, like he'd been crying. "Sam, what are the odds I'd marry an author with experience interviewing others and writing their God-stories, and whose best work comes from wounds?"

I dropped my head, knowing what would come next. His story was so dark, I cringed inwardly just hearing snippets over the course of our fourteen-year marriage. *Please don't ask me to do this.*

I wasn't sure if I directed the plea to Clint or God. Clint's relapse forged a breech in trust only time and effort could mend. Legal ramifications and chemotherapy treatments laid claim to both. There hadn't been space to work on "us."

Interviewing my husband would thrust me into an emotional intimacy that terrified me. Anger and resentment existed where love and trust once resided. Communion stung. *No, please.*

"I want you to interview me. I want you to write my story. How does it work?"

"I interview you and take notes. I record our interviews with an audio recorder in case I miss something. Then I write your story for you in first person, as if I were you. This isn't a small ask."

"When do we start?"

I exhaled. "Probably tonight."

CLINT, FRIDAY, JANUARY 5, 2018
SLEEPY EYE, MINNESOTA

The next morning I stared at my office computer and felt nauseous. Miscellaneous "church debris," bins of Bibles, craft supplies, and some AV equipment laid haphazardly on top of and around chairs I used for counseling. *It's not like anyone should be coming to me for life advice right now, anyway. Maybe I should move my office into the bathroom.*

"Clint." The office administrative assistant beamed at me. "I am so glad you're back."

"Thanks." I tried to smile.

"I think you handled yourself very well. I think people were angry and needed to release it. And I think it's done now."

There's no way I'll be that lucky. "I hope you're right." *What am I even doing here? I'm not a pastor. I'm a fake.*

"Well, welcome back," she said. She settled at her desk in the office next to mine.

Everything felt different, yet some things hadn't changed. One of my church members sent an email informing me about an upcoming pancake and brat dinner. The first sentence of an email from the worship leader read: "Welcome baaaaaaack!" The third sentence was: "By the way, you may have noticed, the five-CD disk changer is in your office."

Another email came from the editor of the local paper, reminding me it was my turn for a column in the religious section of the weekly paper. *Great.*

Then I clicked on two emails from unexpected church members, flabbergasted by the encouragement within.

_____

SAM, JANUARY 2018
SLEEPY EYE, MINNESOTA

I strode into the living room and found Clint standing in a straddle, bent in half, with his head between his knees. Beside him, Trinity stood in the same position. "What did you find out about chemo?"

"I get to take my next treatment in New Ulm."

Only twenty minutes away, rather than the two-hour trips he'd taken this last month. The upcoming round would be his third. "That's amazing news."

"It is, yeah." He unfolded and pointed the remote at the TV, pausing Diamond Dallas Page in the middle of a yoga pose.

Over the years, Clint's broad shoulders stretched the collars of every T-shirt he owned. Now, his clothes hung from him. Chemo forced his body through a reverse Steve Rogers effect. I inhaled and exhaled around the observation.

As if reading my mind, Clint said, "I could only deadlift 400 pounds yesterday."

I bit my lip to keep from laughing.

"It's more than 100 pounds less than three months ago."

"I know, but you hear it, right? How many people can say they deadlift 400 pounds while undergoing chemo?"

Sadness and fear emitted from him in waves. "The girls ask you for help now instead of me. I feel like a liability."

Oh, God, give me wisdom. "I … you're not. We're lucky to have you. I'm proud of you." I backed out of the room and busied myself with dishes so he wouldn't see me cry. I knew his masculinity felt threatened, but I witnessed a strength of character in his perseverance more impressive than any dead lift, squat or bench press. I saw spiritual brawn I didn't know Clint possessed.

Clint returned from Friday's chemo incredibly nauseous and vomiting. I finished bathing the girls, brushing hair, brushing teeth, reading stories, and singing songs. I tucked the covers around Trinity and kissed her forehead, and heard Clint retching in the bathroom.

Most of his spew landed in the toilet bowl, but some splashed onto the toilet lid and floor.

"Clint, go lay down. I can take care of it." After weak protest, he landed on the bed and passed out. *At least I don't have to read books to him or sing him a nite-nite song.* I wiped up his vomit and scrubbed and sprayed. A strand of hair strayed across my face, and I wiped it away with the inside of my elbow. *Man up, Sam.* When the white porcelain shone white again, I leaned back against the bathroom cabinet. "Whew. Done."

The sound of puking came from one of the girls' rooms. I dropped my head. *My real life could be a movie.* That night, Kaylynn and Kelly vomited due to a GI bug. Trinity had diarrhea. Not once did the girls make it to the bathroom. Walls, carpet, hardwood floors, comforters, bed skirts, stuffies … all splattered and caked with puke and diarrhea. Clint took another turn puking the next day, Saturday.

Tomorrow would be his second Sunday preaching since his reinstatement. At least Methodists were notorious for leaving the first several pews empty. Miraculously, probably actually miraculously, I stood at the center of four people expelling germ-saturated body fluids, and I remained healthy.

Clint managed to preach without throwing up on anyone. On Monday, after dropping the older two off at school, I felt like I'd emerged from a strange dream. *Ok. As long as Clint doesn't puke on anyone at court today, we'll be okay.*

CHAPTER THIRTY-SIX

Pastor Clint,

Rita and I have always appreciated the way you care about not only us, but everyone in our congregation, and the people you meet. You use your God-given talent very well. I'm sure you don't even realize the positive effect you have on people. It is a joy to see the way you interact with your wife, children and others. You have had a lasting, positive impact on Rita and me. Thank you. We love you.

Nip

SAM, JANUARY 29, 2018
NEW ULM, MINNESOTA

Gray frost imprinted the edges of the windshield in tiny snowflake patterns. The barometer on the Trailblazer displayed a single-digit temperature.

"It was nice of Greg to rearrange his vacation plans for this," Clint said into the cold silence.

I rubbed my mittened hands along the steering wheel. "I agree."

Twenty minutes later, I passed the metal detector test and strode into the diamond-shaped room with Clint at my side.

"Nip." Clint shook his hand. "Thanks for coming."

With sincerity, he said, "Happy to help."

Clint greeted Greg and followed him to the defense table.

The same judge sat on the same bench and greeted Nip like it were any other Monday and the fate of our life didn't rest with his decisions.

If the felony charge against Clint became permanent, Clint would lose his ministry, our income, and our house. Clint stared down the potential of a minimum of four years in prison, a $3,000 DWI fine, and who-knew-how-many thousands of dollars of restitution for damage throughout the city.

Nip and the judge exchanged stories about their grandkids.

Okay, God. I trust you ... right?

The same eight church members who attended the first hearing sat thigh to thigh in the upholstered chairs behind Nip and me—in the exact same chairs.

"All rise," the bailiff called.

"Go ahead and take your seats," said the judge.

"Your Honor," said Greg, "I am submitting a Nogaard plea on behalf on my client, who does not remember the events of the accident."

Greg read a version of the police report, chronicling every offense Clint committed. I cringed through the retelling, acutely aware of church members sitting behind me.

Greg finished reading the police report of the accident.

Then the prosecution read the charges against Clint:

1. A felony fleeing the scene
2. Gross misdemeanor DWI
3-5. Misdemeanor property damage
6. A petty misdemeanor illegal U-turn

"To these charges, how do you plead?" the judge asked.

"No contest, Your Honor," Clint said.

Each offense felt like rubble crashing down on top of me. The judge, prosecution, and defense volleyed legal jargon and procedures. I would have understood as much of the conversation if they spoke in Latin.

Finally, Greg said, "In regard to the felony charge of fleeing the scene, the defense would like to recommend a three-year stay of adjudication."

Nip leaned over and whispered, "So, the felony will stay on his record for three years and then disappear. If no new charges are filed against him."

Oh, now I remember. Back in October, Greg explained the give and take of the prosecution and defense. "If we are stubborn, they'll play hardball." The Stay of Adjudication gave the prosecution their felony conviction. Three years later, the ruling would grant Clint a back door exit from the charge.

"The prosecution deems the stay of adjudication a reasonable request," said the prosecution.

"In regard to the DWI, the defense suggests a two-year probation period, eighty hours of community service and mandatory, biweekly group counseling."

"The prosecution would also like to tack on jail time to this offense …"

My eyes widened. *What? For how many years?* A cry welled within me.

"… of three days," the prosecution continued, "which, I'll remind the court, has already been served."

I snorted. *Oh.* I waited for a shoe to drop, much less the other shoe. The prosecution didn't demand Clint's driver's license. He didn't utter a word about whiskey plates—a DWI offender's scarlet letter—or a breath-lock, the device which requires a person to blow a negative alcohol test before starting the car.

The judge leaned forward. "And as I understand it, the county has agreed to drop the property damage charges?"

Wait.

"Correct," said the prosecution lawyer, "Your Honor."

"Very well," said the judge. "Then Mr. Evans will receive a two-year probation for the illegal U-turn, as well as a fine of $135, to be paid within thirty days." He inclined his head toward Clint. "Mr. Evans, it appears you'll do fine if you can stay away from alcohol."

"Yes, Your Honor," Clint said.

"I am waiving the three thousand dollar DWI fine, in lieu of Mr. Evans's medical issues."

I didn't notice the background noise, until sound ceased. Chairs creaking, papers shuffling, pens scrawling, keys jingling, computer keys clicking. Even breathing stalled for a second out of time.

Nip gawked.

The judge slapped the gavel against the polished wood. "Court is dismissed."

Movement and sound recommenced.

Nip remained slacked jaw.

No one was harder on Clint than Clint. He was devastated by the people he hurt and embarrassed by the damage he caused. But we serve a God who specialized in "beauty from ashes," and I continued to be amazed at the ways God used the situation for good.

Members of the churches responded with a humbling, Christ-like grace. The event lent courage to church members and even some from the community to be transparent in their own failings and struggles. I was grateful and inspired by our church's support, and for the respect shown to us by New Ulm Police, the Brown County Sheriff's Office, the prosecution and for Greg Handevidt's advocation for our case. God's favor resting on Clint caused me to draw parallels between him and Joseph of the Old Testament. Clint was 100 percent responsible for his crimes, and Joseph went to jail, 100 percent innocent of the sexual assault Potiphar's wife accused him of.

However, in reference to Joseph's hardships, the Bible repeats variations of one phrase eleven times. "The LORD was with Joseph and gave him success in whatever he did" (Cf. Genesis 39-50, Acts 7:9).

I always imagined that when Joseph stepped in faith into a dark nothing, a golden path manifested before him. The same imagery came to mind watching Clint's scene play out in the courtroom. I didn't understand God's plan, but I was confident of His presence.

CHAPTER THIRTY-SEVEN

February 2018
Sleepy Eye Herald Newspaper Article

So, a lot has happened since the last time I wrote an article. It has been almost four months since my alcohol relapse in which I not only made the horrific choice to get behind the wheel, evade police officers, and cause property damage. I thank God everyday no one got hurt. But also when I discovered I have cancer. It has been a long, hard journey, not only dealing with my legal issues, which were resolved on January 29, but also reflecting on how I got to this situation in the first place. I have gone through a great deal of counseling, been attending AA meetings, spent a lot of time reading and prayer in order to improve myself. Through this process, I have uncovered a lot of stuff I kept below the surface, a lot of issues I needed to resolve and work through. I still have a long way to go, but I believe this journey has changed me into a new man.

Physically, I am taking it one day at a time. I started chemo a little bit ago at Mayo and it has not been easy. As a person who was never sick and was very blessed physically, it has been hard seeing my body "betray" me. My famous appetite is diminished. I am more tired than usual. I am no longer in control. But there is beauty in this, as I have had no choice but to surrender and give everything over to God. Am I thrilled with my circumstances? Of course not, but I put myself (and others) in a terrible situation and I have seen God make good things come of it. I am thankful the cancer was detected, as I had no symptoms beforehand. Yes, it is stage IV, but medical advances give me a chance at living for a while. And I have been absolutely flabbergasted at all the love and support I have received from the community. You had every right to kick me to the curb, but you chose to stick by me, and I am forever indebted to you.

But I know all is not well yet. I have been reinstated to work … but I can't go back to work like nothing happened. A lot of healing, a lot of reconciliation, a lot of rebuilding relationships has to take place. My actions not only harmed me, but they harmed my family, my congregations, and the respective communities I serve. There are not enough words to express how remorseful I am. If I have hurt you deeply, please come talk to me about it. Once again, I love you all and am thankful to be part of this community.

Grace and Peace,
Clint Evans

CLINT EVANS, 2019
SLEEPY EYE AND FAIRFAX, MINNESOTA

I clenched the music stand. The congregation waited for me to speak. *I don't deserve to be up here.* I'd stopped standing behind the pulpit and wearing my alb.

Stop making this about you, God seemed to say. *Are we going to preach my message or not?*

I lifted my head and opened my mouth. "I've gotta confess, sometimes when I go home on Sundays after preaching, I imagine you sitting around the table with your family discussing my sermon, and I picture you saying, Pastor Clint's message was 'one of the most insanely idiotic things I have ever heard. At no point in his rambling, incoherent rhetoric was he even close to anything that could be considered a rational thought. Everyone in this room is now dumber for having listened to his sermon. I award him no points, and may God have mercy on his soul.'

"That was a quote from *Billy Madison*, by the way, in case you missed it. God bless, you Erin, for laughing.

"Well, today, I'm going to talk to you about something I understand better than most people in this room: Addiction.

"Addicts have a Stockholm syndrome relationship with their vice. While we are indebted to our master, we can't serve the other. Drug addicts exist in a living Sheol[7]. They are the walking dead, existing in a present-tense hell—desperate for the drug they despise.

"Luke 8 shares the story of a demon-possessed man. Jesus speaks to the man, but the demon within the man replies instead. Not one demon. The demon introduces himself to Jesus as 'Legion,' which is a battalion of *5,000* Roman soldiers. The demon-possessed man is a husk who doesn't even have a say in his own life.

"This story is *not* about addiction. Yet, I guarantee nearly every drug or alcohol addict who reads this passage would agree this story depicts what addiction *feels* like. Addiction consumes the addict, feeds off the addict like cancer. The addiction speaks for the addict. The addict is only a husk.

"According to a study performed by the National Institute of Health, 23 million Americans struggle with drug or alcohol addiction. 46 percent of Americans have a family member or close friend addicted to a substance. Almost half of us. And, thanks to me, 100 percent of you have a personal relationship with an addict.

"I know you love your addict, whomever he or she might be. You do. But your addict has made you angry. Your addict has hurt you.

"And for some of you, your addict is me.

"Maybe your addict stole from you. She'll come over for Sunday lunch and keep her promise to be sober. Because if she can endure two hours of sobriety, she'll have a chance to rob you. You're not inviting the person you love to brunch. You're inviting a puppet, who no longer speaks for herself. The drugs do.

"Do you know why repentant addicts make the most radical Jesus followers? Because they already know what losing life means. They know what slavery feels like.

7   hell

"No place to lay your head? Check.

"Give up everything you own? Check.

"Nothing left to lose? Check.

"Despised by mother and father? Check. Check."

"Redeemed addicts understand grace more deeply than anyone else ever will. Their eager desire to follow Christ regardless of cost and their desperate gratitude for grace is the church's Christmas morning view of following Jesus. That's why God gives you addicts.

"Most of this world writes off ragamuffins[8]. It's easier to feel closer to godly perfection by measuring ourselves against the dirty, homeless and addicted. Clean robes, rather than contrite hearts.

"And I'm about to call you out. If this is you, then you are no different than the first century Pharisees. 'This man consorts with tax collectors, prostitutes and sinners.'

"When the religion of Christianity becomes our master, we idolize the goal to live an unblemished life. How is our idolatry of appearance any different from Jesus accusing pharisees of being 'White-washed tombs?'

"When I'm out on the football field colliding helmets, sweating, bleeding, trying my best—and losing—you know who I don't want to hear advice from? The people on the bench. Don't sit there with your bleached-white jersey and glossy, unscuffed helmet and tell me how to do it better.

"How many of you pay such close attention to a ball snap you understand what happens at the line of scrimmage?

"Few people understand the terminology I just used and fewer can follow the football throughout the entire play when the offensive and defensive lines collide. But follow this. The ball is life and it's your job to get the ball into the end zone. Addicts are the running backs buried beneath a mound of men—burden after burden—who experience more losses of yardage then gains.

"And too many people who claim to love like Christ sit on the

---

8 Ragamuffin—a shabbily-dressed person

sidelines with foam fingers, pointing, gawking, and saying, 'what is the running back's problem?' Christian benchwarmers need to evacuate the stands and run interference. You're better than judgmental condemnation. You *know* better.

"What? You're scared? Shame follows public scandal. Believe me, I know. What if you fail? Take the ball and run with it. And Just. Don't. Slip.

"You might slip. Good thing there's enough grace for all, even the pew-squatter saints.

"Friends, I have three things to say to you:

"One. It's so easy to become a pharisee. Guard your hearts against it.

"Two. What vice do you use to silence God's voice? Some addictions are easier to walk away from than others. Some addictions are easier to hide. If you're shoving an addiction between you and God's call on your life—substance, pornography, food, television—surrender. Because I'll tell you from personal experience, God's plan is greater than your cast-off view of yourself. You can't drink God under the table. I've tried. His plans and ideas for you will be waiting when you wake up. God placed this prodigal behind a pulpit. God's love tromps into the pig pen and rescues the ragamuffins. His grace extends far beyond the comfort zones of any human.

"The third thing I want to say is, 'thank you.' Thank you for seeing me. I would not have been reinstated without you running interference for me with calls and emails to the superintendent and bishop. God set me behind the pulpit the first time, and you brought me home after I'd strayed back into the mire. 'See' others like me, okay? They need you too."

CHAPTER THIRTY-EIGHT

Clint,

I have been to eighteen different countries and talked to very rich and important people, and no one has ever impressed me more than you. I wish I could express how proud I am of you. When I'm around people I always talk about you. You prove every day there is a God.

Whenever you are having a bad day remember where you came from, and how far you have come. I've made a lot of mistakes with you I will always regret. But those are the times when I realize how much I have been blessed with you boys. You and Samantha are special. Thank you.

Love you,
Your dad

SAM, FEBRUARY 2018
SLEEPY EYE, MINNESOTA

Temperatures rose into the high twenties, and I sent the girls outside to play. For thirty minutes, they shrieked and giggled and shouted in delight. When they ventured inside, their hats, mittens, scarves, and coats landed in a heap. Boots caked with melted ice tumbled across the floor. Unzipped snowpants revealed the girls beneath. The three-year-old's hands were bright pink with cold.

I cupped them within my own and blew. "You smell like snow."

"No, I smell like mac and cheese. Mom, can we have mac and cheese for lunch?"

"I don't know if we have …"

Trinity pointed to the open cupboard I'd abandoned when I heard them tromping in. "It's right there."

"Oh, sure. I can make mac and cheese for lunch." I grabbed the box and placed it on the counter.

"Yea. Can I help you make it?"

"Help" meant handing me ingredients. "Sure."

She cheered again and removed the box off the counter.

I set water to boil and tackled dirty dishes in the sink. The three-year-old, already bored, disappeared into another room.

Gurgling water grabbed by attention and I reached for the blue box, which no longer rested on the counter. *Where did she …?*

The cacophony registered.

"A, B, C, D, E, F, G. H, I, J, K, L, M, N, O, P." *What the heck?*

"Q, R, S." Clint's voice rang out the loudest.

He'd been resting in bed following his last bout of chemo. When they finished the song, they started again at the beginning.

I jogged up to our bedroom and found the older two bouncing on the bed, grinning ear-to-ear, and Trinity standing next to the bed, shaking her Mac-and-Cheese box maraca with flourish.

"I'm trying to make lunch."

"Oh, yeah," Clint said. "Little One used the noodles as an instrument. That's how the whole thing started."

Trinity gave me the box, and I returned to the kitchen. The Vontrop family choir moved on to "Mary Had a Little Lamb."

My delight quickly faded.

"We should get more than ABCs, God." I dumped the noodles into the boiling water, trying to keep my tears out of the pot. "Clint should be here for driver's ed and threatening dates, high school graduation, and the chance to walk his daughters down the aisle. We should get more than ABCs."

Later, after we put our Tweedle-three to bed, my husband and I finally faced unnamed fears.

He tried to hold back tears, unsuccessfully. "When this is all over, I just want the people to know I loved them. And yet, through all of this," he cried, pointing at the ceiling, "I know God is still good."

Three months passed. Clint slept more, moved less. One day, on his day off, I spent time with a friend. When I came home, he'd cleaned the kitchen and living room and was dressed to exercise. "I opened all the storm windows like you asked," he said.

I smiled. "Thank you."

That night we attempted sex and failed. It happens to every couple: too distracted, too tired, too selfish. But while he redressed, we both knew it was the cancer.

I stared at his back, where five new moles appeared recently. The sight terrified me. They might not mean anything. *Mention those to the doctor.*

"I need to be alone right now," he said.

I gathered my thoughts and my clothes. "I'm sorry. I love you."

"I don't feel like a man anymore. I need you to know that. Cancer has taken my energy, my strength … " he threw his hands up, "… my body hair. It's taken my dreams of the future and career milestones I hoped to accomplish." He hung his head and whispered, "I don't feel like a man anymore."

"I don't think any less of you," I managed, keeping tears at bay. *What is manhood, anyway?*

Manhood is spending time laughing with your children even when you're exhausted.

Manhood is doing what your wife requests without complaining and then doing more.

Manhood is working forty hours a week to support your family, when you honestly can't remember the last time you slept through the night without waking up in pain.

Manhood is whittling down priorities until all that remains is the desire to see people as people instead of annoyances or step stools or to-do lists—to see people as people—the way God sees them—and to love them until they understand they are loved.

Manhood is having the courage to see and trust and appreciate God's hand in the face of death.

Manhood is opening storm windows and laughing through the ABCs, shouted at the top of your lungs, while staring death in the eye.

Manhood is making the most of every day.

CHAPTER THIRTY-NINE

Dear Evans Family,
  You are so loved.

Carissa

CLINT, JULY 2018
RHINELANDER, WISCONSIN

I stumbled down the gravel road with bleary eyes, squinting against the sun. To onlookers, I might have appeared drunk, but I hadn't touched alcohol for ten months. I barged through the screen door of my father-in-law's cabin. "I need coffee."

"Well," said my father-in-law's wife, Sherry, with a southern twang, "good morning, Clint." She sat by a bay window facing Lake George.

"Good morning, Sherry. Sorry."

"Believe me, I understand."

"Hope tell ya," I said.

She laughed.

I grabbed a Barbie-sized mug from the cabinet, wondering what a teaspoon of coffee could possibly accomplish for anyone, and poured the dark Joe.

"Clint, will you baptize me?"

Sherry's question jolted me like caffeine tapped into a vein.

"I'd love to. I'd have to ask you a few questions first." I slurped my coffee.

Through spiky branches of hemlock trees the sun glittered gold across gentle blue waves.

"When I woke up this morning, Clint, I heard God say, 'it's time,' clearer than I've ever heard Him before. "'Time for what,' I asked Him. I crawled outta bed, sat down in this nook, and stared out over the water. The next second, you burst in, and the words tumbled out of my mouth like they made all the sense in the world."

I'd literally stumbled into God's plan for Sherry.

Later that day, three generations waited on the beach at the time Sherry and I decided.

Sam and I darted around beach chairs, beach towels, and sand pails. Our daughters, who'd been watched by their grandparents, collided with our hips. "Sorry," I said.

"You'll be late to your own funeral." My father-in-law Ed grinned.

"Linemen have no business on paddle boards," I said. A few minutes later I splashed into the water, script in hand, and passed a copy to Sherry, which she wrangled against her blue swimsuit. Ed flanked her. The water lapped against his rounded waist.

Some family members stood on the sand, but most everyone waded into the lake. Witnesses bobbed up and down on floaties— a turquoise toucan head, a pink flamingo, a flimsy silver air mattress. A film of oily sunblock coated the surface of God's holy baptismal font.

This is a first.

And isn't that grace? God asked me. *The messier, the better.*

Alex, my teenage nephew, stood on a paddle board. I imagined him slipping off and smacking Sherry in the head with the board. *I draw the line at mouth-to-mouth on my mother-in-law.* Two of Ed's sisters were nurses. We'd be fine.

Just then, one of Ed's nurse sisters declared she'd warmed up the lake and wondered if I could baptize Sherry with *that* water.

I pursed my lips.

Sam held three-year-old Trinity on one hip. Kaylynn and Kelly, within an arm's length of Sam, shoved water into one another's faces.

"Sit still in the pew and behave," Sam said.

Our daughters scrunched their faces in confusion, but everyone else burst into laughter. The sound rippled across the water.

Better get started before the congregation members float away like little ducklings.

The script flapped flat across my arm with a strong wind. "Brothers and sisters in Christ, through the Sacrament of Baptism we are initiated into Christ's holy Church. We are incorporated into God's mighty acts of salvation and given new birth through water and the Spirit. All this is God's gift, offered to us without price."

Do you see it now? God seemed to say. *My plans are bigger than "should" and "supposed to."*

God was telling me He didn't need a building or clean water or white, frilly baptismal gowns. This baptism, despite paddle boards and pee, was as beautiful as any other baptism God had ever participated in. I felt him smiling.

Clint, you've been right where you were "supposed to" be, all along. With me.

For the span of a wink, I saw my own life through God's eyes—the beauty beyond the destruction. *His* plans and *His* purpose exceeded my wildest imaginations. Fleetingly, beyond knowing in my head God loved me in spite of my great failings, I realized His love in my heart. *There is nothing I could ever do to make Him love me less.*

I focused on the words in front of me with new understanding. "I present Sherry for baptism. On behalf of the whole Church, I ask you: Do you renounce the spiritual forces of wickedness, reject the evil powers of this world and repent of your sin?"

"I do," Sherry said.

I do, too, God.

"Do you accept the freedom and power God gives you to resist evil, injustice, and oppression in whatever forms they present themselves?"

"I do."

Resist evil by Your strength instead of my own? I want to.

"Do you confess Jesus Christ as your Savior, put your whole trust in his grace, and promise to serve him as your Lord?"

"I do."

100 percent. "Yes, Lord, you know I love you," The echo of Peter's voice, following his great betrayal to Christ, overlapped with mine.[9]

"Pour out your Holy Spirit, to bless this gift of water and those who receive it, to wash away their sin and clothe them in righteousness throughout their lives, that, dying and being raised with Christ, they may share in his final victory. Sherry Lewis, I baptize you in the name of the Father, and of the Son, and of the Holy Spirit. Amen."

My forgiveness for you is final, Clint, and My love complete.

Ed took our scripts. Then I lowered Sherry beneath the surface and raised her into the sun.

---

9   John 13:36-38; 18:15-27; 21:15-24

CHAPTER FORTY

Hey Clint,

I didn't have a chance to say bye. But I do remember all the years on and off the field making memories. I appreciate all you've done and stood for. I will see you one day again, sir. Rest with love and peace.

One Love,
Kaleo

SAM, AUGUST 2018
SLEEPY EYE, MINNESOTA

Elbow deep in a pot-scrubbing situation at home, I nodded at Clint over my shoulder and went back to work.

"Sam, I think I need to stop taking hydrocodone."

I swallowed mild panic. "But you've been happier this week."

The opioid separated Clint's brain from knowledge of the pain. In fourteen years, I'd never witnessed Clint so unencumbered—joyful, energetic, hopeful. Friction in our marriage vanished. He took the kids out of the house, performed chores, caught up on work, and exercised. The drug also raised his stamina back to normal in the bedroom.

"My AA sponsor knows about the drugs, but I don't feel right saying, 'It's been ten months since my last drink. I've switched to more dangerous narcotics instead.'"

I tipped my head. I saw his point. "But this is doctor prescribed."

"These patches," he said pointing to the one on his arm, "are so dangerous I'm supposed to flush them down the toilet after wearing one for three days so there's zero chance the girls could touch one. The first patch worked for the full three days, but the second patch barely made it past forty-eight hours. The potency is already wearing off. This is how addicts get hooked."

I finished rinsing the pot and tipped it upside down against the strainer. I dried my hands on a towel. "Feels strange, doesn't it? Me trying to convince you to do drugs?" We'd come a long way since the night I found weed in his shorts.

"You have no idea."

"If you need to stop, then stop."

The next day, I drove our family to the Brown County Humane Society to surprise the girls with a new kitten. Throughout the twenty-minute drive, Clint spoke at rapid-fire speed. I didn't understand one word. Beads of sweat appeared on his forehead and his knees bounced uncontrollably. *This is what withdrawal looks like after five days? Geez, Louise.* Again, my grace grew for the addict.

At the humane society, the employee shut us in a room overflowing with cats, mostly kittens. Black-and-white, gray, tabby, calico, striped and everything in between. The three girls squealed with delight. After reassuring ourselves three-year-old Trinity wouldn't squeeze any kittens to death, Clint and I settled in plastic chairs along the window and watched the girls pick up cat after cat.

An orange tabby jumped on Clint's lap and pivoted so its head rested between Clint's knees. With each firm stroke Clint smashed the cat flat into his lap. My lips parted to say, "gentle," but I noticed two things. One, the cat loved the attention, and two, the repetitive stroking motion soothed Clint's withdrawal symptoms. The force of his stroke eased with the stroke of each minute hand.

After nearly thirty minutes, Kelly pointed to his lap. "Daddy, do you like the orange cat?"

"What?" Clint looked down and noticed the cat on his lap for the first time.

The employee returned. "How are we doing in here?"

The girls' grins answered her question.

Trinity thrust a kitten above her head. "We wah dis wan."

The employee grinned. "And just so you know, it's a buy one, get one." She winked at me and Clint. "I'll give you guys a few more minutes." The door closed.

Clint turned an accusatory stare on me. "Did you know it was a BOGO sale?"

One by one, the girls asked, "What's a BOGO sale?"

Words fell from my mouth as fast as they had from Clint's in the car. "Research says two do better than one because they keep each other company and I didn't say anything, because I wanted to leave it up to you."

"What's a BOGO sale?"

"You're unbelievable." Clint tried not to smile.

"What's a BOGO sale?"

"It means we're getting two kittens," Clint said.

"Yaaaaay."

"We should get these two." Kelly held matching kittens against her belly. "This one is Pitter Patter and this one is Cherry."

Clint stood. "Let me see what you've got there." The girls' gazes were magnetized to his every move. He eased the kittens into his own hands. "What if we name this one Pitter and this one Patter."

Over the top of our cheering girls, he rolled his eyes at me.

tulip

SAM, PRESENT DAY

Luke echoes the same thought twice in Jesus's birth narrative. "But Mary treasured up all these things and pondered them in her heart" (Luke 2:19, 2:51). There were moments out-of-time when Luke's words would roll through me, like God was whispering, "remember this. Save this."

From the time we got married, Clint would comment, "I don't think I'll live past thirty-six." Always thirty-six. Eventually, I shouted,

"Stop saying you'll die by thirty-six." Clint received his cancer diagnosis at age thirty-six.

Clint's need for hydrocodone proved the first of many hints of Clint's timeline winding down.

In September 2018, our church rented an inflatable obstacle course, and Clint and I raced one another. I shimmied through the final tunnel. Clint grabbed the ankle hem of my jeans and yanked. I yelped and wiggled back into my pants while he emerged from the tunnel and thrust his arms into the air. "I am victorious."

In fifteen years, I'd never won a race against him. Ever. My smile faded. *You win all the races you want.*

Clint started playing semi-pro football in 2007. The man was made of pigskin. "I don't know what I'll do when I can't play football anymore," he mused more than once. In truth, I didn't know, either. Each year, he'd say, "I think I'm done. I'm getting too old for this." And every year he re-signed.

In the eleven years he played, he'd never made an all-star team. Several years he suspected league officials passed him over for politics and vented, "I just want one, you know? It's sorta like a bucket list item for me."

In December 2018, one year into chemo treatments, Clint played in the Vikings Stadium in an All-Star game. Afterward, he beamed. "The guys I played with were so impressed. They were like, 'Wait? You have cancer? And you're thirty-seven? And you're still playin? In an All-Star game? Damn man. Nice cojones.'"

I grinned. "Felt good?"

"A perfect ending, Sam. I'm done now."

I understood, for a moment, Clint wouldn't play the following season, because he wouldn't be alive to play. Each time I experienced one of these glimpses, I set the thought aside, unable to comprehend the weight of reality.

In January 2019, my dad gifted our family a trip to Medieval Times. While I drove our family from Sleepy Eye, Minnesota, to Illinois, Clint spent most of the time on the phone with friends and family.

"I know, Darry. I can't believe it. I've always wanted to go to Medieval Times."

But Clint's pain increased throughout the drive. The following night, as we all sluffed on our hats and coats and mittens, Clint laid on the couch, rocking in pain.

Desperation to capture as many memories as possible with him surged within me. "Can you take some pain medication?"

"I already did. It's not working."

I dropped the subject. *When I look back, I'll see this as the beginning of the end.*

I hate staring at the family photo we took because I always see Clint missing.

His workout routine in 2017 was a deadlifting and squatting pyramid of 200-500 pounds. At the end of 2018, he and Trinity did power yoga together in the living room. By February 2019, he followed along to walking exercises. Four-year-old, little Trinity jammed out right beside him, her curls flopping every which way.

I watched it happening but didn't want to believe what I saw. Each step he took brought him closer to heaven and further from earth. From us.

CHAPTER FORTY-ONE

Dear Clint,

I'm not sure how to start this. Whenever I'm thinking of you, it's usually me asking you things. What would you think about this? How would you react? What advice would you give me? What insanely clever yet terrible pun would you make about this?

I miss you. Even though I carry you everywhere, your chair is still empty.

I think about how I was a pretentious little punk. I think about the moments I fell short, could have been better, and could have said something nicer. I try to be better than I was, and I know that's something you understand more than just about anybody.

You once asked me, as a non-Christian, what I believe. It was a gorgeous day, and we were grilling at your place in small-town Minnesota. I wasn't quite sure how to answer. Your face held no judgment but a lot of curiosity. I've learned since then that no matter what life you live, no matter what you do, or what choices you make, we all end up as stories. I'm glad we're in each others', and I hope you're proud.

Fuck did this get deeper than I thought. I feel a little like Chris Farley after being smacked with a two by four by David Spade in *Tommy Boy*. It doesn't hurt here or as much here. But right here. I will always be thankful and proud to be your little brother. Love you buddy.

Korey

SAM, JANUARY 2019
MANKATO, MINNESOTA

Marble pillars stretched toward the vaulted ceiling. Intricate paintings depicting The Stations of the Cross wrapped around the dimly lit sanctuary. I chose a pew far away from the other women on the retreat.

My realities collided like breakers upon the rocks, trapping my mind in the undertow. Sunday morning, 1:30 a.m. "Mrs. Evans, there's been an accident."

Drunk driving.

"Methodist Pastor Arrested." The front-page news included my husband's mug shot.

"Mrs. Evans. We found something on the CT scan."

Stage IV cancer.

Now, fourteen months later, the truth seemed no more real. The spiritual director invited herself into my pew. I rested my head on her lap. "Hey, Stef."

She stroked my hair. "I won't ask how you're doing."

"I feel like I'm suffocating." I closed my eyes. "I'm Peter in the boat, straining to see Jesus through the storm. Frightened, burdened, overwhelmed."

I submerged into a daydream of sorts, imagining myself as Peter.

I hurdle from the boat with enough faith to walk on water. Raindrops slash the darkness and pelt my face. *Where are you, Jesus? Where did you go?*

Lightening streaks across a violet, violent sky. I trip on a wave. My knees buckle.

Water engulfs me.

I strain toward the surface, clawing at currents sliding through my fingers. Darkness spins, pressing against me on all sides. *I can't breathe. I can't breathe.*

Jesus?

The last of my light fades.

Jesus.

I disappear.

Lifeless, my limbs float on the whim of the windswept water.

Void.

Concerted strength punches my chest. The rhythmic pressure resounds like timpani throughout my hollow body.

Warm lips meet my cold-and-grayed ones.

My lungs inflate with someone else's breath. Heat races toward each extremity. Life floods through me; washes over me.

My senses switch on like a fuse box, one at a time.

Smell—briny, fishy murky.

The smell rolls into my mouth, and I taste what I smell.

Thunder resounds overhead. The rumbling seems distorted and muted somehow.

Water laps against my limbs and ripples beneath me.

Peace trickles down and infiltrates the marrow of my bones.

My eyes flutter open.

Droplets clinging to my lashes obscure my vision, but Jesus's profile against the raging sky is unmistakable.

Jesus kneels beside me. Though He is near, He has not calmed the storm.

Confusion parts like clouds.

I am lying atop the sea like a waterbed. I touch my fingers to my lips. Recognition dawns.

CPR.

Jesus brought me back to life.

No. I catapult to my feet. *No. Not me. Him.*

I spin in every direction searching for Clint. Though I can't see him through the blasted rain, I know he is out there, facing the same storm. He is stronger than me, but his strength is waning.

Not me. Go to Clint. Why me? Why not him?

Guilt drags me down like an anchor. I've betrayed Clint by stealing the sustaining breath he needs. He's the one with cancer, not me.

Tears of desperation spring from my eyes. If there must be a choice between us, choose him. *Please choose him. I'd give anything.*

I feel the drag—the pressure of water against, rushing past my face and I am lifted from the depths.

Surfacing from the vision, I stared up at Stef, her hand stilled in my hair. Her eyes and face as drenched as mine. Everything I'd seen, I'd spoken out loud—about my husband. And her close friend and colleague.

I raised my head from her lap and expelled a shuddered breath. She reached for the tissue box. My heart felt steadier, like I'd found my resting heart rate following an intense race. We sat beside one another. In instant calm. The calming of the storm.

For several minutes, neither of us spoke. But the trumpet sounds of obnoxious amounts of snot blown into tissue after tissue echoed off the walls of the empty sanctuary. Together we wept about Clint's diagnosis.

"So," I said, "that just happened."

CHAPTER FORTY-TWO

Sisters and Brothers,

I am writing to inform you Bishop Bruce Ough intends to appoint me, Pastor Clint Evans, to Lydia Zion United Methodist Church and I have affirmed this decision. The new appointment will begin on June thirtieth. My last Sunday at Faith United Methodist Church and Fairfax United Methodist Church will be Sunday, June 16, 2019. Sam and I have made the decision in prayerful discernment and conversation with Bishop Bruce Ough, Rev. Fred Vanderwerf, our District Superintendent.

With as much love as I can muster:

Grace and Peace be with you,

Pastor Clint Evans

CLINT, 2019
SLEEPY EYE, MINNESOTA

A strong support network and social outlets are crucial for the survival of the addict. Several months into our move to Sleepy Eye, awareness of my isolation kicked in. I was an hour drive from close friends. Two hours from family, and two hours from my football team. I loved the congregations of Sleepy Eye and Fairfax more than I could articulate in any sermon or newsletter and the fear of failing hit me like an entire defensive line.

We moved to Sleepy Eye in 2015, and I asked for an appointment change the very next year. I provided valid reasons, but pride and fear of losing my job prevented me from uttering "relapse" or "addiction." Shame writes an alternate version of the truth. *The cabinet*[10] *probably wouldn't understand the severity, anyway,* the devil whispered in my ear.

By 2017, I'd already started drinking. In 2019, with my pitiful flaws and failures utterly exposed, the district superintendents of Minnesota offered me an appointment change close to the Twin Cities.

"Well, Clint," said the angel perched on the shoulder opposite from Legion, "imagine what might have happened if you'd told them the truth three years ago."

---

10 A team comprised of the bishop and the district superintendents

CHAPTER FORTY-THREE

Sunday, March 3, 2019

Dear Samantha,

Morgan was impacted by meeting you last night on the Southwest plane.

Morgan mentioned you are an UNWSP alum, a Dr. Harvey Martin-fan like my husband and I are, and you are a writer and blogger too. It sounds like we have a lot in common.

I can't imagine what you are going through as you and your husband walk this road together. I am sad with you, and for your kids.

I have no perfect words. Your family's story impacted us, and we pray often.

Sincerely,
Jennifer

SAM, FEBRUARY 2019
DISNEY WORLD, FLORIDA

We passed giant teacups doubling as flower planters and found her beneath the shade of a cluster of trees. "Hi, Alice," Clint said. "Are you hiding from the sweltering heat?"

"Shhh. No. I am hiding from the queen." She glanced over her shoulder. Then she grasped the hands of our girls and pulled them into the shade.

"Hi, Alice." Kaylynn thrust her autograph book toward her. "May I have your signature?"

"Why do you want my signature?" She bent down and whispered, "You'll not give it to the queen?"

"Oh, no," Kaylynn said. "Of course not."

With a thick British brogue, she said, "Good, good. Very good." After signing, Alice passed Kaylynn's autograph book back to her. "You do know how to curtsey, yes?" Our three girls demonstrated their best curtsy. "Oh, heavens no." She pressed a forefinger beneath Trinity's chin. "Lift your chin. Straight backs, girls. You cannot curtsy to the queen looking like wilted flowers. 'Off with their heads' and all that nonsense."

With greatly improved form, the girls curtsied with Alice for a photo.

"Father." Kaylynn attempted a British accent. "We are thirsty."

I adjusted the backpacks draped over the Minnie Mouse stroller we'd purchased at Walmart. Trinity hopped in. "We'll find a restaurant as long as you stop attempting a British accent."

Kelly whined. "Mo-om. When do we get a turn in the stroller?"

"Never, if you ask like that." I pushed the stroller around World Showcase Lagoon, alternating passengers. In Future World, the girls tasted sodas from different countries. Kely chose a flavor because of the "pretty" label. "Gross." Kelly twisted her face. "Pleh."

Clint laughed. "Didn't like the cherry flavor, Kel?"

She wiped her mouth, her eyes still squeezed tight. "Pleh. Pleh."

As we left the creation shop, Clint said, "Hey, Sam. I want to ride Test Track, but the girls aren't tall enough."

He'd requested so little on our trip, my yes came quickly. "Oh, go ahead. We'll be right there when you're done." I pointed to a splash pad.

The girls' clothes were yellow, magenta and blue—the primary colors. How perfect will those colors look in photos? I fumbled for my camera and snapped photo after photo of water-suctioned clothing, bare feet, glistening water drops, and unadulterated laughter.

Sadness slammed into me like an oncoming vehicle. I dropped my arms. *This is what our lives will be like soon.* Just us.

Clint returned to us, which wouldn't always be the case. A huge grin plastered to his face, he said, "I liked the ride so much, I went twice. I hope that's okay."

Am I masking my sadness well? "Of course, it is." *Anything you want. At least tomorrow is our rest day.* When planning our weeklong vacation, I intentionally did not purchase park passes for the middle of the trip. We spent the following day sleeping in and ate a late breakfast.

We swam in the hotel pool and shopped at Disney Springs. Interestingly enough, five years later, most of the girls' favorite and most vivid memories—eating ice cream, buying Legos, and trying on funny hats—took place on our rest day.

From a TV in the breakfast nook of our hotel in Kissimmee, Clint and I watched world news bring to light issues facing the United Methodist Church. The LGBT debate fractured our Minnesota conference down the middle, even dividing marriages among clergy. Brothers and sisters together in ministry together for years drew deep lines in the sand. Self-righteous indignation fueled anger on both sides. Those who didn't agree with the conference trajectory left the conference altogether, fracturing the family further.

Clint's conservative theology blended with a liberal love, and he wedged himself in the middle, with close friends on both sides. The issue tore at Clint's heart. After his indiscretion, he'd been lavished with grace. Yet, many of his fellow clergy were denied the same.

His bushy eyebrows furrowed as he stared at the TV. "This world will say, 'Not even pastors can get along? Why would we ever go to church?'"

At every park, Clint asked each Disney character we approached how he or she wanted to pose. "The Evanses will not take boring character photos like everyone else," he'd told us.

Snake-charmer Donald wiggled his fingers. The fairy godmother, who gushed over Clint, wanted to blow kisses. Circus Goofy suggested we pretend to fly. The characters loved the idea and for each photo, our family posed with enthusiasm—everyone except our shy, six-year-old Kelly, who hid her smile behind her fist for every single photo.

Chewbacca wanted to thrust his hands into the air. Kelly stared up at him wide-eyed and terrified. We all posed, Chewie in the middle, Kelly in front of him, flanked by her sisters, and Clint and I on either side.

Clint bent down. "Kelly, please raise your hands?"

She shook her head, terrified.

I bent down and spoke softly. "Kelly, the photos will be so fun to see."

She shook her head.

I straightened with a sigh, resigned.

Without prompting, Chewie bent down with his mouth against Kelly's ear. "WYAAAAAAA."

Kelly jumped, her neck stiffened, and her arms shot toward the sky. The relieved photographer snapped the photo with Clint and I laughing hysterically.

When we look back at the character portraits, we dub them "Before Chewie" and "After Chewie" because Kel posed for every photo after our Chewie encounter. Clint and I decided every parent needs a Chewbacca.

With the rental car packed, we waited in line for "Storytime with Belle," our last event before leaving for the airport.

Clint said, "I can't wait to bring them back here ten years from now." His words faltered as he spoke.

Softer, I said, "That will be fun."

Belle treated our girls like princesses and incorporated the kids into reenacting her story. Her yellow gown billowed as she knelt before Trinity and explained how to portray Belle's horse. House lights dimmed and our daughters filed into place for the dramatic presentation.

Cast in shadow, Clint sat in the front row with eyes glued to our ecstatic daughters. Tears rolled off his cheeks, and he whispered, "We made it."

The girls lined up with Belle and the other kids and took the most uncoordinated bow I've witnessed. Clint rose to his feet, cheering and clapping louder than any other parent.

What a perfect last.

We packed Clint's pain medication into our checked bags and part-way through the flight he experienced horrible abdominal pain. Across the aisle from Clint, Kelly, and Trinity, I sat in the middle seat of three, with Kaylynn on my right and a stranger on my left. Across from me, Clint sat in the aisle seat with the other two girls to his left.

Turbulence caused flight attendants to survey each passenger. One attendant said to Clint, "Sir, you need to buckle."

"Okay." Clint pretended to click the buckle, and the stewardess moved on.

But, feeling slighted and disrespected, she returned. Multiple times. I suppose she valued feeling important in her narrow aisle of influence. "Sir, you need to buckle."

Defend him. No, don't make a scene. She'll leave eventually. My brave id and wimpy id argued about the best course of action. Sarcastic Sam also chimed in. *What? She's afraid he's going to die?*

With "Miss, my husband has cancer and he's in an extreme amount of pain" on the tip of my tongue, Clint blurted, "I don't care about the damn seatbelt. Leave me alone."

Scene successfully caused, the stewardess sputtered and scuttled back to her seat. I said to the college-aged girl on my left, loud enough for other passengers to hear, "He has cancer and he's in a lot of pain. His meds are in his checked bag."

The girl and I made small talk. Her father sat in front of her and her mother was seated several rows back. "Where do you go to school?" I asked.

"Northwestern in the Twin Cities. It's a small, Christian college."

"3003 Snelling Avenue N," I said. "I have a youth ministry degree from there."

The girl's face brightened. "My parents too."

Her dad leaned around the seat. "Wow. Small world."

"Dr. J.E. Harvey Martin?" I posed the name of my most memorable professor as a question.

He grinned. "We still talk to him. Are you still in youth ministry?"

"Pastor wife," I said. "I'm a writer now."

"Oh, so is my wife, Jennifer."

Another Christian author who graduated from my same college, sitting on the same plane during one of the most difficult times in my life. That's how God introduced Jennifer Dougan and me to one another.

⌁

SAM, FEBRUARY 2019
MINNEAPOLIS, MINNESOTA

We landed in Minnesota, in February, wearing shorts and flipflops, and lumbered toward baggage claim. We lugged Kelly's three-foot-tall stuffed Minnie Mouse through the airport like a fourth child. I opened a suitcase and withdrew sweatshirts and pants for the girls.

Kelly crossed her arms and pouted. "I don't want to wear pants over my shorts."

"I don't care, Kelly. "

"Sam," Clint said. "Shuttle. Come on."

I frowned at Kelly and stuffed her pants into the suitcase. At 9:00 p.m., the shuttle dropped us at our Trailblazer, walled in by three feet of snow behind the rear wheels from snowplow passes.

As the driver removed our bags, Clint asked, "Do you have a shovel with you?"

The man pretended he hadn't heard Clint, jogged back to the driver's seat, and drove away.

Clint yanked the phone from his pocket, scowling at the taillights of the vanishing shuttle.

"Mommy. I'm c-c-cold," Kelly said.

Yeah. I bet. The girls erupted into a conglomeration of whining, crying, and begging. "Alright, girls. Our adventure isn't over yet. Dad and I are going to fix it. Stop whining so I can think." With mild panic, I envisioned Kelly tromping through thigh-high snow in shorts. "Stay right here." I pointed to the compacted snow beneath their feet. "Don't move." The circumstance bordered dangerous with temperatures in the lower teens.

While Clint spoke with his dad on the phone, I tromped toward the car in my flipflops, running through a mental checklist.

Start car.

Girls into car.

Hats, mittens, coats, and boots … in the back.

With bare toes, I kicked iced-crusted snow away from the runner on the driver's door. I slid into the driver's seat—freezing leather—started the engine and hopped out again. I opened the rear passenger door as wide as the snow would allow—about eighteen inches. Youngest to oldest, I swooped up each girl beneath the armpits and slid them into the narrow opening. "We'll get you warmed up, girls. Hang in there."

Behind me, Clint spoke with another traveler who offered to drive to a building in the distance and ask for help. I opened the hatchback and snow tumbled away from the car.

Leaving winter gear in Minnesota rather than lugging everything to Florida and back had been an intentional choice. We'd laid all the coats and boots in the cargo area of the SUV for easy access upon our return. I hadn't expected to be barricaded by snow, but I should have. *I can't believe I didn't bring a shovel and kitty litter.* I flung coats and mittens to each girl over the backseat. "Socks, girls. Here. Get these on your toesies."

"My coat is cold," Kaylynn said.

"It won't be in a minute."

Clint threaded his arms through his leather coat and shoved his blaze orange hat on his head. "Whew. Better. Where's kitty litter when you need it, huh?"

I handed Clint his hunter orange mittens. "I thought the same thing."

"My dad will be here in fifteen minutes with shovels."

"Oh, awesome. Well, come wait in the car."

Chuck arrived and approached the driver's door where I sat. "Betcha you guys wish you'd stayed in Florida, huh?" He laughed.

Kelly cried, "Gran'pa Shuck. Grand'pa Shuck." Her sisters joined her chorus.

"Hey girls," he said. "You stay warm." He patted me on the shoulder. "You, too, Samantha. Clint and I will take care of this."

At 11:30 p.m., we pulled into a Taco Bell drive through near the airport. The backseat was one giant plush pile of coats, blankets, pillows and stuffed animals with our daughters buried alive beneath them.

CHAPTER FORTY-FOUR

Dear Clint,

I didn't know how hard this would be, for you, but for me, and for everyone else. I never understood the saying, "you never understand how much you have until it's gone." I didn't expect to bond with you as much as I have, and I didn't expect this to take such a big toll on me. Honestly, I hated your dad jokes and sermons, but I didn't realize how much I would miss them. I guess I kind of feel betrayed because you are the one I looked up to. You were my mentor, the one who conformed me. I understand you're not perfect and I'm not angry or sad. I forgive you, but I will not forget.

Teen From Church

CLINT, PRESENT DAY
SLEEPY EYE, MINNESOTA

When I read the letter, the words made me laugh. This girl constantly rolled her eyes at my corniness. Fine by me. The words made me cry. I ached insurmountably, knowing I'd caused her and others so much pain. The words made me proud. *You never cease to impress me. You are so smart and well-articulated.* Also, I'd created an atmosphere in which this girl knew I welcomed her honesty, as difficult as it may have been for me to hear.

SAM, WEDNESDAY, FEBRUARY 10, 2016,
CLINT'S FIRST ASH WEDNESDAY AS A PASTOR
SLEEPY EYE, MINNESOTA

The crunch of his bulletin between his meaty paws clued me into his nerves about leading his first-ever Ash Wednesday service.

The lights dimmed. The sanctuary quieted. The line to receive ashes formed.

"From dust you were created and to dust you shall return."

Clint dipped his finger into the damp ash and swiped the forehead of the next person in line. I ushered our older daughters forward while balancing our sixteen-month-old on my hip. I cringed at the soot stain soaked into Clint's alb. *That's gonna leave a mark. And who gets to wash it? This girl.*

Clint turned toward the altar.

And how did the oaf manage to smear ash on the back? Amazing. My sardonic thoughts flipped off like a switch, eclipsed by the awe of the position God raised Clint to. Adoration for both God and Clint flooded through me like chills as I scooted forward in line.

Clint wore the honor of his call with humility. Somberly, he whispered to each congregation member by name, repeating, "From dust you were created and to dust you shall return."

Finally at the front of the line, my eyes met Clint's. His mask slipped. For a flash, a giddy smile spread. His eyes sparked with glee. *We made it, Sam. Can you believe it?* I read his thoughts easily, because I shared them. I'd never witnessed more determination or grit in one single person—qualities uniquely blended with his gentle spirit. *He's finally living out his God-purpose.*

Clint's reverend-self flickered back into place. His warm finger brushed against my skin. "Beloved, from dust you were created and to dust you shall return." He covered our baby with the same promise. "Hey, little one. From dust you were created and to dust you shall return."

I dipped my forefinger into the ash and whispered, "This is really wet."

"Next year, I need to use a lot less water."

I stared into his eyes and pressed my finger to his forehead. "Clint Evans, I am so proud of you. From dust you were created and to dust you shall return."

After the service, Clint learned ashes blended with water burn the skin. *Oops.* He showed me memes about rookie pastor mistakes. The following years, he used oil.

SAM, WEDNESDAY, MARCH 6, 2019
SLEEPY EYE, MINNESOTA

Fourteen months into chemotherapy treatments, Clint stood at the front of the sanctuary as congregation members formed a line. The shapeless alb obscured the evidence of his thirty-five-pound weight loss. His jaw line was more pronounced. The shadows beneath his eyes, deeper. Treatments and fighting to live exhausted him, and still he preached, and taught, and visited, and served.

To the left of my pew, church members lined up. "Angie." He brushed ashes on her forehead. "From dust you were created to dust you will return."

I'm so proud of you, Clint. He'll pull through. Patients with stage IV cancer live for years, all the time.

Clint called each person by name and brushed ash across each forehead. "From dust you were created and to dust you shall return." The black stains on his alb from his first Ash Wednesday service never washed out, but I doubted anyone else noticed. I appreciated the stains on his garment now. Following the drunk driving accident seventeen months prior, he refused to wear the alb. "I disgraced the pulpit, Sam. I'm not worthy."

"None of us are. That's why we're 'clothed with Christ.'"[11]

Now, he wore the robe for special services. The garment reflected God's work in Clint.

....
11 cf. Galatians 3:1-5, 26-27

People in the pew before me rose and filed into line. I stepped into the aisle behind them. Trinity, four years old, tugged at the hem of my sweater. "Mommy, can you carry me?" I swept her into my arms and glanced over her shoulder where her two older sisters colored furiously, paper and crayons scattered everywhere. "Are you coming?"

"I don't want slimy dirt on my forehead." Kelly's declaration caused church members on the opposite side of the sanctuary to chuckle.

"Me either," Kaylynn said.

Not worth the battle. Trinity and I reached the front of the sanctuary, and my thoughts reeled. Clint and I mirrored a sad knowing as our eyes met. *From dust to dust? This is too real. How much time do we have?*

He marked Trinity with ash first, murmuring her name. My eyes closed when his cold thumb spread ash across my forehead. "Beloved, from dust you were created and to dust you shall return."

I opened my eyes and stared at him while I pressed a finger into the perfectly blended paste and rubbed his forehead. "Beloved, from dust you were created and to dust you shall return." *How soon?* I gritted my teeth against the threatening tears, squeezed Trinity tighter, and scurried back to my pew. *His forehead felt so cold.* Clint used to joke my hands were "cold like death." The joke wasn't funny anymore.

Part Five

For I know that through your prayers and
God's provision of the Spirit of Jesus Christ
what has happened to me will turn out for my
deliverance. I eagerly expect and hope that I will
in no way be ashamed, but will have sufficient
courage so that now as always Christ will be
exalted in my body, whether by life or by death.
For to me, to live is Christ and to die is gain.

Philippians 1:19-21 NIV

CHAPTER FORTY-FIVE

My Dearest Clint,

Thank you for inviting me to your wedding in Chicago. Seven of us drove back to Minneapolis together in a minivan. Every time we stopped, we looked like a clown car.

I loved when you moved out to Oregon and got to know you as an adult. Sharing life with you and Sam was so special. Andy still talks about running into you at Oregon State and eating lunch with you. I loved watching your football games and seeing you at the Oregon State Fair. I got to watch the moment you became a father, as you talked to and 'cooed' and bathed your first born. God brought you so far. Thank you for inviting me to Kaylynn's dedication and talking with Brady when he struggled. It meant more than you will ever know.

Thank you for the love and gospel you share with everyone in your life. Thank you for your love and God and for being the Prodigal Son.

May God grant you peace and comfort, Clint. Until we meet again.

Love,

Bev

CLINT, MAUNDY[12] THURSDAY, APRIL 19, 2019
FAIRFAX, MINNESOTA

Tires of my gold '94 Buick Regal crunched atop the snow-caked street outside the church. Houses along 4th Avenue SE remained dark. *No*

....

12 "Maundy" translates "mandate" or "commandment." Maundy Thursday is the Thursday before Easter. In the Bible, this is the night Jesus eats the last supper with his disciples. At the last supper, Jesus gives his disciples a new command: "love one another." John 15:17

one's home from work yet. I cut the engine and punched the headlight switch in. With no streetlights to speak of, peaceful darkness enveloped me.

The driver's side door creaked open and probably alerted anyone within a half mile of my arrival. The soft-white dome light popped on—about the only feature still functioning in addition to the engine. Lord knew the heat didn't work. Hadn't since I bought the boat. *This car suits me. I don't deserve nice things.* The bag rustled as I shoved the grape juice and Hawaiian loaf back into the plastic. Thin vapors of my breath coalesced around me.

I straightened and slammed the door, feeling the prickle of a blackout coming on. *Must have stood up too fast.* My heart hammered like pistons. *In. Out. In. Out.* Despite the concentrated effort on breathing, I couldn't fill my lungs with a satisfying breath. *I wish Sam was here.*

Shaking off my fear like a coating of snow, I tucked my Bible and worship materials beneath my arm. Light from the sanctuary's stained-glass windows flipped on and lit the sidewalk. *Maria.*

I entered the sanctuary. "Lamb of God" hummed through the organ's pipes, Maria's fingers sliding across the keys.

Fairfax United Methodist Church had been built in 1915. The room was diamond-shaped, with the pulpit and organ resting on a stage that spanned one corner. Three rows of walnut pews created a semi-circle of seating. I dropped my coat on the pew nearest the stage.

A petite woman joined Maria and me in the sanctuary. She patted her thin brown-and-white bob and shed a purple coat so large three of her might have fit inside it.

"Evening, Faith." I grinned at her. The simple greeting tightened my lungs. *Why can't I breathe? What time did Sam say she'd be back from Mankato?* She'd scheduled three-in-one teeth cleanings for our daughters at the dental school and warned me, depending on timing, she might miss the service.

Maundy Thursday observes Jesus's Last Supper, the night He took the place of a servant and washed the feet of His disciples. Tonight, I'd be washing the feet of congregation members who wanted to come forward.

I started down the steps toward the kitchen at a jog and stalled. *In. Out. In. Out.* I squeezed the wooden railing. *Is this it? Am I dying right now? No. The least I can do is wait until after Holy Week.* "God, help." Moments later, I climbed the same stairwell with a full basin of hot water. I paused on the landing and squeezed my eyes shut.

My tears dropped into the basin I balanced on the railing. *Please.* I exhaled. "All right, Clint. Get it together." I exhaled once more, and even though my lungs left me wanting, the breath worked to reset my emotions.

I ducked my head into the crook of each arm to wipe my face and continued my eight-stair climb up Everest to the sanctuary.

The bulletin encouraged people to enter the sanctuary in silence, setting the stage for the somber service. Tonight, the normally boisterous community of believers greeted one another with nods and shy smiles.

After the opening song, I stretched out my arms to the congregation in invitation. "With the words found in … your bulletin, pray with me?"

"Holy God, draw us into worship with a spirit of humility," I started the congregation off and let my voice fade away as they continued, "let us gather with open hearts prepared to love, even to the point of breaking, as we seek to receive this story with our whole selves."

I glanced at the bulletin. "Please turn in your hymnal to number 504, 'Old Rugged Cross.' No one in the room needed the hymnal or the notes. They sang the familiar tune with the affection of greeting an old friend. The harmonies gave heaven a run for its money. Their voices pointed toward the pulpit where I stood. The melody engulfed me.

"To that old rugged cross I will ever be true, its shame and reproach gladly bear; then he'll call me some day to my home far away, where his glory forever I'll share. So I'll cherish the old, rugged cross, 'til my trophies at last I lay down. I will cling to the old, rugged cross and exchange it some day for a crown."

As the song ended, my heart burned, wanting for oxygen. *This is not good.* "The gospel reading this evening is," I paused to breathe, "from John 13." *Inhale. Exhale.* "Now before the festival of … the Passover,

Jesus knew that his hour had come to depart from this world and go to the Father. Having," I paused again, "loved his own who were in the world, he ... loved them to the end ..."

Joyce gripped the pew in front of her and leaned forward. "Pastor Clint, are you all right?"

"My chest feels tight, like I finished a hard half of football. I'm fine though." But I'd said the words "chest" and "tight" to a group of people whose median age was seventy.

"I'm calling 9-1-1," someone said.

I inhaled to protest but couldn't draw enough air. *Okay, so maybe 9-1-1 would be best.*

A guy about my age sidled up to me and escorted me to the back of the sanctuary. "Let's get you some fresh air."

"Thanks ... Jason."

"Save your breath, Pastor Clint."

My leather coat landed atop my shoulders. I threaded my arms through the thick lining. Someone tugged my orange beanie onto my bald head. A small, but firm hand landed on my shoulder.

Someone nearby spoke in a hurried tone. "Sam. Hi, this is Janet. Clint's having trouble breathing. An ambulance is on its way."

"Um. Okay ...." I heard her voice, and the way she shifted from concern to problem-solving between syllables. I would have laughed if I could breathe.

Geez. Janet's age showed with the volume of her receiver.

"Do you know which hospital they're taking him to? I'm between New Ulm and Sleepy Eye, and I have the girls in the car. I can turn around."

I imagined Sam behind the wheel of our Trailblazer, arranging details like a puzzle. "No. Have her ... have Sam get the kids home. Ask her which hospital I should go to."

Apparently, Sam could hear me, too, because she said, "Mankato is where his oncologist is."

A few minutes later, paramedics fitted an oxygen mask on my face. *This is my first ambulance ride. The first one I remember.* Shame pummeled me with a jolt of adrenaline as I recalled past drunk driving accidents. One negative thought spurred another. *If I don't even have enough stamina for Holy Week, I'm in trouble.*

"Mr. Evans," said the paramedic. "Mr. Evans, try to relax. We'll get you help as soon as we can."

At the hospital, an X-ray revealed fluid gathering near my lung, essentially shrinking the lung cavity. When the doctor drained the fluid, I breathed like normal, but the accumulation of fluid worried doctors and they keep me for a few days for observation.

On Easter morning, I posted this message to my Facebook page:

So, it is Easter morning, and I'm stuck in a hospital room. I feel a lot like the disciples the weekend Jesus died. After giving up their lives to follow Him, they thought they had it all figured out. Then Jesus was arrested and died a most humiliating death. Had they made a mistake? Had they given their lives up for nothing? What do they do now? But then Jesus flips the script by coming back. Death is defeated, what can stop us now?

CHAPTER FORTY-SIX

Dear Clint,

   You came into my life like a whirlwind. I don't remember deciding to like and trust you—I just did. Everyone who met you noticed your charisma, humor, and loyalty, but I'm most grateful to you because you saw me. It sounds trivial, but as a young mother my whole identity was dependent on motherhood and what I did for others. But you didn't focus on what I could do for the church or for you, and you made me feel valued. Even when it was clear you were struggling with your own hurts, you always saw me and clearly cared. I am so thankful you came into my life. I am grateful to you even today.

Love,

Emily

SAM, TUESDAY, APRIL 30, 2019
SLEEPY EYE, MINNESOTA

Light from the hallway bled into the bedrooms where exhausted toys lay carelessly strewn about the floor and three bath-fresh, little girls snuggled down with their stuffies.

His wide frame momentarily eclipsed the doorway.

"Daddy!" High-pitched delight burst forth from girls with rosy, cherub cheeks. Small hands grasped the back of his neck. He kissed each daughter's forehead and sang the "nite-nite" song in a mellow tenor.

"Good night, sweet princesses, it's time to take your rest.

"Lay your sweet heads upon the Savior's chest.

"We all love you, yeah, but Jesus loves you best,

"So, we say, 'Good night, good night, good night.'"

"I love you, Daddy," they each said.

"I love you, pun'kins."

Trinity, four-years-old, snuggled into her father's embrace. His cut-off tee accented the lion tattoo covering one delt and the lamb on the other.

"Leave the door closed so no monsters come out of the closet."

"There are no monsters," he assured them.

"But Daddy, what if there are?"

"Then I'll fight them for you."

Clint eased the door closed, leaving a crack wide enough for light to spill through. He dropped onto the disheveled comforter in our bedroom. The façade of strength he entertained for the girls' sake exhausted him. He mumbled into the mattress, "I'm so tired,"

"I know, sweetheart." I eased our bedroom door closed and walked downstairs. *He'll be asleep within seconds.* "I know." *I wish I could fight your monsters for you.*

Early the next morning, our neighbor arrived prior to any hints of daylight. I glanced around her at the street. "Did you drive here?"

"It's cold."

"It's less than a block." We smiled. "Thank you."

"We'll take care of everything here."

Minutes later I climbed behind the driver's seat to take Clint to an appointment at Mayo. Headlight beams shone eerily upon empty roads and endless acres of farmland.

Please no deer.

After several attempts at conversation during the hourlong drive, I faded into silence. I tried the radio. Shallow lyrics glorifying materialism and lust annoyed me. Peppy songs portraying life as sunshine and unicorns provoked actual groans. I grinned. Clint despised country music. Purely to incite a reaction, I switched to country. Clint's lack of response disturbed me. *Okay, no radio.*

His head lolled against the headrest. Denial outweighed the fears swelling within me. *This next line of treatment will alleviate the symptoms.*

Fluid accumulation in the cavity beneath his right lung sent us to the doctor every few days. At our last visit, our family doctor withdrew more than two liters of bloody fluid. The catheter insertion would allow us to remove the blood serum from home.

We parked at the cancer center, and Clint trudged in. Shadows lifted from the sky but deepened beneath his eyes. I flanked him in silence. The elderly man behind the information desk instructed us to walk to a different part of the hospital.

A feral growl of annoyance rumbled in Clint's chest.

Because an elderly man is healthier than he is. I hesitated, knowing the answer before asking. "Do you want me to get you a wheelchair?"

"No. Let's just get there."

Up an elevator, around the corner, over the river and through the woods, we eventually arrived at the proper desk.

"Clint Evans, checking in for a surgical procedure."

The receptionist clicked through several screens on her computer. "Oh, Mr. Evans. We canceled your appointment." Her voice carried a not-our-problem tone.

He glared at her. "When?"

"Fifteen minutes ago."

Oh, Lord. My nervous fingers scrape through my hair. *He'll be angry.* I jolted at the vehemence of his words.

"What the hell do you mean, you cancelled fifteen minutes ago? I live *an hour* from here."

"I'm sorry, Mr. Evans—"

"You're sorry, you're *sorry?* You're wasting what little time I have left on this earth. I'm fucking dying and you're sorry?"

"Clint." I reached for his arm. He shoved my hand and rational thought aside. "I will not be quiet. This is the third time I've driven all the way here and these assholes told me I have a canceled appointment and 'oops, they forgot to tell me.' I don't have time for this shit."

Even with muscle deterioration and weight loss, his appearance intimidated people. Patients skittered past.

I leaned over the counter. "We drove an hour to get here. We had to find a babysitter for our kids. Is there any chance he can be seen?"

"I'll see what I can do." The receptionist strolled through intake questions.

Clint's punctuated replies revealed his crescendoing impatience. He exhaled hard through his nose, struggling to rein his anger.

I covered my mouth with my fingertips. *Lady, you need to speed this up.*

Her fingers slowed and she stared at her magic screen, which granted her authority to dole out infuriating answers. "I'm sorry, but we have no openings."

Hulk smash. Clint's fists slammed the counter. "Do you have any idea what it took for us to get here? Call the doctor. I want to talk to the fucking doctor."

The woman stared aghast at Clint. She reached for the phone.

I hope she's not phoning security.

A surgeon emerged from behind the secured doors. "What seems to be the problem?"

Clint shouted through his explanation.

The receptionist said in a stage whisper, "Should we call security?"

I wanted to hurdle the counter and hit her myself.

The doctor stayed her with his hand. "Not yet. Give us a second." He spoke to Clint. "Let me talk to my colleague and I'll see what I can do." He disappeared behind secured doors.

The receptionist continued her torturously slow interrogation. A mercenary ripping off my fingernails with pliers would have been less painful. "And how many doses of antibiotic have you taken?"

"Two days' worth."

Her eyes darted up to my husband. She didn't need a computer for this one. "Doctors won't do the procedure unless you've taken six doses. You've only taken four."

"The prescription came through two days ago."

I cringed, remembered, and tilted my head. *Technically he's only taken three.*

When I glanced up, Clint's glare waited for me in warning. I widened my eyes in collaboration. *You think I have a death wish?*

The receptionist finally answered. "I'm sorry, but—"

"Fuck youuuuuuu." He stretched flexed arms to the sides—the motion of rending a garment, expanded his chest, craned his face toward the ceiling and growled at the top of his lungs. Fury visibly surged through his veins. Like the Hulk.

I blinked. Not imagining. This nightmare was happening in my real life. Mary Shelley couldn't have dramatized the scene better.

"Clint, please." I cried. "Please. Let's talk to the doc—"

"Mr. Evans, I'm going to call security."

He growled at the top of his lungs, a feral animal.

Please.

He stormed toward the elevator and slammed his thumb into the button. The elevator took too long. With fisted hands, Clint growled again. He punched the door of the elevator and when his hand recoiled, I spotted the dented metal. The doors eventually parted, thank God, and he disappeared behind them. Everyone in the room sighed.

"Here." Another receptionist joined the shaken woman. "Let me take over."

The idiot gladly stepped back, but hovered.

The new receptionist glanced at me and lowered her eyes back to the computer. "My husband went out of his mind when he had cancer. I didn't even recognize him."

I hesitated. "Is he still alive?"

"He died three years ago."

"I'm sorry."

When Clint returned fifteen minutes later, calm…ish, I relayed the good news: "The doctor will insert the pleura catheter."

All the tension deflated from his body, expelling the monster within. "I'm sorry."

"I know. It's okay. You're the one facing cancer." I waited for him to look me in the eye. "I know you're scared."

"I'm so scared." He cradled his head in his hands and shattered into sobs. "I don't want to die."

"I know. I'm so sorry." I stepped forward and pressed my mouth into his bloodied knuckles. I wanted to weep with him. Instead, I tapped into a reservoir of strength he's freely lent me for so many years.

He dropped his head to my shoulder and wept like a child.

I wrapped my arms around his back. *There is so much less of him than there used to be.* I wanted to tell him everything would be okay, but I refused to lie. "I love you so much."

Jesus, why is this happening to us? To him? He's so tired; we're so tired.

I held his shaking body, grateful for Clint's vulnerability. In the last eighteen months Clint shielded me from the brunt of his fears. He allowed me to remain in denial about the severity of his prognosis. And in the midst of this fire, his most precious gift to me had been the endurance of his steadfast, Shadrach faith.[13]

"Sam," he'd said a couple weeks prior, "I know God can heal me, but even if He doesn't, I know God is good. God is killing all the garbage within me and resurrecting something new."

I'd locked snippets of conversations like those securely within my heart.

Twenty minutes later, doctors prepped him for the surgical insertion. The drugs they administered eased Clint's anxiety and granted him momentary reprieve.

I held his hand. He squeezed back. "I'm right here. You've got this."

The doors opened and closed, separating us.

I returned to the prep room, slunk into a chair, and cried so violently my stomach convulsed. The sound resembled a suffocating person gasping for breath, an accurate interpretation of how I felt.

....

13 In Daniel 3, Shadrach refuses to bow to an image of the king. He tells the king, paraphrased, "Our God can save us, but even if he doesn't, we will not worship you."

CHAPTER FORTY-SEVEN

Hey, Clint.

I can't believe we've been friends for twenty-plus years. We've come a long way since our backyard wrestling days—power bombs on stained mattresses and thumbtacks. I'm grateful to have you as a friend. You're the most loyal friend I've ever had—you had my back when people wanted to stab me in it. Our friendship has survived through marriage and kids. Whenever my family experienced problems, you reached out with prayer and words of comfort—or you'd drive eight hours just to be with us.

You're an amazing father, husband, and God-loving man. I am so proud of you. You became part of our family, a brother. My brothers and sister talk about you often, how we've watched you fight through adversity and come out on top. That's the measure of a man. You and your family will always have a seat at our table.

Love ya, Big Nasty.
Sincerely,
Travis "The Franchise"

SAM, MAY 2019
SLEEPY EYE, MINNESOTA

A disconnect forged in my brain. I couldn't say when the divergence occurred. I hoarded moments into jars like fireflies, collecting as many as possible before Clint died. Also, I didn't believe Clint was dying.

One of the moments I wanted to collect was a memory with Clint at my mom's new home near the ocean. My mom and her husband,

Marc, moved to Oak Island, North Carolina, three blocks from the Atlantic. Each sibling couple created a stepping stone with their hands or feet. I wanted my darn stepping stone with his footprint beside mine. I wanted time at the ocean to breathe. I wanted a memory of Clint in Oak Island, so he'd be there with me after he died. But how do you tell your husband that?

You don't.

Instead, we argued.

Moving boxes used in preparation for our move to Lydia transformed hallways into mazes. I wove through the cardboard jungle and found Clint and Trinity mirroring exercises on the TV.

Clint paused his walking workout. A triangle of sweat stretched from his collarbones to navel. Sparking eyes with brown circles beneath glared at me. "Sam, the trip will mess with my chemo schedule. Do you *want* me to die?"

I couldn't hear Clint's fear with the words he didn't say. "Not to mention, I have to get permission from my probation officer to leave the state."

Don't remind me.

"What about the fluid drains?"

I thought of all the other fires I'd extinguished in the last several years. *This one's simple.* "We'll bring bottles with." But I'd missed the point. Clint wasn't concerned about space in our luggage. "I just want one …"

"Fine," he shouted. "Book the trip."

I got my way, so I clamped my mouth shut on the words … *last family vacation.*

I turned to leave the room.

"Sam, I didn't tell you." I braced myself as he continued, "I got an email from Greg. Read it three times to make sure I understood. The judge changed my time frame for my stay of adjudication."

Oh, no.

"From August 2020 to August 2019."

"What?"

"By the end of this summer, the felony drops from my record. I'll be clear."

"Clint, awesome." I waved in his direction. "I'd hug you, but ..." Phew. "That is really, really good news."

Maybe then we'll have time to work on our marriage.

Often enough, Clint's energy seemed normal. He worked, he brought the kids on outings. He laughed and snuggled with them. Even on our journey from the airport security check-in circus to our gate at the opposite end of the terminal, nothing about his health alarmed me.

We landed in Myrtle Beach, greeted our parents with hugs and laughter, and stopped at a restaurant for dinner. *See? I was right. You're fine.*

We divided into two vehicles for the ninety-minute drive—boys and girls—with Marc and Clint leading the way. The cars' headlights illuminated tall evergreens along State Highway 57.

My phone pinged with a notification— a text from Clint.

I think I'm going to be sick.

Well, ask Marc to pull over.

I didn't want the girls to overhear, so I didn't say anything to my mom.

"Oh, Marc's pulling over." My mom flipped on her right turn signal. "I wonder why."

"Mom, pull in front of Marc. Please." Apparently, my words didn't compute. "Mom, Clint's going to be sick, please ..."

Marc's passenger door flew open, and Clint's bent form stumbled into the brush. The headlights of my mom's Jeep gave us the perfect view of Clint hurling up his burger and fries.

"Oh, poor Clint," my mom said. "We should have pulled ahead of Marc."

I pressed my lips into a thin line.

Kelly asked, "Is Daddy puking?"

I dropped my forehead into my cradled palm. *Well, you won, Sam, didn't you? You got him here.* "Yes." *Don't argue with him about anything else while you're here.* For the most part, I kept my promise. I felt guilty for dragging him to the coast, but not guilty enough to regret my choice. The living have the burden of living after the dead die.

He slept most of each day while the girls painted, swam in the pool, and took trips to the beach. Once, he ventured outside and, from the upper balcony, watched the girls swim—he didn't have enough energy to come downstairs.

"Hi, Daddy." Kelly waved, her brown eyes lit with playfulness and mischief.

"Hey, pun'kins."

We visited the USS North Carolina and our family posed for a photo with a gun turret. Clint trailed along for dinner at a restaurant, two walks on the beach and the opening festivities for a new splash pad in the area. At Clint's request, we visited a marine wildlife rescue, but by the time we got to the parking lot, he was too tired to enjoy himself. Instead, we argued with one another and returned to my parents' home with promises to the girls we would take them to a marina another time.

Fluid accumulated faster than we anticipated and when we ran out of bottles, we stopped at the nearest hospital for a quick fluid drain. The visit felt as routine as a trip to the grocery store to purchase a gallon of milk. In the exam room, I showed nurses how to use the bottle.

On a dinner date at The Fish House along the intercostal, we dined on the patio. Clint hadn't eaten all day. After several bites of his cup of clam chowder, he slid the saucer toward me.

Behind him, jewel tones and sherbets lit the sky. The color spilled over Clint's shoulders, casting an ethereal glow. An Oscar-winning movie could not have set the scene better. *You recognize this, don't you? You're an author too. This is a farewell.* I felt like God orchestrated the Act III conclusion just for me.

When we returned to our parents' place, Clint went straight to bed.

"You want an Island Cooler, Sam?" Marc asked.

I glanced at the stairs. *He won't be coming back down tonight.* "Sure. Okay."

Marc made a drink for each of us, and we sat together on the balcony. "I warmed up the hot tub for you."

"Thanks."

Marc crushed his cigarette into an ashtray on the table. "Sam, you don't want to hear this, but I wish someone told me when Pam got sick. Your mom thought you should know."

I steeled myself. "How long?"

"Two months. At most."

"I hope you're wrong."

"Me too."

The next morning, I stood on the balcony and stared out over the ocean. The door cracked open, and Clint stepped outside. *Don't argue with whatever he says.*

"Sam, I think I should turn down the Lydia move. I don't have enough energy to give a new church what it deserves."

"I agree."

The thing about 'lasts,' is you don't know they're lasts. You can guess, suspect, but it's impossible to know for certain.

The last time Clint saw the ocean.

The last time he watched his daughters swimming.

The last time he and Marc embraced.

I didn't know those would be lasts, but I captured the fireflies and added them to my jar. *We're getting closer to the end.*

CHAPTER FORTY-EIGHT

Before car seat laws and enforced seat belt regulations, I blasted Sandi Patty on the cassette player in my station wagon. I looked over and little three-year-old Clint stood on the front seat, eyes closed, head tilted toward the sky, with hands raised to heaven, worshiping his little heart out.

Dawn Evans

CLINT, MAY 2019
FAIRFAX, MINNESOTA

I parked along the street, behind the dumpster parked in front of Millie's house, and walked up the narrow sidewalk to the front door. I pressed my thumb against the broken doorbell, and let myself in. "Millie? You awake? It's Pastor Clint."

Sunlight poured in through the open curtains. A hospital bed had replaced the burgundy recliner, and someone traded towers of newspapers for walking space. I noted the visible color difference between the old walking path and the new.

"Cold hands, Millie." A male hospice nurse pressed two fingers against Millie's translucent wrist. He finished counting. "Hey, Pastor Clint."

"Mike." I nodded. "If she's sleeping, I can come back another time."

"Nah. She's actually been asking for you." He adjusted the stethoscope around his neck. "Millie, Pastor Clint is here."

She barely opened her eyes. "Pastor Clint. Help yourself to some cookies."

"I sure will." Mike and I shuffled around one another in a limited space. I unzipped my brown leather communion kit. "Millie, how 'bout we serve you communion?

"On the night in which He was betrayed, Jesus took the bread and broke it … " After the wafer melted on her tongue, I tipped the cup of grape juice to her lips. "… the blood of Christ, shed for you. We do this in remembrance of Him, until the day we feast with Him in glory at our great homecoming banquet." I reached for her hand, warm to the touch.

"It won't be long now, Pastor Clint. Won't be long."

"Oh, yeah? How can you tell?"

"This world starts to fade away, fade to gray, and you'll long for the one home rather than the other. I'll see you."

I leaned down and kissed her forehead. "Aw, Millie. You and Jeff save a seat for me, k? And my kids. Tell my kids, daddy's coming home." Millie drifted off to sleep before our conversation ended. I imagined the moment Millie would meet Jesus and was suddenly filled with inexplicable joy at the prospect of seeing my Savior's face. Would He be proud of me?

I already am.

I squeezed Millie's hand. "I'll see you, soon."

CHAPTER FORTY-NINE

Dear Clint,

In a very short time, it's obvious God gifted you and used you to ful-fill your purpose. Many were blessed by your ministry. You lived well.

Though the body fail, the spirit triumphs as death allows us to transition to the heavenly reward awaiting us. And God says to you, "Well done, my good and faithful servant."

Aunt Thelma and oncology nurse

SAM, SUNDAY, JUNE 2, 2019
SLEEPY EYE, MINNESOTA

The front door opened and slammed. "A congregation member com-plained to me because I haven't visited her as often. They should be visiting me." A week had passed since our return from Oak Island.

Tongue-in-cheek, I said, "That's amazing. People are amazing." Mirth faded to sadness. No one comprehended Clint could die. *The strongest man among you will live forever.*

"Fred sent us the link for the video chat," I said. "My laptop is set up in the sunroom."

A few minutes later, we greeted Fred and Cynthia through the video screen. Cynthia was a district superintendent, like Fred, but for the district that Clint's upcoming church appointment was located in. Jet-black spirals of hair framed her face. "How are you guys doin'?"

"We're okay," I said.

Clint swished his hands back and forth. "Just want to hear what you have to say."

"I understand." Cynthia led us in prayer.

After a pregnant pause, Fred said, "Well, Clint, we've decided to place you on medical leave."

Clint stilled. Thoughts and emotions crashed down like a glass bowl falling from the top of a China cabinet. Their decision made complete sense but still managed to surprise me.

Fred and Cynthia explained what medical leave would look like practically and financially. Fred said, "The new pastor for Sleepy Eye will live in New Ulm, so your family is welcome to stay in the parsonage as long as necessary."

"Do you have any questions?" said Cynthia.

"No." Clint clapped in frustration. "I want to end this call."

"All, right, well, we'll be in touch. Blessings."

"Thank you," I managed and closed the laptop.

"And just like that, I'm not a pastor anymore."

"Clint, that's not …"

Clinching his first, he bolted from the room.

Later, I sat on the couch in the living room with him. I flipped through photos on my laptop of our Oak Island Trip and smiled at a shot of him and Trinity with the sparkling Atlantic behind them.

"Sam, there are youth director openings on the conference website. You should see if you can apply for some supplemental income."

I opened Google Chrome and navigated the link. "Do you have a preference?"

"Rochester. One of the openings is at the church my mentor goes to."

I studied the posting. "Today is June 2. Applications are due June 3." The next day, I talked to a woman named Jenny in the office. "If you can get your resume to me by tomorrow morning, I'll add your application to the others."

"Thank you." *First, I need to write it.*

The next day, Jenny called. "I received your resume and cover letter. How would you feel about interviewing on Thursday evening?"

Same day as Clint's surgery. "Can you give me a second to check with my husband?" I muted the phone and dashed up to our bedroom where Clint and Kelly snuggled. "Clint, Christ UMC, interview Thursday."

"Do it. We'll figure out the rest." He stroked Kelly's back. "Shhhh. Mom's on an important call."

I inhaled a deep breath, tapped 'unmute,' and said, "Yes, Jenny, thank you."

Two days later, dressed in a skirt and blazer, I drove Clint to a surgery in Mankato where he would have a pain pump inserted. I watched his patient number slide from "operation prep" to "in surgery." My knee bounced up and down. *Please change to "in recovery."*

I didn't want to leave him, and I didn't have a choice. West to East, Sleepy Eye, Mankato and Rochester are all dots along Highway 14. I drove eighty-two miles in under seventy minutes, arriving at the church in Rochester only four minutes late.

"Did you get rerouted with construction?" the pastor asked.

"I did." I had not made a single wrong turn.

"So, how are you? How's Clint?"

The occupation of ministry blurs personal life and professionalism. I should not have been asked a family-related question during the interview, so I felt zero guilt responding with an ambiguous answer. After the interview I headed West back to Mankato, back to Clint. I dashed into a TJ Maxx to buy a pair of pajamas and stopped at a Burger King drive-through.

As I darted into the waiting room, I clutched the grease-stained Burger King bag and soda in one hand and pinned my laptop case to my side with the same arm. I half-jogged. The plastic TJ Maxx bag coiled around one leg. and I balanced my purse and my backpack on the opposite shoulder. The word "recovery" appeared beside Clint's number on the screen above my head.

Still performing my juggling act, I approached the counter and brushed hair from my face that had escaped from my sagging bun. "Clint Evans?"

The receptionist eyed my frazzled state with veiled amusement. She clicked the mouse through options on her screen. "Just waking up, actually. We'll call you back in a few minutes."

"Thank you." I sat in my same seat, unceremoniously dropping my armloads to the floor. After a breath, I dove into the brown paper bag and shoved three still-hot fries into my mouth. My tongue watered as I bit into my original chicken sandwich. I tilted my head back against the wall and sighed.

Twenty minutes later, when the receptionist called Clint's name, I rose with aplomb. With only my purse and my backpack to carry, I followed her through the double doors. She drew the curtain back and left.

Clint appeared groggy, but awake.

"All right, Mr. Evans," said the attending nurse. "Let's see your incision site." She shifted his hospital gown, exposing his abdomen. "Oh, you have so much meat on your bones, you can hardly tell it's there."

The pain pump reminded me of a circular tobacco container.

"So, we'll keep you here overnight, make sure everything looks good, and then you can go home."

"How're you feeling," I asked.

"Great, right now." He smiled sloppily. "How'd the interview go?"

"Good? I don't remember most of it."

He giggled.

"Wow. You *are* feeling good."

"Very good."

"You want to have them do a drain while we're here?"

"Probably should."

Friday and Saturday were incident-free, and I looked forward to attending Clint's farewell party after church. He surprised me before the service by saying, "I'm in a lot of pain. I want to go to the hospital."

"But Clint, your party." *My party.*

"I'm going to the hospital. Are you taking me or not?"

We zipped over to the hospital five minutes from our home. I still clung to hope of attending the celebration. *Why am I obsessed with the party? Oh. Because I want to feel loved right now.*

After X-rays, the nurse escorted us to the largest exam room. *I wish I wasn't familiar with this room.* I glanced at the clock on the wall. *We still have time.*

The on-call doctor strode in. "Well, Mr. Evans, let's drain the blood serum and then I ordered a CT because I want to confirm our X-ray results." His tone instilled calm but he wasted no time with his movements.

"Thanks, Dr. Dhaliwal."

I checked the time. A CT scan would mean we'd miss our own party. "But we drained fluid yesterday."

I missed the doctor's shocked expression until I replayed the moment later. Nurses scurried around Dr. Dhaliwal. He pointed, corrected, confirmed. He wiped Clint's catheter site himself and connected the tube with practiced fluidity.

Blood serum wound through the thin tube and poured into the bottle at an alarming rate. With two liters of blood serum drained, the doctor slowed the flow.

"Two liters, Clint," I said. "Do you feel like you got the wind knocked out of you?"

"A little, but keep going, please."

My eyes widened. The serum continued draining from his pleura, the membrane surrounding his lung.

The doctor stopped at three liters.

The facts lined up in front of me, but I couldn't add the sum of them. Even when the doctor returned with the results of the CT and said the words out loud, I couldn't grasp the implications.

"I'm sorry to be the one to tell you this, Mr. Evans, but the cancer is growing."

My mouth fell open. "They checked him on Thursday. Are you saying his cancer has grown noticeably since *Thursday*?"

"Yes."

And still, my brain could not fathom the bottom line. "Well, we have a follow-up appointment at Mayo tomorrow. We'll talk to them then."

At home, Clint went upstairs to rest. Three church members stopped by—Shirley, Erin, and Gina—to present Clint with a gift, a thin rectangle, at least three feet long and two feet wide.

Shirley ducked into the bedroom and said quietly, "Hey, Pastor Clint."

Shirley's husband, Greg, had driven Clint to almost every chemotherapy appointment. "We'll just be a minute."

Clint's eyes opened to slits. Erin and Gina followed her in, each holding one end of the present. Gina glanced around the room and then dropped her gaze to the package in her hands. I didn't know whether to laugh or cry. *I feel awkward with you in my bedroom too.*

I looked at Clint. "Do you want to open the gift?"

Clint opened his eyes wider but made no effort to get out of bed.

I forced cheer into my voice. "Okay. Why don't I open it for us." I tore at the paper, revealing a sign that read "Have I not commanded you? Be strong and courageous. Do not be terrified or dismayed for the Lord your God will be with you wherever you go. Joshua 1:9." Words lodged in my throat for a minute. "Thank you. It's beautiful." I accepted the gift from them and leaned it against the dresser.

"We love you, Pastor Clint," said Gina.

"I love you too."

The rims of Shirley's eyes were red. Erin didn't make any Adam Sandler jokes. Gina held her breath like if she exhaled, she would release the emotions she held back. The ladies gracefully bowed out, and I walked them to the door, watched them leave. That was the last time they ever saw Clint.

I trudged back up the stairs to check on Clint. "You need anything? "No."

I eased the door closed.

"Sam?"

I whipped the door open. "Yeah?"

"I think I finally love myself."

His palpable statement hit me square in the chest like a linebacker does a running back. A thousand responses flew through my thoughts, each one inadequate. Clint and I studied one another and let fifteen years speak for themselves. Arguments. Encouragements. Disappointments. Triumphs. Pleas.

"I think I finally love myself," he repeated.

"I've prayed you'd love yourself for a very long time."

"I know. I love you, Sam."

This might be the first time he believes me. "I love you too. Good night, Clint."

"Good night."

In the hallway, I leaned against the doorframe, the way movies taught me to, and let the tears come.

⧓

SAM, MONDAY, JUNE 10, 2019
SLEEPY EYE, MINNESOTA

In the small exam room, the paper on the table crinkled beneath Clint's restless energy. "Would it be possible to up the amount of pain medicine being released?"

"Of course," said the surgeon. "We got that oncology appointment scheduled for you for forty-five minutes from now. Just enough time to walk over there."

Another day, another doctor. In a closet-sized exam room, the surgeon flipped back and forth between multiple CT images. I couldn't see his computer screen, but somehow I knew.

The hospital staff's speed in scheduling an appointment with Clint's oncologist would have been another red flag, had I paused to notice.

"I need to use the bathroom, first," said Clint.

I watched the door close. "Can you tell me what you see?"

"I can't, actually. Only your oncologist can interpret these scans."

"It's not good?"

"It's not good."

When Clint returned, I rested my face in my hands.

"What's wrong?"

"It's hard to watch you going through this." I turned to the surgeon. "Eight months ago, he was deadlifting 400 lbs."

The surgeon's eyes widened.

"Sam." Clint waited until I faced him. Quietly, he said, "It's okay. It's gonna be okay."

I gathered my hair into a ponytail. The oncologist tapped images on a monitor with a fine-tipped pointer. "This is the first image we ever took. These are your ribs here, Clint. There's the original nodule, and there you can see the cancerous tissue spread across two, almost three, ribs near your right lung."

I saw gray and darker gray, but I took his word for it.

He switched images. "This was taken Sunday." He slid the pointer up along the rib cage. "Here, the cancer has grown around five, six ribs."

"Okay," Clint said, "so, what's our next step?"

"I want to try a radiation pill. We'd need to do an EKG tomorrow to make sure your heart is strong enough for this third line of treatment."

My ears keyed in to "third line of treatment." When Clint first received his cancer diagnosis, my aunts explained that cancer is not a "save the best for last scenario." Doctors use the most effective medicine first. So, when patients move to the second and third line of treatment, doctors don't expect as much success.

I drove home from the hospital knowing the radiation drug would work, and I wouldn't have to think about Clint's death for two more years.

The day of poking and prodding exhausted Clint, I dropped him off at home and drove three extra blocks to Randy's, the local pharmacy, and picked up his prescriptions. While I walked toward the car, my phone rang. I shuffled through my purse and spotted an unidentified number on the caller ID. "Hello?"

"Hi. Sam? This is Karla, from Christ UMC."

The second my call ended with her I dialed Clint. "Clint, I got the job."

"You got the job?" I heard more inflection and relief in his tone than I'd heard in months. It made me want to weep. "Good job, sweetheart."

"Yeah. I'm on my way home now with your medicine. I'll see you in a few minutes."

I tossed the white bag on the passenger seat. Reality struck.

Now we need to buy a house.

CHAPTER FIFTY

Tuesday, June 5, 2018

Dear Clint,

Today you rolled out of bed and received a chemo treatment. Then you ate lunch with a pastor-friend walking through a divorce. You met with your boss, lifted weights, and watched Kaylynn and Kelly's softball game. You encouraged them each time they failed and each time they succeeded. you told me I am a better person than you and you meant it with all sincerity.

I remembered. Maybe God reminded me. In high school, I laid on my bed in Naperville, Illinois, staring at my bedroom ceiling. A friend had held up a mirror to my ignorance and judgementalism. In that moment, I knew my husband would be the flipside of the coin—the prodigal son to my elder brother.

And I found you.

So, here it is. And it is honest. I am a better person because of you. You...

Push me when I want to give up.

Free me to chase dreams.

Pinch hit when I am tired.

Want what's best for me.

Confront my anger when I am in the wrong.

Show me how to love people who don't look like me.

Lead by example with patience toward our children.

Are forthright with others and temper grace with truth.

Are accessible to society's unwanted and escort them to the cross by your own hand.

I watch you. You may not know. Every day. And I am inspired by you. Your grace for others is greater than mine. And in all these things, I strive to be more like you. I love more effectively because I love like you. I am a better person because of you. My fury has subsided, like waves stretched thin across the shore.

Love,

Sam

SAM, TUESDAY, JUNE 11, 2019

I don't remember how the girls got to school. Seven miles into our forty-four-mile drive, Clint doubled over on the passenger seat with pain.

"I want to go home." He groaned.

I eased my foot off the gas pedal and scanned the road for a place to pull over.

"No. Go." He flipped his hand forward. "I'm so sick of the hospital sending me home. They can get me medicine and …" His words trailed off with another groan. He leaned his head against the window, then against the headrest, then curled into his abdomen again, unable to get comfortable.

I frowned at Clint and dialed his oncologist. "We're still coming to the EKG, but he's doubled over in pain."

"Do you need an ambulance?"

"Uh." The question threw me. "No?"

"What's the question," Clint asked.

"Do we need an ambulance?"

"No. Sam, you're from Chicago. Drive like it. Just drive."

Now you know how I felt when I was in labor with Kelly and you were driving like a grandma. I shot a glance at Clint, remembering my labor pain, and applied weight to the gas pedal. *Oh, wow. Kelly's birthday is in two weeks.*

When I curved around the ER entrance, Clint accepted a nurse's help into the wheelchair. My mouth fell open.

Logic and hope branched into two parallel universes coexisting in the same space. I was walking with Clint as far as possible, but at his end, our paths would diverge. I was his wife in our past and his widow in my future. I knew he was dying, and I believed he would live. My identity was inexplicably tangled with his, and unwinding. I simultaneously thought: *does this mean he's getting closer to death?* And: *they'll fix his medicine, and he'll be fine.*

His surgeon and oncologist were already in the room when I arrived after parking the car. The oncologist smiled at me. "Hey there, Mrs. Evans. I think we should admit your husband until we can get the pain under control."

Clint exhaled. "Thank God."

"Hang in there, Clint," said the oncologist. "We've already sent orders for dilaudid."

I'd translated "admit him" to mean "check him in for his EKG appointment." Because EKG equaled hope. I drew my gaze away from the doctors and stared at Clint on the hospital bed. "What about the EKG?"

"I think we need to admit him and get his pain under control first," the doctor repeated with the utmost patience.

I nodded, but we were still having two different conversations. "Right, get him some pain medication and then do the scan." I glanced from Clint to the doctor. "What time is the EKG scheduled for?"

"Mrs. Evans, we canceled the EKG for now. We're admitting him for pain, and we'll go from there."

Hope refused to hear what the doctors were not saying.

"Admit him? You mean, overnight?"

Ding. Ding. Ding. Logic chimed in. *We have a winner.*

I replayed the conversation. "I'm sorry. I didn't understand."

"No worries."

"How are you doing, Clint," I asked.

"Better. Much better."

"Good. I wasn't ready to spend the night."

"I know. And I want you to be with the girls." He looked for his phone. Not finding it within arm's reach, he gave up. "Can you call my dad?"

"Of course."

I called Chuck and explained what was happening.

"Absolutely, I'll be there, Samantha," he said. "Is there someone who can sit with him until I get there?"

"Yes."

I sat in a corner chair and called to mind all of Clint's colleagues within a forty-five-minute radius. One of his closest friends, Nick, lived two hours from the hospital but I included him too.

Tuesday, June 11, 2019, 3:49 p.m.

Doctors believe the tumor has grown since Sunday. His chemo treatments these last several months have done nothing, it seems, except facilitate the growth of a highly aggressive cancer. The pressure of the fluid in his pleura (lung cavity) pushed his heart toward the left and there is now fluid in the cavity beneath his heart. Doctors recommend keeping him in Mankato overnight. Clint wants me to return to the girls, but he's scared. Can any of you rotate visitation? His dad is coming from the Cities. I'm so tired of dark hospital rooms. Your dear friend, Sam

3:52 p.m.

I'm on my way ... — Terri

3:56 p.m.

J.J. here. I will be there at 8

4:06 p.m.

I'll be there by 5. — Nick

He lived two hours away, so I laughed at his message.

7:26 p.m.

Tumor shows noticeable growth since Sunday. "Growing at twice the normal rate," says the oncologist.

7:32 p.m.

We prayed for Clint in the room.
— Terri and Dan

8:37 p.m.

Praying from Washington D.C.
— Matt

8:41 p.m.

Fred prayed with Clint.
We're leaving now. Dad is here.
— Nick

After I left, hospital staff moved Clint to the hospice wing. "Why the hospice wing?" I gripped my phone. My voice sounded harsh, even to my own ears.

"Because the hospital had larger, more private rooms available there," the oncologist said.

"Oh, okay."

Bomb defused.

The second morning into his stay, I arrived at the hospital after getting the girls to school and scurried up to the hospital room. Clint's dad stood beside Clint, encouraging him, hugging him, rubbing his back. I'd missed something.

A doctor turned, clipboard in hand. "Your husband signed a DNR, Mrs. Evans."

"What is a DNR?"

"Do Not Resuscitate. It means, if your husband's heart stops, medical personnel will not try to revive him."

"Oh, okay." My eyes flitted to Chuck, where I found reassurance. *Thank you, Chuck for being someone Clint can speak hard truths to.* But I shrugged off the DNR as an unnecessary precaution. I couldn't comprehend the need for 'Do Not Resuscitate' conversations. I couldn't understand he was dying, but my brain knew he was dying.

Later, I sat beside Clint's bed and shook my head. "Clint, I don't know if I have the mental capacity to start a new job right now."

His eyes hardened. "You will absolutely take that job."

At the time, neither of us knew how our finances would shake out. Clint needed his wife to have a job so his family would be provided for. His demand required me to house hunt while he remained in the hospital.

One evening, I stayed with Clint's cousin, Joe, and his wife, Lindsay, overnight—the same cousins Clint stayed with following his first chemo.

I'd received a letter from the Methodist annual conference regarding death benefits as pastor's widow and was convinced I was reading a foreign language. Joe and I leaned on adjacent sides of the kitchen island, murmuring sections of the letter.

"I think it means you'll receive this *and* this," he said.

"It means I'll be okay."

"It means you'll be okay."

Lindsay got their three littles down and joined us in the kitchen. I pressed my palms into the counter. "Thank you, Joe. I know this can't be easy—talking about money I'll receive after your cousin dies."

"His death is the hard part, Sam. Knowing his young family will be taken care of makes it easier."

My sister, Meredith, drove from Chicago and met me at their house. The next morning, Meredith, the realtor, and I would survey several homes before I returned to the hospital.

"Whatever you need," Lindsey said.

You've already done it. Driving Clint home from his first chemo appointment. Hosting my sister and I overnight. Helping me with finances. "You've been amazing, Lindsey. Thank you."

I returned to the hospital the following afternoon with photos of houses. Clint's dad was excited to see them, but Clint refused to look at the pictures. I stuffed the photocopies into my purse. *He doesn't want to see photos of a house he'll never cross the threshold of.*

Clint's youngest brother of two, Darry, and his wife Yesi arrived. They'd hoped Clint could officiate their wedding, but his health declined too quickly, so they'd opted for the Justice of the Peace instead.

Darry learned over the side of the bed. "Yesi's pregnant. We're going to have a baby in November."

Clint smirked. "Nice work, Darry."

Darry grinned. "Thanks."

I rolled my eyes.

In the hallway, Darry told me, "People keep asking me how I'm doing. I say, 'How the fuck do you think I'm doing? My brother's dying.'"

I returned to Clint's room after they left.

Matter-of-factly, with a hint of resignation, Clint said, "I'm never going to meet my nephew."

November is only five months away. Of course, you will.

Clint and the doctors comprehended what I and others struggled to grasp. His sudden, sharp decline left little time to acclimate to ever-changing realities.

As each day passed, he slept more and ate less. The first Sunday following his admittance was Father's Day. I navigated the path I'd memorized to his room. The girls, armed with presents, towed behind me.

Clint greeted the girls with a forced ear-to-ear grin. Eight-year-old Kaylynn presented him with a teddy bear nearly as big as her. Trinity, four, giggled and bounced. She placed a gift bag on the bed beside him. He withdrew a Mario Brothers beach towel.

Clint's face lit up. "This is awesome. Thank you."

Kelly gave Clint a cellophane bag of chocolates.

"I will definitely eat this," he said. Then he withdrew the card she'd chosen.

The card had a gold plastic unicorn bust glued to the front. Bold letters across the front of the card spelled out "Life Trophy." Fighting back tears and shaking his head, he said to me, "She gets it. I don't know how. But she gets it."

The following Tuesday, I typed into the group message: Friends, this morning Clint chose to enter into hospice.

Clint's hospital stay overlapped with the 2019 Annual Conference, a three-day gathering for worship and business with representatives from three hundred United Methodist churches across Minnesota. Every pastor in the group message attended the 2019 Annual Conference.

During a point of privilege, Fred read an announcement to a room of 800 people. "Pastor Clint Evans, one of our clergy, cannot be in attendance today because he is in the hospital with cancer. He is thirty-eight years old. Just this morning he entered into hospice."

The collective gasp reached the rafters. Pastors understand "hospice" better than most. The messenger group of Clint's colleagues grew exponentially following the announcement.

After we'd left on Father's Day, I realized I'd gotten a photo of Clint kissing Trinity, but not the other two girls. Dawn and I arranged to meet at the hospital and for her to bring the girls to her house from there on the following Wednesday. I planned to get the photos then. Dawn knew this.

When we were still on our way, Wednesday, Dawn sent a text:

Clint's sleeping. I'll meet you in the lobby.

Fury boiled within me. *Clint can sleep when he's dead. She is not protecting her son from his children.*

She met me us in the lobby, took Trinity's hand. "I'll take them to my house. They don't need to go up."

I took Trinity's hand and yanked her away. "This is my girls' *father.* You will not keep them from him." I stormed past her with my kids. She trailed behind, sputtering.

A thought occurred to me. Each of the girls have a journal. I'd left the journals at the hospital and asked *both* Clint's mom and grandma to have Clint write last words to his daughters. I spun on her. "Did you show Clint the journals?"

"No, he's been so tired."

Of course, he's tired. He's dying. A week ago when I brought them he would have had more energy.

If they'd shown Clint the journals and he was too tired to write in them, I would have understood. But they robbed him of the opportunity by making the choice for him.

Kelly strode into Clint's room first. Her dad greeted her with a cheerful "Oh hey there." Kaylynn sat quietly and rubbed his legs. I got my photos before Clint drifted off to sleep.

After the girls went with their grandma, I did a double take when I saw Clint's bed. Trinity had tucked her stuffed dalmatian up beside him. After awhile, Clint stirred. I pulled out the journals and sat beside him on the bed, facing him. "Do you think you could write words for the girls?"

"Sam, he's really tired," his grandma said.

I glared at her. "Did people bully you and insert themselves into *your* marriage when your husband was dying?" I shouted at Clint's grandma. "You and Dawn do not get to dictate how this happens. This is *my* husband. *My* one-flesh."

She left the room, thank God, to go to the cafeteria, or China… I didn't care.

By the time I mentioned the books, he was too weak to write the words himself. I opened the journal and reached for the pen. "What if you tell me what you want to say to them?" I wept for what was stolen from his daughters.

After I wrote Clint's last words to his girls, he said, "We should probably plan the service, huh?"

The thought pummeled me, honored me. *He trusts me to talk about life after his death.* I squeezed the tears away. "Of course."

I pulled his funeral template up on my laptop. "Okay, opening song?"

"This Little Light of Mine."

I laughed while I typed. After sharing fifteen years of marriage and ministry, we'd collaborated on hundreds of events. Planning an order of worship felt as normal as eating a meal or sitting next to him to watch a movie.

For the next thirty minutes, the hospital disappeared, the machines, the diagnosis. For a blink in time, we were two old friends planning a service together.

CHAPTER FIFTY-ONE

Clint,

Since I first met you, I have found joy in your dynamic personality. I've enjoyed our time together. You have brought a wonderful energy, not just to your churches, but also to us as clergy.

It has been an honor to hold you in prayer in this season of your life. Thank you for being a blessing to so many people in your churches and in the greater world.

Of God's Promise,

Tony Fink

SAM, THURSDAY, JUNE 20, 2019
MANKATO, MINNESOTA

Each time Clint mentioned communion, he spoke of the elements and Jesus's presence with such reverence listeners would salivate for a taste of the Bread of Life. He brought his communion kit to every home and hospital visit he made. Clint basked in the resurrection of Christ and the grace of God alive in his ragamuffin heart.

Which is why, despite his request for no visitors, I invited all the pastors from the Facebook Messenger group to come and administer communion to Clint. I felt strongly what Clint wanted and what he needed were two different things.

Following the annual conference, pastors gathered in the chapel of Mayo in Mankato, Minnesota. Katie, the Mayo chaplain, arrived first.

"How are you?" she asked.

"His grandma is angry I'm inviting visitors and now I'm questioning myself."

"Sam, you're his wife. You're the one he trusted to be his Medical Power of Attorney. *You* know him better than anyone. *You* know how much communion means to him." She paused, debating whether or not to say the next part. "And you know he's dying."

I stilled. "You don't think they do?"

Several more clergy entered, and we greeted them with waves.

"He's lonely, Sam, because he can't talk to anyone he loves about what's happening next. You're not going to upset him by acknowledging his death. If anything, he'll be relieved."

We surrendered the conversation to more intentional greetings.

Eight pastors arrived, and one clergy spouse. Four of them wore their albs, everyone wore their stoles. "High church" as Clint called it, and he loved the imagery of garden-variety sinners being clothed by Christ to share the story of God's love.

"I have the elements in my car," said Josh. "Wine or grape juice?"

I glanced at Jo Anne, who'd visited him in jail after the accident.

"Well, it's not like the alcohol can do any damage at this point," I said. "But he'd want to say he died twenty months sober."

Katie's smile seemed to say, 'See? You do know him best.'

I walked with Josh toward the parking lot and saw the sign for the cancer wing of the hospital. "I'll meet you back here in a second, Josh." I veered off. At the reception desk, I asked, "Is Jim working?" *Please, God.* A moment later, he emerged from the back. *Thank you.* "Hi, Jim. I'm Clint's wife."

"I remember you." He smiled.

I opened my mouth and closed it again. Patients and their family members sat in the waiting room, still fighting, still hoping. "We're, uh, some friends of Clint are giving him communion right now, and I wanted to invite you to come."

By the tone of his answer, I knew he knew. "Of course."

Josh entered the building on cue, and we met up with the others.

We navigated the halls between the chapel and Clint's hospital room. Heads turned at the sight of our entourage. I glanced at Josh and laughed. His stole floated around his shoulders as he walked. Alb unzipped, jeans and T-shirt beneath. Baseball cap firmly in place. I nodded. *Perfect.*

Clint's eyes were open, but he wasn't really seeing the world around him. When we entered, he was confused and disoriented.

"It's okay, Clint," I said. "We're here to give you communion because we love you."

Clint's grandma pursed her lips and stormed out of the room. I held fast to my faith. This was the right thing. *She's going to miss the miracle.*

Josh and Nick positioned themselves on opposite sides of the bed. Gathering courage, Josh unwrapped a stole. Leaning forward, Josh said, "Brother Clint, this is Josh. Josh Doughty." My eyes narrowed. They'd been close friends for over eight years. *Why is Josh introducing himself? Oh.*

Oh, no.

Among these eight pastors' years of service, they'd performed thousands of hospital visits with the dying. Josh recognized where Clint was, or rather, where he wasn't. Clint stood closer to heaven's threshold than earth's.

"Clint, this stole has been blessed by the bishop and pastors of the United Methodist Church. Hundreds of prayers are woven into this garment."

Josh and Nick rested the stole about Clint's shoulders. "It's been an honor to serve with you."

Dianne, whom he'd been in ministry with us in Pequot Lakes, kissed his forehead. "This is Dianne. I love you." She straightened and spoke from memory, "Clint, you remember that the night Jesus was handed over, he gathered around with his friends."

There were twelve of us, including Clint. Twelve disciples of Jesus.

Dianne continued, "Those who he ministered with. Those who walked and journeyed with him, listened to him, and learned from him. Knowing he would be handed over, Jesus took the common element they had eaten together many times and broke it, saying, 'brothers, [and sisters] this is my body which is given for you. As often as you eat this bread, remember me.' Then he took the cup 'This cup is poured out for you and for many for the forgiveness of sins. As often as you drink of it, remember me.'

"So, today, Clint, we come. We come to this table with you, knowing Christ is here among us. That Christ is right beside you, holding you, walking with you. And we, too, come as your brothers and your sisters, asking Jesus to hold you. To bring you all the way to the other side, that you may be victorious with Jesus on your day." She looked at us. "I invite you as brothers and sisters join together in the Lord's prayer."

We all intertwined our voices with hers. "Our Father, who art in heaven, hallowed be Thy name. Thy kingdom come. Thy will be done, on earth as it is in heaven ..."

Clint's eyes remained closed as he murmured the prayer. Dianne broke off a piece of bread, dipped it in the cup, and passed it to me. I touched the bread to Clint's lips. He opened his mouth. My fingers brushed against his dry lips as I placed the bread on his tongue.

While others around the room received communion, I opened my Bible to John 14. "Clint, I've been reading this passage from the perspective of Jesus talking to someone who is about to crossover from death into life and join him on the other side." Emboldened by our friends' presence, and Katie's encouragement, I read parts of John 14. "Peace I leave with you. My peace I give you. I do not give you the world gives. Do not let your hearts be troubled and do not be afraid.

"You heard me say, 'I am going away and I am coming back to you.' ... I have told you now before it happens, so that when it does happen you will believe. ... Come now; let us leave."

I closed the Bible that Clint gifted me years prior. "Clint, you have touched so many lives. I'm proud of you, and I'm excited for you to go see Jesus. You have my blessing to take the next step in your journey, okay? I wanted to bring Jesus into the room today because I know how much communion means to you. I wanted Jesus to be present here with you in this room." I blinked back tears. "I love you."

Clint opened his eyes, alert and aware. One by one, his friends stepped toward Clint, leaned down and introduced themselves. They grasped his hand and whispered assurances. He reached for his colleagues as they approached.

"Jim!" Clint exclaimed when his oncology nurse approached. The room exploded with laughter.

Prior to this moment everyone tiptoed around the word "die," like the news would shock Clint. But ignoring the truth isolated Clint even more, robbing him of his ability to honestly process the path before him. So many friends and church members wanted to visit, and I'd said 'no' to all of them, honoring Clint's wishes. But these, these were different. They ushered him forward rather than pulling him back.

We sang "The Servant Song" with harmonies. When the song ended, I wrapped my palm around the metal doorknob. *This is their stop. They've traveled with Clint as far as they can go.* With silent nods of acknowledgment, everyone shifted toward the door.

"I love you guys."

We all spun, startled. For a blink, happy, healthy Clint returned— smiling generously, alert.

"We love you too," they echoed.

"Like a brother," said Nick. "You're my brother."

Sleep pulled Clint under as I stepped into the hall and eased the door closed.

We shared a moment of silence. After a breath, Jeff said, "All right. Whose room should we visit next?"

Pent up emotion spilled into laughter.

"Sam, do you have time for dinner?" one of them asked.

After checking with Clint, I accepted their Perkins invitation for dinner. When I returned to the hospital, Clint opened his eyes to the sound of the door, sighed, and whispered. "There we go."

I rushed to his side and his grandma graciously eased away from the bed. "I'm so sorry I took so long. I tried to be quick. Our friends were taking care of me."

His eyes closed. "You're taken care of?"

"I'm taken care of."

"Well, good. If you're taken care of, I'm taken care of. If you're taken care of, I'm taken care of."

"I'm taken care of."

He mumbled his mantra again and again and faded into sleep.

CHAPTER FIFTY-TWO

Dear Clint,

    I hope you understand your impact on all of our lives, especially mine. You've always been an amazing mentor to me. Always challenged me to grow in my faith and led me to a deeper faith in Christ. And you took the time to not just be my pastor, but my friend. You gave me advice to help me become a better father, husband, and Christian man and I'm so thankful for you. I will truly miss being able to spend time with you. Our early drives to men's group, talking about life ... getting deep in conversation and then laughing at you dad jokes. Times together like Walk to Emmaus and men's retreat in Bricelyn. Having lunch at Subway and talking for hours. I will cherish your friendship forever and will miss you more than words can say. You did what God called you to do and so much more. We all love you so much.

Jaime

SAM, FRIDAY, JUNE 21, 2019
MANKATO, MINNESOTA

Wait a minute. By Clint's second Friday in the hospital, I realized Clint's oncologist placed Clint in the hospice wing intentionally.

Every time I called someone, I heard an intake of breath on the opposite side of the receiver, so I started quoting *Monty Python and the Holy Grail.* "He's not dead yet." But conversations couldn't begin until I'd assured listeners this wasn't *that call.*

The days blurred together and became snapshots of moments rather than individual days. I'd often open the door to Clint's hospital room and find Clint's soldier brother Darry keeping silent vigil.

"I can't wait to get Clint home and let him rest," Dawn said, when the two of us were alone in the room with him. We'd agreed that home hospice should happen at his parents' so our daughters wouldn't watch him die, but Dawn's attempts to control my access to my husband and my children's access to their father were finished. She could take a flying leap.

"The girls will have unlimited access to their father. You understand, right?"

"Unless he's resting."

Hell no. "I need a key to the house. If Trinity wakes up in the middle of the night and wants to see her daddy …."

Someone knocked and a female doctor with long, brown hair entered the room.

"What time does he get to come home today?" Dawn asked.

I gritted my teeth.

The doctor glanced at the monitors surrounding the bed and lowered her gaze to her clipboard. "Actually, I'm not sure he'll be up for the travel today."

"Oh," Dawn said, crestfallen.

"Why don't we see how he's feeling Monday?"

"Oh, okay" Dawn perked up.

I didn't. I calculated linear equations. His constitution had been in steady, hastening decline since our arrival the previous Tuesday, and if I were honest, for the prior three-to-six months. Refused a wheelchair. Accepted a wheelchair. Only got out of bed to use the restroom. Didn't need to use the restroom because he barely ate.

If Clint's not feeling up to travel today, then why would the doctor suggest …oh. She expects him to pass away over the weekend. My eyes widened. *Should I tell Dawn?* I cast her a sidelong glance. *No. She's not ready.*

I followed the doctor out of the room. "Tell me more."

"The cancer is crawling all over his body. Honestly, an older, weaker patient would have passed by now, but your husband's young, healthy kidneys, liver, and heart are working double-time to save him."

My jaw shifted. "Thank you." I stepped back into the room and eased myself down on Clint's bed. "I'm here, Clint." He reached for my hand. I reached for his.

"I don't want to do the drains anymore," Clint said.

I expelled the implications on an exhale. "You don't have to."

"What?" Dawn shrieked. "That means ..."

"That's exactly what that means," I said with finality. "I'm taken care of, remember?" I told Clint. "I'm strong. I'll be okay." With a voice fortified by the prayers of others, I said, "You're dying well, Clint. This is the hardest thing you'll ever have to do, and you are so brave."

"I just want to be done."

Grandma clutched his hands. "You're all finished. You've nothing left to do."

"Your to-do list is finished, Clint," I added. I'd find his chicken-scratch to-do lists all over the house. He often commented that his to-do lists were never complete. While the world would miss Clint's grace, his compassion and fierce defense of the underdog, it would not miss Clint's handwriting.

"I want to go." Clint's words jerked me back to the present. "Why won't He take me?"

I don't know. "It won't be long now, Clint. You're doing great," I said. "Jesus will be here soon."

"Why don't you come over here, Sam?" Grandma suggested.

The simple gesture was a balm to my heart—her way of recognizing my place as his wife. *Finally.*

Clint struggled to take a full breath, and the sound held a watery quality to it.

His mom begged, "Clint, please do another drain."

"No." I glared at her. "That's not what Clint wants."

"You brought visitors when he didn't want visitors."

This isn't a damn contest, you child. "That wasn't about me. I brought *pastors, trained* in end-of-life etiquette, to give Clint communion and encourage him on his journey." My jaw quivered with anger. *She's a mother losing her son. She's a mother losing her son.*

"Come on, Dawn," her mom said. "Let's give Sam some time alone with her husband."

The moment the latch clicked, I sighed.

He whispered, "I don't want to leave the hospital. Please don't make me leave."

He waited for his mom to leave? "It's okay, you can stay here until … until it's time for you to leave."

He expelled a breath, relieved.

He can't even die the way he wants because she's making his death about her.

With closed eyes, he said, "Why won't he take me? Why isn't he taking me, Sam?"

"I don't know, sweetheart."

"Dear God," I whispered. His hospital gown felt cool beneath my palm. I didn't recognize my husband's shape as I slid my hand across his abdomen to his heart. Tears soaked my face with the words I was about to speak. "Dear God, please stop his heart."

I pressed my forehead into folded hands and wept.

✝

One of the Evans boys—I couldn't even tell you which one— knocked the tray table, spilling Clint's barely-touched, vanilla milk-shake all over his hospital gown and sheets. I pressed the call button. A female nurse responded quickly.

Korey, who lived in Brooklyn, and Travis, hoisted Clint out of bed and into a chair while I ripped off the dirty sheets. Clint decided to use the bathroom, oblivious to cords and lines and wires.

With NASCAR pit crew efficiency, we rescued strained cords, replaced vanilla ice cream-coated sheets and sweaty pillowcases with fresh, clean linens, assisted the tipsy Mr. Evans with his briefs, and exchanged his gown with a clean one.

Clint slept soundly and peacefully after the ordeal.

Later, I sat on Clint's bed, and we read Luke 15, the Prodigal Son. A nostalgic sense of homecoming washed over me. The image of the prodigal running to his father carried new meaning as Clint took his final steps toward home.

After speaking with the nurse, I returned to our house in Sleepy Eye, still filled with moving boxes, and found my girls, a church member and a room-sized fort in my living room. After arguing with the girls about toothpaste, I tucked them in and sang their "nite nite" song.

At 5:00 a.m., Kelly woke me. Patter, the fatter cat, jumped into a wardrobe box and couldn't get out.

At least things at home are normal... ish.

CHAPTER FIFTY-THREE

I met Clint at seminary, and we became fast friends. His love for Jesus was evident with every word he spoke. I was truly blessed to be one of the lucky people in life to meet him. May God continue his legacy through his children, and the gospel Clint lived each and every day.

Matt Carter

SAM, SATURDAY, JUNE 22, 2019
MANKATO, MINNESOTA

Clint heard the door open and sprung out of bed wearing nothing but a diaper. My mouth froze in place. No one included "your thirty-eight-year-old husband is wearing diapers" in the updates I'd received. His frame reminded me of photos I'd seen of Auschwitz victims, with the shape of his bones visible beneath thin skin.

"I've gotta go," he said.

Go? To the bathroom?

"Whoa, Clint. Whoa." Chuck, several inches taller than Clint, muscled him back to the bed. "It's okay, son. It's okay. I've gotcho."

"I've gotta go."

"I know. I know. And you will. This is the way. There you go." Chuck held his son in diapers and spoke to him with the tenderness and patience a father uses with a young child. "It's okay, son." Chuck eased Clint back into bed and drew the sheet to Clint's chest.

Chuck shook his head. "He got up a couple times when Dawn and Mary Lou were in here with him. Once Mary Lou was by herself."

Both Dawn and his grandmother Mary Lou barely crossed the five-foot threshold and the image of them wrestling Clint back to bed amused me and terrified me at the same time. They'd kept faithful watch over Clint for the prior ten days, sitting with him in silence and in prayer throughout a cyclone of movement. Their presence with Clint made it possible for me to be present for our daughters, and search for our new home.

Throughout the next hour, the entire Evans clan arrived. We caught our breath in an unplanned moment of togetherness.

Sunlight streamed through the windows. Kaylynn tucked herself beneath Korey's arm. Chuck and Dawn wrapped their arms around each other and stared lovingly at Clint.

I nudged Darry with my elbow, and smirked. "How are you doing?"

"About as good as you."

We all stepped into the hallway, and I found Paul and Deb Marzahn, long-time friends, dressed in Harley Davidson gear.

"We know you told us not to come, but we ignored you."

I smiled. "I'm glad you did."

"Where do I know him from," Dawn asked me.

"I don't think you've ever met," I said. "Paul, Deb, and I worked together at CrossRoads Church in Lakeville."

"No, I know him." She stared. "I swear."

My energy for the conversation expired.

Paul and Deb greeted Chuck and Dawn. "I'm so sorry you're going through this," Paul said to us.

Chuck shook their hands. "Thank you."

"Do I know you?" Dawn asked.

I shook my head.

"You do, actually," said Paul. "I brought Clint to your home to visit with you when he was staying at Teen Challenge."

I was wrong. I smiled at Deb. "Of course, they've already met. I forgot we were talking about Paul for a minute."

Deb laughed and hugged me. She and Paul followed me into Clint's room. When I'd been nineteen and single, Paul took it upon himself to "discourage" suiters he deemed unworthy.

I frowned at Paul. "So, when I introduced you to Clint, you'd already met?"

"Yeah. And I couldn't break his confidence, so there was no way to ask how much you knew about his past."

"He *told* me everything before we started dating. The alcoholism, crack addiction, Teen Challenge, Midwest Challenge. But I didn't comprehend marriage to an addict." I sighed. "I think this was supposed to be my story."

"It's going to be a powerful story," Paul said.

Our gazes both gravitated to Clint, whose eyes remained closed.

I wasn't convinced. More goes into writing a book than most people realize. First, I'd have to write the story. Edit. Reedit. Send it to an editor. Edit the edited version. Swear at the editor under my breath. Choose independent publishing or seek a lit agent. Create a cover. Doubt myself. Battle imposter syndrome. Pray. Edit the edits of the edited version. Pray some more. Call my mommy, and finally, dub the entire manuscript "this stupid book" and consider setting the entire document on fire.

So, if you're reading this and there's a cover on the front—then God took the pitiful offering of my obedience and used it for a glory far greater than I could ever ask for or imagine.

Back to Saturday.

Paul reached for Clint's hand, and Deb's. I did the same. "Well, he certainly impressed me. It's been amazing to watch the two of you grow in the sharing of your faith."

After praying together, we stepped into the hall. Following a flurry of activity, Korey, Kaylynn and I were alone with Clint. Later that evening, my dad and Sherry arrived to say goodbye.

Sherry grasped Clint's hand. "I cherish the memory of my baptism."

Clint murmured, "My privilege and my honor."

My dad choked out heartfelt words around a sob. "Love you, Clint."

In an alcove at the end of the hall, we found eight-year-old Kaylynn playing with toys, and laden with gifts. Prayer shawls, teddy bears, books, and blankets multiplied by three for her sisters. *You poor, sweet girl. I hate this story for you.*

My dad and Sherry took Kaylynn to my house so I could stay with Clint overnight. I reentered Clint's room.

"Please don't bring the girls back here anymore," he said.

"I won't." *He's facing heaven.* The silence nagged me like a leaky faucet. Clint smelled like body odor and vinegar. His fingertips were pale blue. *There's no manual for this.* "My mom's plane gets in tomorrow. But if you don't want to wait for her, she'll understand, sweetheart."

Silence. I lowered myself to the bed by Clint's feet. Lying on his left side for the first time in months, the fluid shifted and pooled, giving his chest an inflated, watermelon-shaped appearance. I touched his chest and shoved my shock into my back pocket for another time.

"We've had a lot of fun together, haven't we?" I asked.

"It's true."

"We are blessed, aren't we, Clint?"

"'S true. 'S true." He stopped answering my question and started speaking of Jesus. "It's true. It's true. It's true. It's true, it's true, it's true."

"When I went …" *Ooh, too high.* I adjusted my pitch and started again. With a firm hand, Clint grasped mine and joined me singing "Down in the River to Pray." We sang all the verses—multiple times. Everyone ended up by the river to pray. Brothers, sisters, mothers, fathers, aunts, uncles, kittens … you name it.

I sang "Come by here, My Lord," otherwise known as "Kumbaya." It required effort to shove away the cheesy stereotype, but the words never seemed more applicable.

"Someone's singing, Lord. Come by here …

Someone's praying, Lord. Come by here …

Someone's begging, Lord. Come by here …

Someone's dying, Lord. Come by here. Someone's dying, Lord, come by here. Someone's dying, Lord, come by here…Oh, Lord, come by here."

I rubbed Clint's leg. "Do you see him, Clint? Do you see Jesus?"

"Yeah."

"What's he saying, sweetie?"

"Come. He's saying, 'come'."

I recited Psalm 23 and yanked my Bible from the bedside table to read Psalm 84.

I sang "In the Garden," a hymn quickly becoming one of my favorites. The sterile hospital room with its stark fluorescent lighting faded to gray. The garden came into focus. Forest green trees stretched to a height where darkness mingled with light. I saw Clint and Jesus walking, talking, smiling together, but I lagged behind, cherishing the gift of the vision, yet knowing the conversation and the space wasn't meant for me. Light emitted from Jesus and from somewhere beyond the woods, but the rest of the trees and flowers fell into shadow.

While I sang, I knew there was a door in the garden, though I couldn't see it, and I'd not be allowed to enter through.

A person can only repeat the chorus so many times. I clung to the image of the garden when I opened my eyes and the hospital room came into focus.

Clint appeared more muted than he had prior to the song, unresponsive. Clint loved the book of Habakkuk, so I opened to Habakkuk 1:1. Partway into chapter two, a wave of exhaustion hit me. I glanced at Clint. *He'll never know.* I skipped to the last verse of chapter three. "The Sovereign Lord is my strength; he makes my feet like the feet of a deer, he enables me to tread on the heights" (Habakkuk 3:19 NIV).

"Is that it?"

I startled at the sound of Clint's voice, and rolled my eyes in disbelief. "No. I missed a part. Sorry." *Who memorizes Habakkuk?* The man couldn't even remember to remove sweaty game jerseys from the trunk of his car.

I flipped to chapter two and started reading.

CHAPTER FIFTY-FOUR

Dear Sam,

This is the meditation for June 22 from *Twenty-Four Hours A Day*. "I would do well not to think of the Red Sea of difficulties that lie ahead. I am sure when I come to that Red Sea, the waters will part and I will be given all the power I need to face and overcome many difficulties and meet what is in store for me with courage. I believe I will pass through that Red Sea to the promised land, the land of the spirit where many souls meet in perfect comradeship. I believe when that time comes, I will be freed from all the dross of material things and find peace." This is Clint. This is what he knows.

Love,
Cindy

SAM, SUNDAY, JUNE 23, 2019
MANKATO, MINNESOTA

I glanced at the screen on my phone to check the time. Again. Urgency spurred an excessive string of texts. Mom's plane landed. She'd rented the car. She was only forty-five minutes away. I'd received minute-by-minute updates since her flight touched down at Minneapolis-St. Paul. When I triple-checked the time, another text came through.

I'm only thirty minutes away.

The question "Am I too late?" wove into each update.

Look forward to seeing you.

Veiled behind each response I said, "There's still time."

I dropped my phone onto the bed and flipped to Revelation 1. "I'm going to read descriptions of Jesus, so you know what He looks like when He comes to bring you home. This is the Jesus you'll see."

> Among the lampstands was someone like a son of man, dressed in a robe reaching down to his feet and with a golden sash around his chest. The hair on his head was white like wool, as white as snow, and his eyes were like blazing fire. His feet were like bronze glowing in a furnace, and his voice was like the sound of rushing waters. In his right hand he held seven stars, and coming out of his mouth was a sharp, double-edged sword. His face was like the sun shining in all its brilliance. ...
>
> When I saw him, I fell at his feet as though dead. Then he placed his right hand on me and said: "Do not be afraid. I am the First and the Last. I am the Living One; I was dead, and now look, I am alive for ever and ever! And I hold the keys of death and Hades.

My phone rang, jarring my thoughts. *Please nothing bad.* I pressed the green phone button with my thumb. "Hello?"

"I'm in the parking lot." She panted. "I'm on my way up."

"Mom. Breathe. He's waiting for you."

"Did he tell you that?"

"He doesn't have to." She exhaled built-up tension into my ear. "I mean, don't stop for coffee, but he's waiting."

"Oh," her voice hitched, "Saman—"

"We'll see you in a couple minutes, Mom. We both will."

I propped the door open and stood in the hallway. Pinning her purse to her side, my mom all but sprinted toward me. At her first sight of Clint, her hand came to her mouth and tears sped down her cheeks. Three weeks prior, she took photos of our family smiling with the Atlantic Ocean at our backs. Now, I saw Clint the way Mom saw him.

He'd rolled onto his back at some point while I read to him. His frame had deflated so profoundly his body no longer created a mound in the middle of the mattress. The shapes of the bones in his arm were visible beneath his skin, and his lips were a pale, blueish gray.

My mom scooted a chair closer to Clint. "Hey, Clint. It's Jennifer."

"Hah," he said.

His hand came up, and she grasped it. She darted a glance at me, her eyebrows pinned together.

"Hey," I said quietly. "He was saying, 'hey.'"

She mouthed, "Are you sure?"

I nodded. "He can hear you, Mom. He knows you're here. He was waiting for you so you could say goodbye. Because he loves you."

My mom's bottom lip jutted out while she held back tears. "Well, Clint." She sniffed. "I'm proud of you. The way you put yourself through college, the way you overcame your addictions, all the work you did to become a pastor. And you're an amazing father. I've loved watching you with your girls. They'll be okay." She stopped. Cried. "Marc and I will make sure they have everything they need, okay? So, you can rest. Your family is going to be well taken care of. Provided for." She kissed his forehead. "I love you."

Clint grunted.

"I love you too," I translated.

My mom backed away before her tears fell onto Clint's face. She squeezed his hand and struggled to release it. Struggled to release him. Finally, she stroked his hand with her thumb and lowered his arm to the bed. "Goodbye, Clint. I love you."

After my mom left, I laid beside Clint on the bed. "Can I do this, Clint? Am I strong enough? I'll try to be patient with them like you are. And I'll try to make the decisions for them you would make."

When his nurse entered, I asked her to check his feet. The tips of his toes had a blueish tinge and the pulse in his foot was faint.

Eventually, I slept.

A blaring beep and soft moans woke me after 2:00 a.m. Clint thrashed in his sleep. I pressed the dilaudid button and nothing happened. The screen on the medicine dispenser said EMPTY.

I darted into the hallway, approaching the nurse's station in unflattering jammie pants and a sweatshirt. "He's out of pain medicine and I can tell he's in pain. I pressed the call button, but I didn't want to wait."

"We'll check the machine and put a call into the pharmacy right away."

Call the pharmacy? Don't you have drugs up here, in a closet somewhere? Since *ER* and *Grey's Anatomy* provided the full extent of my medical training, I remained quiet.

"The drugs should be up here in hour." She tilted her head. "Maybe."

My eyes popped out of their sockets. "What can you do for him now? Until then."

"We have to check with his doctor before we give him anything different than what he's already been prescribed."

I slammed my hands on the counter. "Then check." Not following proper protocols could lead to a person's death. Then again, Clint was dying. What would the wrong cocktail do? Kill him? "Please hurry." I strode back to his room.

The smell of vinegar knocked me back. Clint pinched his eyes shut, and he shifted uncomfortably. "They're going to get you more medicine as soon as they can." I eased down on the bed. The shift in weight caused him to cry out. I jumped up. "Sorry. Sorry." I eased away. "Oh, God, this is a nightmare."

I inched down atop the arm of the chair. *Is this going to tip on me? No. Okay, good.* Eye-level with Clint, I studied the blue-black circles beneath his eyes.

The nurse came, checked the readings and explained to Clint they'd already phoned the on-call doctor.

I sat beside him until the medicine came and placed his hand on my knee. I didn't want to reach for my Bible, so I quoted passages I'd memorized: 1 Corinthians 13, Philippians 1-2, James 1, and Matthew 6.

I sang a bunch of praise songs, half in my sleep. Then I reached for my Bible, and I read from Genesis about the formation of Adam and Eve, the remembrance of "dust to dust." My body felt thick with sleep.

I fingered the wedding band on his finger. For the briefest moment, I considered removing the band. *No. We're still married.*

"I'm not sure how to say goodbye to you. Can you tell me how to do this?" I dragged the sleeve of my sweatshirt across my face to mop my tears. I leaned down and kissed his forehead. I rambled, feeling like if I kept talking to him, I could keep him on earth. "I love you, Clinty. It's okay. We'll be okay. You don't have to fight this life anymore. Jesus told you to come, so you should go."

My voice cracked. "Good night, sweet Clinty, it's time to take your rest. Lay your sweet head upon the Savior's chest. We all love you, yeah, but Jesus loves you best, so we say good night, good night, good night."

When I could no longer stay awake, I said, "Tomorrow I'll read about Jacob wrestling with God. The nurse will be here any minute with extra medicine. I'll be right beside you, but I need to sleep so I have enough strength to face tomorrow."

My eyes watered when 'see you in the morning' wasn't a promise I could make. "I'm right here, if you need me. I'm right here." I rested his hand on the mattress, lay on the bed beneath the dark window, pulled the white sheet up to my face, and cried myself to sleep.

Clint groaned.

With heavy eyelids, I fumbled for the pain button that can only be pressed every fifteen minutes. Contented by the sight of his chest rising and falling, I let my eyes flutter closed, knowing Clint was alive beside me.

Hours later, dim sun came through the blinds. I felt pressure against my shoulder.

"He's gone," a female voice said.

Another nurse flipped buttons on machines.

Her words didn't register. I opened my eyes and stared up at a woman I'd never seen before. *Who are you? Where am I?*

"He's gone," she repeated.

Nurse. Hospital. I remembered Clint jumping out of bed Saturday. "Where'd he go?"

"No. He's gone."

Oh. "Oh!" I sat up and stared at his body.

My first, true feeling was relief. *Our fight is over.*

The nurse took a steady hold of my upper arm. "Are you okay? I mean, are you going to pass out?"

"No. Is that a thing?"

"Yes."

I couldn't take my eyes off Clint's peaceful expression. "Can I have a minute? Please?"

"Of course."

The two female nurses scooted out of the room. My gaze dropped to Clint's left hand. I removed his wedding ring from his finger and slipped it onto mine. Then I just stared.

No whirring machines. No beeping.

No rasping breathing, loud conversations to Clint, or whispered words we hoped he might not hear.

Just silence.

I stood. His face appeared younger, almost glowing. I felt each breath wade in and out of my lungs. *One breath you're there and the next you're not. How does a person vanish?*

Awestruck, I observed a total absence of sorrow or fear. I felt a peace beyond any logical explanation. Though I never saw anything with human eyes, my awareness came with the sense that I was not alone.

The veil thinned. I felt them watching me watch Clint's body. I inclined my head toward Clint's body, and in faith, spoke out loud to Jesus. "Not there anymore."

No, not there.

"But alive and well?"

Yes, Sam.

"And happy?"

Blissfully.

A laugh bubbled up from my chest at the word blissfully, a personal joke between me and Clint. The sense of someone else's presence in the room faded. But … the peace remained.

After a moment's hesitation, I turned toward the bathroom. Because living people pee.

Clint died four weeks shy of his stay of adjudication.

At his last, Clint Evans died tatted with a lion on one deltoid, and a lamb on the other. Etched across his forearms were the words: Prodigal Son. He died a pastor and a felon—the culmination of every Christian redeemed by Christ.

On Facebook, I wrote:

> Strong as a lion and gentle as a lamb, Clint Evans crossed into heaven this morning around 6:15 a.m. I'm so proud of him and honored to have been his wife these last 15 years. Peace be with you.

The news of Clint's hospice care and death spread, jolting friends and family like a bucket of icy water to a hot face.

Part of me had grieved Monday, June 24, 2019, since Sunday, October 1, 2017. I'd rebelled against his decline even while I grieved his impending death.

The week following Clint's death, every time the doorbell rang, it seemed a friend or family member from another state had arrived.

Clint died the day before Kelly's seventh birthday and the entire community came together to throw a party bigger than I could have imagined. There was even a litter of new puppies waddling around our front yard. The event gave Cirque du Soleil a run for its money. Everyone threw their helplessness into effort for the celebration.

The next afternoon, I sat across the table from Fred. He shifted his weight forward onto his elbows and grinned. "So. Who do you want to officiate the service?"

Immediately, 300 names came to mind, and we laughed. "Um. Probably you or Bishop Ough if he's available, so there are no hurt feelings."

"I was thinking along similar lines. I've already talked to the bishop, and he said he absolutely would have, but he's out of state. So, I guess you're stuck with me." He chuckled and looked down. His hands hovered over a printout of the email I sent. "Your service outline was pretty thorough."

"Clint planned out the service."

"Clint … when?"

"Last week." I exhaled. "Just another Sunday service, right?"

The brims of Fred's eyes filled with tears. "This will be the hardest funeral I've ever performed. I've never buried a peer. Not like this."

Fred's tears and his admission of Clint as a peer swiped his position as Clint's boss off the table. His damp eyelids, a beautiful portrait of his vulnerability, were a bittersweet gift to me.

I'd just laid my purse on the table when the doorbell rang again. A female friend and her eight-year-old son, who was my daughter's classmate, stood on my front stoop.

"Hey there," said my friend. "We have something we want to talk to you about."

I ushered them to the dining room table. Seated, the boy looked to his mom for reassurance.

"It's all right," she said. "She'll believe you."

The boy described the hospital room he'd never been in with details that transcended lucky guesses. "The morning Pastor Clint died, angels and demons fought over his body."

No matter how this ends for me, Satan ain't gonna win.

"There were three demons and two angels," the boy said. "But the angels won."

EPILOGUE

Clint,

Dear friend, I pray you receive a balm to your soul and refreshment for your heart. You have been in my prayers for many weeks. I pray you are being lavished in the love of the Father, that you are being healed and freed.

I hope you know how deeply you are loved. I pray you have felt it deep into your bones, down to the very marrow. I pray God has met you in your laughter and tears, joys and frustrations.

Friend, I believe in you. I believe in your ministry and your work, and the beauty of your life. Even more, I believe in God, who offers us more love and forgiveness and abundance than we can ever fathom. And, I believe through God, your story is being written to be a story of resurrection and triumph.

There is so much goodness in you. I pray you hear the voice of God louder than the shouts of the enemy. May life and hope be spoken over you and may you hear God's loving truth above the noise and chaos.

I pray for your health, that wholeness and healing will be yours, that you can testify to the mercy and love and power of the Creator.

I am praying for you, because you are my friend, my fellow traveler on this journey, my brother in Christ.

We are here for you through this journey and always.

Blessings,
Stefanie

Messiah United Methodist Church, one of the largest Methodist churches in Minnesota, offered to host Clint's memorial service.

Football players in jerseys of black, white, blue, red, and green poured through glass doors lining the front of the building. Pastors in street clothes carrying garment bags filed down a stairwell. Pastors wearing robes and albs ascended the stairs. Erin, wearing a Wrestle-Mania shirt, and Heather, Clint's favorite living Catholic, posed for a photo. Heather's green T-shirt depicted the pope riding a bicycle.

Each of my daughters wore Renegade football jerseys that hung below their knees. Trinty's reached her ankles. I wore Clint's red all-star jersey—to a funeral—and tried to let that feel normal. Each of Clint's brothers wore one of his Evans jerseys as well. Angie, a church member and friend, wore an ugly Christmas sweater depicting a tyrannosaurus rex with a Santa hat and a glittering disco ball above his head. Clint had worn the matching sweater the previous Christmas.

Everyone in attendance was adorned with leis. *The only thing missing from this circus is a trapeze. Do you love this, Clint? Do you see how much love and life surrounded you?*

The sanctuary filled. While the worship team sang "This Little Light of Mine," Clint's family filled ten rows.

Clergy on both sides of the LGBT debate set down swords and banners beyond the sanctuary and joined in processional into the room as one, unified body. The 120 pastors filled nearly an entire section, and for a few sacred hours, the lines vanished. Clergy emulated Christ's "thy Kingdom come, thy will be done, on earth as it is in heaven." The celebration of Clint's homecoming boiled Christianity back down to the basics: Love God. Love your neighbor.

Fred stepped to the center of the stage and covered the mic at his cheek with a cupped hand while he cleared his throat. His eyes briefly closed. "I think it's important you know Clint, to use an expression of Paul, had a thorn in his side called addiction he came up against many times throughout his life. Sometimes submitting, only to find rock bottom.

"Clint made ministry as simple as loving people. Clint's charm as a pastor was that he was down to earth, not pretentious. He was a pastor, and he was just Clint at the same time. With Clint, what you see was what you got.

"Much of his own call to ministry came from his witness of the damage the church caused when they put on airs. He wanted to be a different kind of pastor and create a church atmosphere more accepting, more loving, more gracious, more authentic.

"Sam describes Clint as 'having a fierce heart to defend the underdog.' He'd been the underdog himself, you see, and found that no one was outside the bounds of God's grace.

"Clint's fierce love for the underdog took him to places like Standing Rock and helped him embrace outsiders who came into his church. It emboldened him to share about his own past for the sake of new pilgrims on the Minnesota Walk to Emmaus. His fierce love for the underdog is even why he chose to play the offensive line.

"He felt like if he was on the defensive line, his job would be to tear the quarterback to pieces, but on the offensive line, his job was to make sure no one else did.

"They say every pastor has one good sermon that comes out in different ways. Sam said Clint's sermon was, 'Love no matter what. Love until it hurts. Love no matter who they are.'

"Often, when a pastor sits with the family to discuss the Celebration of Life service, deciding on a Bible passage is challenging. Let me tell you, choosing the story of the Prodigal Son for Clint's service was a cinch. After all, this parable was so important to Clint's understanding of his own life journey, he tattooed the phrase across each arm.

"…If you're not careful you can get so enamored in the story of [the prodigal son] that you can forget the audience to which it was told. Scripture reminds us the tax collectors and sinners gathered around Jesus and the Pharisees, and the teachers of the law muttered, 'This man Jesus welcomes sinners and eats with them.'

"I love that line because it comes off the lips of those appalled by Jesus and the company he kept. Little did they know that in their very mutterance, is that a word? In their very mutterance, 'this man Jesus welcomes sinners and eats with them,' that's the summation of the gospel.

"On the lips of bullies and chastisers the central message of the gospel is being expressed. 'This man Jesus welcomes sinners and eats with them!' To which Jesus then responds in the parable, 'Yeah. You get it.'

"Most of us here have glimpsed Clint's big forearms. Sometimes he was tired and stretching or yawning, or wiping away laughter, or waving at you.

"On one occasion, admittedly not his finest moment, I sat directly across from him in jail. Past demons reared their ugly head, and Clint made bad choices. There was Clint, resting on his elbows in front of me, with his face buried in his hands.

"I grabbed hold of one of his arms and prayed for him with my eyes open, looking directly at him. And I could see the powerful phrase, one word on each arm, 'prodigal son.' I saw in this moment, in this context—and this one person— a dual reality, a dual identity. On the one hand, I knew Clint's story and how he identified with the younger son, the prodigal, which means, by the way, 'recklessly, extravagantly wasteful.'

"Clint identified with the life lived by the younger son. On more than one occasion, he found himself in a far-off country, had squandered his last dime, worn out his last welcome. He fed slop to the pigs. Clint tattooed the words 'prodigal son' on his body because of how seemingly impossible it was to think anyone could welcome him back home, let alone God himself.

"In a miraculous act of loving kindness in 2003, while Clint was still far off, Clint would tell you that the grace of God hit him like a two by four. And on that day, Clint found out that the only one living a more wastefully, extravagant life than he was God himself, with his extravagantly wasteful, reckless love found in the person of Jesus Christ.

"After all this man Jesus welcomes sinners and eats with them. How reckless!

"Sitting across the table from Clint, praying with my eyes open, I could see not only Clint's identification with the rough, reckless nature of God's son gone wild, but also but the other reality— the identification of a father even more reckless and wild with his love.

"In that moment, I wanted to reach out across the table with a sharpie and add an 's' to the word "prodigal." Because he and you and I are all prodigal children and absurdly, at the same time, children of a prodigal God, recklessly wasteful with His infinite supply of grace and love.

"And I think Clint already knew this, because this informed his ministry. One reality always difficult to escape from, an adjective, the prodigal son, but the second reality always unfathomably true: a prodigal God's son, an adjective about who we are changed to a possessive noun about *whose* we are.

"The party has begun for our brother. The fatted calf has been prepared, and he has been welcomed home to His father. And Clint has been fully welcomed at the table. This brother of ours was dead and is now alive again. Lost and now found.

"Because of the truth of the gospel, this man Jesus welcomes sinners and eats with them.

"The reason you have all been adorned with leis today is because today is a celebration of the prodigal's homecoming. The story of Clinton Marvy Evans is a celebratory story. It's a story of a life redeemed, of a God who will go to great lengths, reckless, extravagant lengths to run after His child."

If standing ovations were appropriate at a funeral, Fred would have received one.

ACKNOWLEDGEMENTS

Jorie, the layout of this book is gorgeous, and just as Clint always contested that there should be more statistics for linemen, you deserve so much credit.

Mom, for listening. You endured years of my word-vomit venting which enabled me to sift through the pain and formulate intelligible thoughts.

Terry Whalin, for mentoring me, believing in me, and all but marching this manuscript into the *New York Times* office yourself.

Larry J. Leech II, for demanding excellence, and for stating emphatically, "This. This is your last line."

Clint, I wish you could see how many lives your testimony will reach and enrich.

Chuck, Clint's dad, for the bravery required when you said, "Write this story the way Clint wanted it written." As long as I knew Clint, you were always the first person he turned to for help and advice—his loyal, trustworthy, loving father.

Tim, my husband. God gave me you. Thank you for your patience and support on this *Moby Dick* of a project.

My Savior, for the avalanche of miracles required to place this story in front of readers.

And to you, the reader on the mirror-side of my keyboard. Thank you for entrusting me with your time. Possibly, this story has changed you, as great stories should. May you see the breadth of God's love for you.

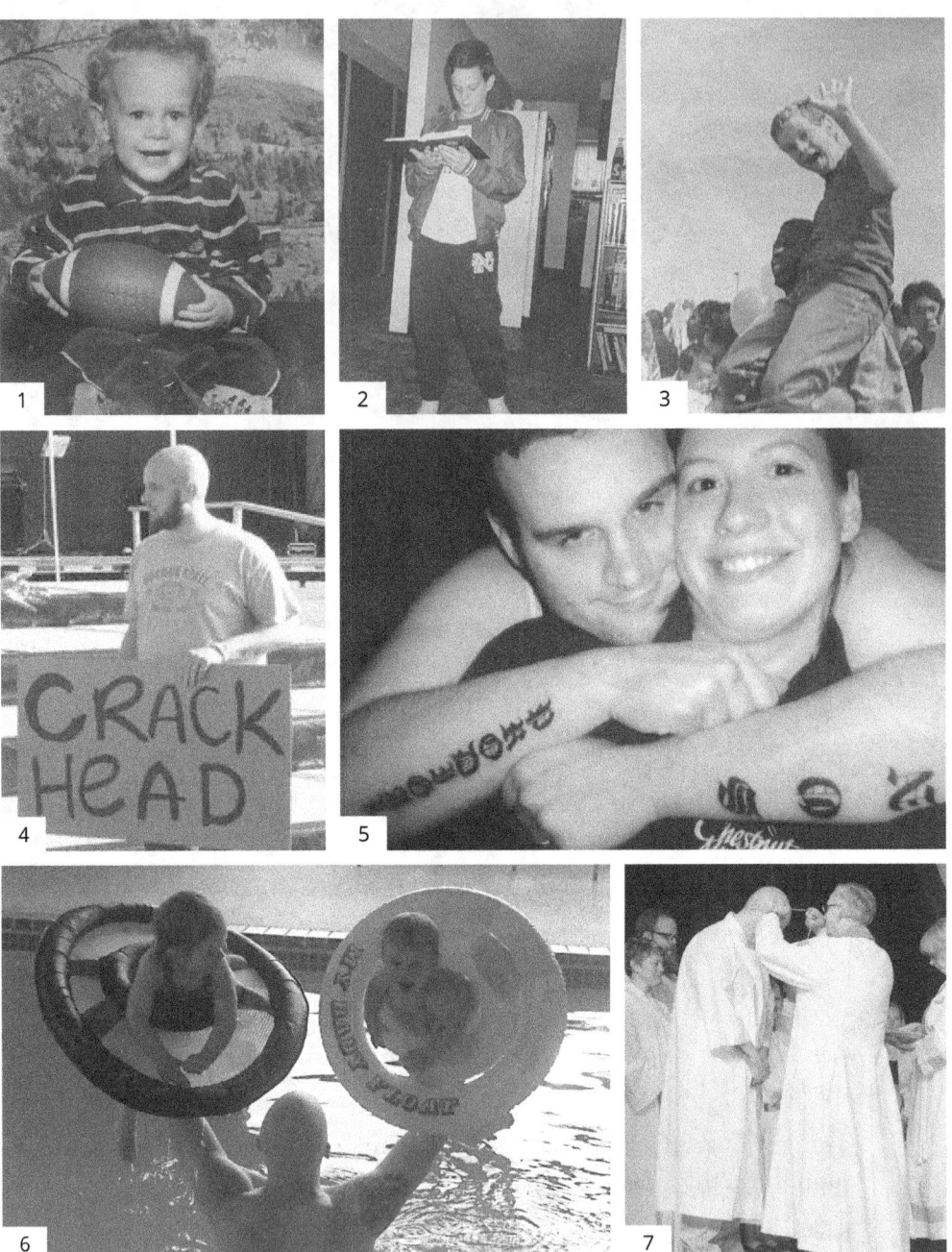

1. 1982, Clint
2. Clint reading the Easter story, 1993
3. Families wait while the U.S.S. Jason (AR-8) pulls into port
4. 2011, Cardboard Testimonies, Lebanon, Oregon
5. 2008, Clint and Sam, Lebabon, Oregon
6. January, 2013, Clint with Kaylynn and Kelly
7. June 2016, Minnesota United Methodist Church Annual Conference

8. 2016, Standing Rock Pipeline Protest, North Dakota
9. July 2013, Clint with Kaylynn and Kelly at Sonshine Music Festival, Willmar, Minnesota
10. Summer 2017, Sabercats Offensive Line
11. August 2018, Clint baptizes Sherry in Rhinelander, WI
12. February 2019, The Evans family at Disneyworld
13. Winter 2018, Warhawks, U.S. Bank Stadium
14. Father's Day, 2019, Clint and Trinity

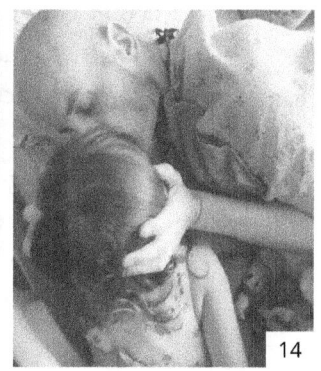

ABOUT PIGS

When I set out to write *The Prodigal's Son*, I spent days studying Scripture and commentaries about the prodigal. My eyes were still bleary with sleep, skin blissfully warm beneath the covers, the morning I heard God say, "Pigs."

"Pigs?" I grabbed my phone and Googled 'Bible references of pigs.'

Before the search results materialized, I guessed what I'd find—at least one Leviticus reference to God deeming pigs "unclean," Legion begging Jesus to cast him into pigs, and the prodigal son wishing he could eat what the pigs ate.

The last thought snagged me. "Oh. What do you want to teach me about the prodigal son this morning?"

I'd finished reading Henri Nouwen's *Return of the Prodigal Son* based on Rembrandt's painting "The Return of the Prodigal Son." For an entire week, God showed me new facets of the Luke 15 "Lost" parables I'd never seen before.

The Google search yielded two surprising results from Isaiah.

> a people who continually provoke me
>   to my very face,
> offering sacrifices in gardens
>   and burning incense on altars of brick;
> who sit among the graves
>   and spend their nights keeping secret vigil;
> who eat the flesh of pigs,
>   and whose pots hold broth of impure meat;
>
> Isaiah 65:3-4 NIV

"Those who consecrate and purify themselves to go into the gardens, following one who is among those who eat the flesh of pigs, rats and other unclean things—they will meet their end together with the one they follow," declares the LORD.

Isaiah 66:17 NIV

Both verses mentioned pigs and graves. *Graves? Legion was among graves, wasn't he?*

A picture formed, the contrast and compromise of the Israelites.

- God deemed pigs unclean, therefore, God's people had no business raising pigs.
- The Israelites, aware of God's instruction, raised pigs beyond the walls of the city—because pigs were unclean. Out of sight, out of conscience.
- Israelites constructed graveyards—also unclean—beyond the city, near grazing pigs.
- Jesus and Legion, speaking among the tombs, could see pigs grazing from where they stood.

When Jesus cast Legion into a large herd of pigs, the Israelites were more distressed by the eradication of unclean animals than joyful about the clean, restored human.

Folding the story of the man possessed by a Legion of demons lent a richer picture of the prodigal son. Jesus couldn't have chosen a filthier animal for the prodigal son's parable.

The younger son had been a wealthy, well-known heir, lavish and comfortable. By a series of poor choices, he traded affluence for debasement and became unrecognizable. Shame replaced pride. Humiliation; glory. His gold was long since spent and he'd pawned robes, chariots, jewelry and other valuables to scrape by.

Bright, cinematic color faded to muted grays. Ragged and cold, he shoveled pig manure. Hollow, he wished he could eat what the *unclean* animals *ate*. Beyond sight of the city's exuberant nightlife, silhouettes of the graveyard marked the dwelling places of the humans he bore the closest proximity to.

Jesus tells the Pharisees this wretch, "got up and went to his father."

When the Father saw his child returning, he didn't care about his son's appearance—only that he'd returned home. While his son smelled of pig excrement and stale urine, wore tattered rags, worn for weeks on end, had lice-infested hair and bloodied, bare feet, the backstabbed, broken Father kissed his child.

In the 'lost' parables, Jesus demonstrates love as pursuit. The shepherd pursues the marginalized sheep. The woman pursues her friends to celebrate the discovered treasure. The father sprints toward the younger son.

Teachers of the law were known as shepherds, so Jesus is essentially asking, "Would you go out for the lost sheep?"

Here's something new I noticed the152nd time I read the story of the prodigal son. The father pursues the judgmental elder son too. Jesus is telling the pharisees, *You* are lost too, and God the Father is looking for you."

Both sons need the Father, Nouwen points out. And the Father loves both in equal measure—pursues both, invites both to the banquet.

Jesus concludes his story without telling His listeners if the elder brother joined the celebration. He leaves the question hanging as an open invitation.

Sunday mornings in twenty-first century churches are packed with elder brothers who turn their noses down at the world's prodigal sons. Wouldn't the elder brothers be appalled to realize that it's the Prodigal Son extending the invitation to heaven's banquet?

Because 2,000 years ago, Jesus, the wealthy, well-known heir, left home, lived among the unclean, and traded the lavish comfort of heaven for the graveyard beyond the city.

TELL THE WORLD WHAT YOU THINK WITH A REVIEW!

The Best Way to Say "Thank You."

 Did you appreciate this book? Reviews are currency for authors. The more reviews a book acquires, the more visibility the title receives. Especially with independently published works, the numbers matter. The best way to thank your favorite authors is by leaving reviews.

PRAY FOR YOUR PRODIGAL WITH
PRAYERS AGAINST ADDICTION

Purchase
Prayers Against Addiction

WELCOME, ADDICT. Or maybe you landed here because you want to support a loved one battling addiction. You are not alone.

Prayers Against Addiction: Praying for Your Addict Where the Needle Pierces Skin meets addicts on the battlefront of sobriety. During an arrest. In jail. When our prodigals battle depression and suicidal thoughts. At the moment of relapse, and through a withdrawal. *Prayers Against Addiction* prays God into the darkest moments of our beloved prodigals' lives and calls them home.

This addiction recovery resource is like no other. *Prayers Against Addiction* is written by addicts on their recovery journey who understand the importance of seeking treatment and maintaining sobriety. These prayers describe withdrawal symptoms, address the correlation between addiction and mental health, and include pleas for relapse prevention, safe harbor, and strength to walk away from the vice.

SPECIAL FEATURES
Within the pages of *Prayers Against Addiction* you can:
- Read prayers written from the perspective of both addict and addict's loved one
- Hear personal recovery stories

- Write your own specific prayers for healing
- Record evidence of the answered prayers
- Receive hope on the path to sobriety
- Meditate on encouraging Bible verses
- Pray about addicts' every day struggles like preventing relapse, addiction in family members, and battling suicidal thoughts.
- See captivating images and quotes from *The Prodigal's Son: Crackhead to Jesus Freak*
- Read excerpts from *Radiance of the Moon*, a Christian fiction book that depicts the battle of alcoholism.

OTHER BOOKS BY S.E. TSCHRITTER

Do you feel helpless, watching a loved one grieve a loss that you can't fathom? Written by a griever, these books reach the heart of someone in grief. Give the gift of words when you can't muster them yourself.

She Told Them They Were Loved

Someone grieving a loss will find themselves saying, "Yes, this" when they read, and ruminating on the words long after they close the cover. "When I leave this earth, that's what I want people to whisper about me in my absence—'She told them they were loved.'"

~S. E. Tschritter

Until the Day We Meet Again

Unique Features Include:

• The journaler becomes the author of his/her story • Designed by a mom of three heaven-born babies • Journal prompts listed in the table of contents • Thoughtful gift for grieving mothers • Captivating photos • Coloring pages • Open-ended journal space • Excerpt from *Love Letters to Miscarriage Moms* • Encouraging Quotes • Bible Verses

Love Letters to Miscarriage Moms

In this book, over 40 men and women lend vulnerable insight into their experiences with infant loss. With raw honesty, Sam shares hard-won lessons learned during her darkest days. From practical suggestions to spiritual encouragement, *Love Letters to Miscarriage Moms:* Validates unique grief experiences, provides ideas for self-care and healthy coping strategies, and lays bare legitimate, complex spiritual doubts.

2023 Golden Scroll Award, Advanced Writers and Speakers Association
2023 International Book Awards, Finalist, Health: Women's Health
2023 International Book Awards, Finalist, Best Interior Design
2010 Orange County Christian Writers Conference Award

ABOUT THE AUTHOR

Sam Evans Tschritter

Multi-award-winning author S. E. Tschritter (pronounced Shridder) specializes in articulating grief and loss, leading grievers toward hope and healing. Whether poetry, fiction, or non-fiction, Tschritter writes content that will stick with readers long after they close the cover. Her 20-plus years of leadership experience and contributions to over 30 books enable her to serve others, speaking truth with transparency, humor, and love.

Tschritter grew up in Chicagoland and has also lived in Minnesota and Oregon, granting her widespread views of people all over the country. She currently resides in Simpsonville, South Carolina with her husband, their three teen and preteen daughters, cats named Pitter and Patter, and their Siberian husky whom she lost the vote to name Onomatopoeia. Nothing refreshes Tschritter's soul like gardening. She gardens to work through plot holes, writer's block, character development, and book ideas. Tschritter spends a great deal of time gardening.

The Lakeshore's Secret
Lakeshore Mysteries Book One

S.E. Tschritter's Debut Novel
Spring 2026

For more information join Tschritter's newsletter
and follow the series on Facebook.
https://Linktr.ee/LoveSamEvans

Can they discover who betrayed her before anyone else is killed?

After multiple break-ins to her Chicago apartment, Tasha Baker flees to her grandma's small town in the Northwoods of Minnesota. But just after her arrival, her grandma is poisoned, and three million dollars goes missing. The killer believes Tasha holds the key to finding the money. Seven people are dead and without the help of her ex—who broke her trust and her heart—she'll become the next victim.

Jake Parsons excels at assessing security deficits of prestigious companies. So why, when his ex-girlfriend breezes into town with a killer on her tail, is it so hard to keep her alive? Will he discover her attacker's identity before he loses Tasha forever?

Don't miss out!

- The latest news
- Giveaways
- Encouragement
- Inspiration
- Only two-ish emails / month